T0331998

Land, Investment and Migration

Land, Investment and Migration

CAMILLA TOULMIN

OXFORD
UNIVERSITY PRESS

OXFORD
UNIVERSITY PRESS

Great Clarendon Street, Oxford, OX2 6DP,
United Kingdom

Oxford University Press is a department of the University of Oxford.
It furthers the University's objective of excellence in research, scholarship,
and education by publishing worldwide. Oxford is a registered trade mark of
Oxford University Press in the UK and in certain other countries

© Camilla Toulmin 2020

The moral rights of the author have been asserted

First Edition published in 2020

Impression: 1

All rights reserved. No part of this publication may be reproduced, stored in
a retrieval system, or transmitted, in any form or by any means, without the
prior permission in writing of Oxford University Press, or as expressly permitted
by law, by licence or under terms agreed with the appropriate reprographics
rights organization. Enquiries concerning reproduction outside the scope of the
above should be sent to the Rights Department, Oxford University Press, at the
address above

You must not circulate this work in any other form
and you must impose this same condition on any acquirer

Published in the United States of America by Oxford University Press
198 Madison Avenue, New York, NY 10016, United States of America

British Library Cataloguing in Publication Data
Data available

Library of Congress Control Number: 2019955945

ISBN 978–0–19–885276–6

DOI: 10.1093/oso/9780198852766.001.0001

Printed and bound by
CPI Group (UK) Ltd, Croydon, CR0 4YY

Links to third party websites are provided by Oxford in good faith and
for information only. Oxford disclaims any responsibility for the materials
contained in any third party website referenced in this work.

Preface

Why this book, a longitudinal study of a small mud village in Central Mali? It is not a well-known country, as it formed part of the French colonial territories. It lies like a huge butterfly in the heart of West Africa, the northern half a desert vastness, the southern half with enough rainfall to grow crops and support live-stock. It is twice the size of France, with the great River Niger running through it. Better known is the fabled city of Timbuktu, which lies on the bend of this magnificent river as it cuts into the desert and before it turns down to flow into Niger and Nigeria. If you are keen on world music, you will have heard the *cora* playing of Malian masters such as Toumani Diabaté, throaty *wassoulou* singers like Oumou Sangaré, soft love songs of Miriam & Amadou, and rhythms of Salif Keita. However, you may also have seen Mali figuring on the news because of ongoing conflicts between jihadist groups and the army, supported by France's troops and a range of other Western and African forces. This may seem a long way away and have little to do with us, but the jihadist groups were greatly helped in late 2011 by the British, French, and US decision to dislodge Muammar Gaddafi of Libya, in an ill-judged move to bring democracy to a country that had only known strongman rule for the previous 40 years.

These jihadist groups are earning much of their money by controlling the traffic of cocaine across the Sahara Desert as it makes its way to the European market. Also familiar to press and TV audiences will be the boatloads of young men and women, many of them from Mali and neighbouring Niger, attempting to cross from North Africa to the southern shores of Europe. Each one of those faces, peering out from a blanket on board a rescue ship—if they are lucky—has a story of hope and hardship, as they have trekked from villages and towns on the far side of the desert, using up hard-won cash on the services of people smugglers. From being described as a geopolitical backwater, West Africa has become strategically very important to Europe, with large sums of money now invested in the fight against jihadism and illegal migration. Donor agencies have grouped together to form the Sahel Alliance, which aims to address the intertwined problems of poor governance, lack of jobs, climate change, migration, and insecurity.

While these problems are hugely significant, and set the wider scene, this book is mainly about how life in the Bambara village of Dlonguébougou has changed. I was fortunate to live there from May 1980 to March 1982, carrying out research for the International Livestock Centre for Africa. It was my first proper field research, after 2 years of teaching Economics at Ahmadu Bello University in Zaria, in the north of Nigeria. I had come across people doing research in villages near Zaria, and it gave me an appetite to understand rural life better. When Duncan Fulton, an anthropologist, and I went to live in Dlonguébougou, the purpose was to collect detailed economic data on agricultural production and household budgets. For various reasons, including ambivalence towards highly quantitative approaches, and the enormous size of many Bambara households, we abandoned questionnaires and opted for participant observation combined with in-depth enquiries once we had established greater confidence with the population. From walking about, sitting to chat, eating meals together, trying to wield the hoe, a cotton spindle, a threshing flail, or a plough-team, we established ourselves as slightly odd but respected members of the community. You make friends over a 2-year period, and by the end, there are people you want to keep in touch with, whose lives and prospects matter to you. So, recently, I went back to find out how lives have changed.

I have many reasons for writing this book which I hope will resonate with my readers. First, it is really interesting to see how people's lives play out in different places, over more than 35 years. Think about the pleasure of meeting someone you have not seen since school. Going back to Dlonguébougou is a bit like a condensed version of the BBC Radio drama 'The Archers'. There is so much to catch up on. I also wanted to go back and see friends, get their thoughts on prospects for the future, and find out if some of their children are among those trying the boat route to Europe. In 1980–1982, I had tried to understand the pattern of life, choices made, and differential ability of households and individuals to cope with risk. I had recognized the pressures on grazing and the potential for the farming system to run into trouble, so I wanted to see for myself how these trends had evolved. Following the fortunes of people in Dlonguébougou has also made me more curious about how life has treated small rural communities in my own country over a similar period. I am planning in my head a study of rural life in the borderlands of North West England to explore the interplay of population, climate, policy, and technology over the last 40 years, to see what we can learn, and to provide a point of comparison with the Mali study.

Second, while every place is distinct, because of location, history, and people, the village of Dlonguébougou is also a microcosm of common forces and trends which have played out in similar ways across the world. Exploring these trends throws our own society into focus. The power of consumer culture has been all-pervasive everywhere, but especially here, where the shift in values from a strong collective tradition to a much more individualized pattern of production is really marked. As Hawa says, 'we've discovered all sorts of wants and needs we never knew we had before'. The threadbare days of the early 1980s have given way to a delight in consumer goods and smart clothing, so that even a small child wanders around with a plastic replica of a mobile phone. And while a shift in values is less visible to the eye than the introduction of new technology, or the impact of climate change, it has reshaped choices and restructured relationships. Old people say, 'young people no longer respect their elders'—well, there is nothing new there. But from the perspective of younger folk, they revel in their liberation from parental obligations, and most are itching to set off and explore the world away from the village. Older people worry that the web of mutual obligations which assured the family support is eroding away. While the structure of the large domestic group still stands, much of the glue holding it together is thinning, and it is hard to imagine these big groups will survive the next 35 years. Faced with multiple risks and uncertainties, these domestic groups offer significant mutual support and social insurance, in exchange for contributions in kind and cash. These large households of more than fifty people stand in stark contrast to our own domestic arrangements, with many people living alone, and old people herded into residential care to be managed by nurses who have travelled from the other side of the world.

Third, the study speaks to broader concerns about 'how to feed the world'. It shows the difficulty faced by dryland farmers in a warming world, faced with shorter farming seasons and more intense rainstorms. But climate change is often not the most important stress on farming systems. Government neglect and disdain make the farmer's life harder. Farmers and herders must come to terms with the shift from land abundance to scarcity, and seek new ways to address these challenges, such as 'regreening' techniques tried out elsewhere. The study also shows the hardship of farming for the poorest families; assets and equipment are needed to survive and prosper. People invest considerable sums in their farms and equipment each year, yet receive no recognition nor support from government. The neglect of family farmers offers a contrast with government's pursuit of 'agricultural investors', large commercial operators who are courted, provided with generous tax breaks, and offered cheap land. I make the case that reliance on large-scale irrigated agriculture will not solve many of the food-security problems faced by countries like Mali. Government and donors focus their investment on irrigation, while rain-fed farmers and herders are turned off their land without any compensation, and many of the simple low-cost public investments which might be made in dryland farming systems just do not happen. Social justice and value for money demand a better balance be sought for the millions of farmers struggling to make ends meet across the Sahel.

Fourth, the study shows the importance of establishing arenas in which to seek collective solutions to common problems. Traditionally, villages like Dlonguébougou had control of the land, water, trees, and grazing resources stretching in all directions, through ritual gifts to the spirits of the landscape. They maintained a tight hand on who could draw water from the few wells around the settlement and, hence, those seeking land and grazing. The combination of colonial conquest, freeing up of land access on Independence, establishment of decentralized local government, and abandonment of the local gods in favour of universal Islam have meant that this customary control has slackened, so there are few if any means to manage these key resources. Mali's new Agricultural Land Law offers some prospect of creating greater order, but it is hard to see any progress made while conflict and tension deepen and scar relations between different ethnic groups sharing the same space. Small sparks if ignored can turn into great conflagrations. Strengthening local dispute resolution mechanisms to bring different groups and interests together will be key to re-establish trust and agree how to manage scarce resources more effectively.

Fifth, this is the story of one village and its multiple connections. When we first settled there, I had no inkling that we would find some many connections between this small settlement and the rest of the world. Living in Edinburgh, I have a soft spot for the Scottish explorer Mungo Park, who travelled across this region in the 1790s, and came from the Scottish borders. Whenever I go through Selkirk, close to the farm where his family were tenants, I ask myself how he felt tramping through the Sahel, driving his sick horse before him, and whether his heart ached for the drizzle and mist of his homeland. His two journeys also epitomize contrasting approaches to travelling in strange places. The first journey showed if you put yourself at the mercy of local people, you may go hungry and even be kidnapped, but you can also find great warmth and generosity. The alternative approach, adopted for his second journey, which ended in a fatal shootout on the River Niger, involved arriving with an armed escort, keeping his distance from local powers, and firing off guns to repel strangers.

Sixth, and most of all, I feel a debt to the people of Dlonguébougou. I want this book to celebrate the energy, persistence, and generous nature of people in this and neighbouring villages, who have been keen to share stories of their lives, both the good things they are proud of and the difficulties they have faced. I have much enjoyed getting to know the Bambara language, its proverbs and tight structure, and how it absorbs the French language into its own format. I have learned that people are both different but also much the same around the world—some make delightful companions with so much to discuss; others are so annoying that everyone tries to escape when they see them coming. I wanted to describe the mixed emotions of people from Dlonguébougou who have left the village and made their home in the capital, Bamako, yet feel the tug from nostalgic references to childhood back in the village. I felt compelled to describe the consequences associated with the sugar cane plantation set-up by a Chinese company with Malian government support, the corners they have cut, the damage they have wrought for miles around, and the absence of any response by government or the company. It is one of too many land grabs across Africa, in which presidents and government officials seem much readier to help foreign investors than offer protection to their own citizens. I have been deeply impressed by the courage with which farmers evicted from their land have set off looking for somewhere else to sow their crops. I have asked myself why people in government maintain such disdain for the women and men who farm the land. How would they cope if they had to balance their belongings on a donkey cart and walk for 3 days? And I am discouraged by the likelihood of further large-scale land allocations by the government, which seems to have no interest in learning from past mistakes. It is painful to see the country and broader Sahelian region wracked by conflict, much of which is rooted in the corrupt, venal behaviour of some of those who have been in positions of power. Jihadist forces have found a ready audience amongst people marginalized over decades by a system which works against them, in which they are unable to get a fair hearing over land disputes, and where they see others flourish while their own prospects diminish each year. I hope you read on and enjoy this book.

Acknowledgements

Deli kanyi nka a fara ka ko.[1]

It is now 39 years since I first went to Dlonguébougou (DBG) as a 25 year old. As the villagers say, it is not today, nor is it even yesterday. For me, this connection to DBG has provided a fascinating journey over many years, keeping in touch, and seizing opportunities to spend a few days in the village. I hope this book will be of value to the people of the village and wider region, by providing a narrative which demonstrates the energy and innovation displayed by the villagers over the last 4 decades, but also the complexity of life within the village and its interactions with the wider world. Before publication, I would have wished to present my findings and the conclusions I have drawn to the people of DBG myself, in order to get their reactions, corrections, and perspectives. One of the things I have liked most about people there is their robust approach to discussion. They have a self-confidence, humour, and willingness to argue which are admirable, if sometimes very animated and noisy. I am working with my long-standing research assistant and friend Sidiki Diarra to get the main findings back to them, talk through problems with the farming system, compare the change in attitudes over time, and consider ways both to strengthen land rights and reduce conflict between groups over access to land, water, and grazing. I wish to recognize the open, warm welcome I have always received from people in the village, and from the three village chiefs I have known—Dafé, Babo, and Danson Dembélé. I want to thank them all for their willingness to put up with another lot of questions, and for the persistence of DBG's women in trying to teach me how to pound millet, farm a fonio plot, winnow the grain after harvest, and spin cotton, none of which I mastered with any degree of finesse.

I have received much encouragement from friends and colleagues in Mali, most particularly my research assistant Sidiki Diarra, with whom I originally worked in 1980–1982, and who has continued to provide steadfast, constant help, whether it is visiting the village with me, keeping contact with and supervising research by Makono Dembélé and his team of young assistants, or explaining the ins-and-outs of village life. Makono Dembélé from DBG village has also been of great assistance, by keeping track of major events, monitoring the sesame harvests and sales, measuring the rainfall, and travelling to meet me in Ségou when it

---

[1] 'Getting familiar with people is a good thing, but when you have to leave them, it feels bad.'

Photo A. Sidiki Diarra and Makono Dembélé, in Ségou, discussing our findings, 2017.

was not deemed safe for me to get out to the village. Both Sidiki and Makono have been a delight to work with over the last 3 years, and I am very grateful for everything they have contributed to this project. Sitting in Ségou with Makono and Sidiki, I became very familiar with Schubert's Trout Quintet, the ring-tone of Makono's mobile phone, as this has now become an invaluable research tool for checking information.

Opening up a trunk full of notebooks and maps from the 1980s has unearthed many memories and rekindled many conversations. Duncan Fulton, with whom I did the 2-year fieldwork in 1980–1982, has been very generous with his time, reflections, and materials from our shared time in DBG nearly 40 years ago. I would like to acknowledge the research assistants who accompanied us on the first 2-year period in DBG: Sidiki Diarra, Karounga Coulibaly, and Baba Konaté, fed and watered by Sidiki's estimable wife Bintu Coulibaly. Jeremy Swift was the original instigator of this research, and he has remained a strong supporter of my work and a friend with whom to pick-over old and new perspectives on drylands and pastoralists and the hurdles they face. Sara Randall has challenged easy assumptions about domestic groups and illuminated a range of demographic issues. Her detailed survey in 1981 of populations in DBG and many neighbouring settlements in the commune of N'Koumandougou remains a great asset which we should find ways of exploring further. Thanks are also due to Mary Martin, who had the task of taking up residence in DBG as we moved out in 1982, and digging into a detailed understanding of food provision and nutrition in the village. I am also very grateful to Karen Brock, who lived in DBG and led the Sustainable Livelihoods Research project in Mali in the late 1990s, for sharing her detailed findings and reflections.

In Mali, Yacouba Dème at the Near East Foundation (NEF) has been a generous, loyal supporter of my research, and has insisted on providing a car and driver to take me out to DBG, whenever possible. The NEF drivers have a particular brand of indefatigability, whatever the circumstances. We have been stuck in deep mud or caught by a huge rainstorm, in the middle of nowhere. Yet the cheerful banter, preparation of tea, and gossip continue unabated. They have always been ready to find string and nails to rig up my mosquito net, to help me improve my Bambara, or to insist on my trying a local snack of fried fish or sweet fritters. I wish to thank them all—Amadou, Vieux, Aba, and Amidou—and express the hope we have other bush travels ahead of us.

Youba Sokona, with one foot firmly in Mali and the other in global climate research, has offered his interest, friendship, and support, questioning my findings and opening doors to his network of family and friends. Béchir Sokona, Youba's brother, became my landlord, or *jaatigi*, in Ségou during my visits in 2016, and thanks to his indefatigable wife Tata, who provided a delicious dinner every evening, which ran through the gamut of Bambara cuisine. Moussa Djiré, Rector of the University of Political Science and Law, has always offered good counsel and hospitality in Bamako, and advice on chapters. His generous manner, friendly home, and uproarious grandson have made visits to Bamako very special. With Djeidi Sylla, our long friendship has allowed for regular discussion of how the pastoral livestock dimension fits into the bigger picture, and I have enjoyed working with him on options for better grazing management on the North Bank of the River Niger. Adam Thiam has provided a critical eye and wise commentary on Mali's politics. Tiébilé Dramé has always been interested to hear about life in Dlonguébougou and problems with the sugar cane plantation. Mary Allen has offered very helpful comments on draft chapters. And Alice Walpole introduced me to her fellow ambassadors in Bamako.

Chris Reij has been a source of inspiration and advice, as a long-standing advocate for supporting local people in Africa's drylands, building on their knowledge and ways of working. Pierre Hiernaux has walked the fallows of DBG and helped me understand the patchy mosaic and pace of ecological change in the Sahel. Gray Tappan has provided generous access to satellite images, which have made me gasp with wonder at seeing DBG from the skies. Mark Haywood and Matt Turner have shared ideas and materials which illuminate ecological change and demonstrate the importance of taking a landscape approach. Chris Field, Gemma Gubbins, and Andy Harfoot have gone out of their way to help me interpret the satellite images available, given my inability to master the software, despite instruction. Myles MacInnes has provided valuable funds with which we could develop a Local Convention for managing land, grazing, and water resources in N'Koumandougou Commune.

Regular visits to Paris and Montpellier have allowed me to benefit from the friendship and comments of French friends and colleagues, who have kindly read through chapters and commented on the overall findings, especially Vatché Papazian and Alain Rochegude. Thank you to André Marty, Patrick Caron, Marie-Jo Demante, Philippe Lavigne Delville, and Jean-Marc Pradelle, for all the counsel, ideas, and references which have extended my understanding of the Sahel's history and institutions.

My 30 years at the International institute for Environment and Development (IIED) have been almost as long as my relationship with DBG, and I have gained greatly from colleagues there working on similar subjects and topics, especially Ced Hesse on drylands, Lorenzo Cotula on land tenure, Jamie Skinner for everything to do with irrigated agriculture, and Simon Anderson on climate resilience. Liz Aspden talked through my plans and kept track of my movements in Mali, encouraging me not to stray too far into the red zone. Andy Norton my successor as Director of IIED is owed special thanks for his continued support of this research project and shared interest in Mali.

I have wanted to bring my research findings to life through use of figures and infographics. Many of the illustrations in this book have been designed by Kate Lines, who has shown great imagination in identifying with me what needs to be said, and then exploring how to present this simply and clearly. Anna Mill has drawn beautiful maps and diagrams, when she had many other deadlines to meet.

Mike Mortimore was always ready for quizzing me about my latest visit to DBG, and I am sorry he is no longer alive to give his considered verdict on my findings. Mary Tiffen's work with Mike Mortimore and insights from her own earlier study in Gombe, Northern Nigeria, have helped me understand the importance of bottom-up investment, and how decentralized government can unleash a different kind of energy and action. There is a singular generosity of researchers who have worked on Bambara society and village life, and I must acknowledge the help and friendship of John van dusen Lewis, who did his fieldwork south of Ségou in Doukolomba, and Larry Becker in Soro, now on the eastern edge of Bamako. It has been wonderful to share interpretations and findings with them. It is a tribute to Bambara society that the warmth, engagement, and energy these people embody have been absorbed and expressed by those who study them. I would also like to thank Richard Roberts for his very kind speed-reading of my history chapter, which I hope has helped me avoid too many pitfalls.

With a part-time base at the Lancaster Environment Centre, my colleagues there have been a willing audience for several presentations on DBG@35, and have encouraged me to get the book finished, as have my friends and colleagues Virginia Beardshaw, Felicity Bryan, Andrew Cahn, Nathalie Delapalme, Nick Gestrich, Bara Guèye, Tim Jackson, Susie and Julian Leiper, Kevin MacDonald, David Nissan, Jeff Philipson, Kate Raworth, Ian Scoones, Nick Stern, Adam Swallow, Michael Whitaker, Steve Wiggins, and two anonymous reviewers. I also benefitted from advice and suggestions at seminars on this work given at Cambridge, Oxford, Edinburgh, the UK Department for International Development, and University College, London.

I am very grateful to the Open Society Foundations (OSF) for providing a 12-month fellowship grant, which they were willing to stretch over 21 months. Their support was critical in providing the means to get started and carry through my project. OSF colleagues in New York—Akwe Amosu, Steve Hubbell, Milap Patel, and Zach Seltzer—offered a supportive and interested audience. Gerald, Margaret and Joe Elliot gave a very generous grant to support this work through the Binks Family Trust in Edinburgh. This hugely helpful supplementary funding enabled me to undertake things outside the strict remit of the OSF fellowship, such as digging deeper into the establishment of the N-Sukala sugar cane plantation, and consequent impacts.

Finally, my deepest thanks go to my husband Mark and my children, who have had me nose-buried in finishing off this book for some time. It was a huge pleasure to take William and Agnes out to visit DBG in 2006 and 2009, respectively, as well as improving my credibility amongst the villagers in having managed to rear these young people to adulthood. I wish I could have included my eldest son Luke on a visit to the village and given his architectural training, take him to see the astonishing mud mosques of Djenné and Mopti, before travel to this region became too risky. My hope is that the current turmoil and conflict across Central Mali will find its resolution soon, in a just peace which recognizes the many failings of current and past administrations and seeks to do things differently. I would like to continue work in the neighbourhood of DBG, following the proposed Daouna project, which is planned to begin in 2019, understanding the history of the region better, and documenting oral testimony from the many settlements in this fascinating region of West Africa. I have promised to help Makono Dembélé produce a history of the village in the Bambara language, and I hope to get published a French-language version of this book, so it becomes accessible to the many Sahelians for whom French is the main language of education.

I am also grateful to many other people who have helped in multiple ways, but wish to absolve them all for any responsibility for mistakes and misinterpretations I may have committed.

Camilla Toulmin

Edinburgh
April 2019

Contents

List of Figures

Central Colour Plate Section

List of Tables

List of Boxes

1

Introduction to Dlonguébougou

Jirikuru be men ji la, a te ke bama ye.[1]

Introduction

This book presents the study of a village in the dry Sahel region of Central Mali and the people who live there. Lying between the desert and savannah, the settlement of Dlonguébougou (DBG) nestles in a saucer-like depression, surrounded by gently rolling sandy plains (as shown in Figure 1.1, see the colour plates section[2]).[3] Its name means the village, or town of Dlongué, who was the founder of the settlement and forefather of the chiefly Dembélé family. The village is a cluster of sandy-grey, mud-brick houses, which are home to more than 1,600 people today. I first went there in 1980, when I was a young researcher doing my first proper fieldwork. At the time, it felt incredibly remote, but despite this apparent isolation, I was to find that its people and history have been linked to the wider world for centuries (see Figure 1.2). Aerial photos from the early 1950s show DBG as a tiny speck lost in an ocean of empty bush, but this landscape has long been traversed by traders, explorers, and military expeditions. Settled 3 centuries ago, the village's history has been connected to political events near and far, such as establishment of the Bambara kingdom of Ségou in the eighteenth century, the French colonial conquest in the late nineteenth century, and jihadist conflict today. The villagers feel the full force of twenty-first-century globalization, for good or ill, in what land people can call their own, their ideas and aspirations, the clothes people wear, the crops they grow, and the mobile phones they have come to rely on.

This first chapter introduces the village and its people, describes my first and subsequent visits to DBG, and outlines the methods and aims of this book.

---

[1] 'A log of wood may stay a long time in water, but never turns into a crocodile', meaning that you can stay a long time in a place but never become a true native and therefore know and understand the local people.

[2] The colour plates are found in middle of the book.

[3] I have abbreviated the name of the village to DBG throughout this book.

Land, Investment and Migration. Camilla Toulmin, Oxford University Press (2020). © Camilla Toulmin.
DOI: 10.1093/oso/9780198852766.001.0001

Figure 1.1. The village nestles in a saucer-like depression, 1981

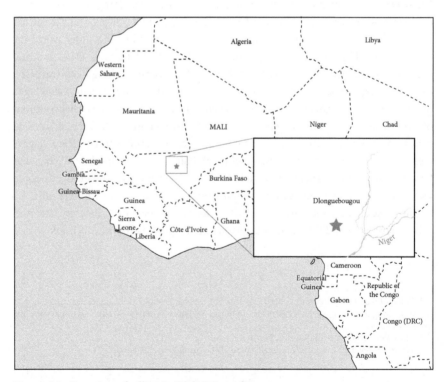

Figure 1.2. Location of village in Mali, West Africa

The village

Walking about the village today, mud walls shoulder-high knit together a series of compounds, containing flat-roofed mud dwellings, each with a thatched shady area at the front, where people seek shelter from the midday sun. If you walk through the entrance hall, or *blon*, into the open courtyard of the compound, you find donkeys tied up, sheep and goats tethered to posts astride a carpet of dung, and a collection of big wooden pestles and mortars for pounding grain. Washing is drying on the line; a calabash containing groundnuts is perched on a trestle; there are a couple of carts akimbo; large and small granaries stand on a stone base; chickens squawk; and dogs pant under the shade trees. A stack of wood is piled next to a mound of blackened metal pots and a three-stone hearth where women take turns to cook (see Figures 1.3 and 1.4). A trio of plastic kettles,[4] a couple of bicycles, a motorbike, and several solar panels complete the household inventory. In the early morning, one of the women will sweep the sandy ground, sprinkling it with water to keep down the dust, and collecting up the rubbish, which she throws onto the waste heap to be taken out to the fields later.

You can visit DBG by Google Earth today, and zoom in to view who has been building a new house, digging a well, or cutting a new field. But visiting DBG in

Figure 1.3. Big household granary stands in the courtyard, DBG, 2014

[4] Plastic, though highly dysfunctional for a kettle's original purpose, makes this the perfect vessel for the regular washing of hands and feet, before prayer.

Figure 1.4. The kitchen fire and pots, DBG, 2011

1980 was much more of an effort. When I first went there, it was a day's drive from the capital Bamako, the last 2 hours along a rutted, dirt track. Today you still bump along the dirt tracks, which snake their way across the landscape, but the road from Bamako to Ségou is greatly speeded up. And soon, a bridge across the River Niger at Ségou should cut the travel time further, opening up the North Bank of the river for 'development'.

In 1980, the village still bore many traces of the fortified settlement from precolonial times (see Figure 1.5), when continuous raiding and warfare brought the risk of being captured into slavery, and destruction of the village.[5] When I first visited DBG, its surrounding mud wall had lost much of its height and protective mantle, but there were still three main entry points leading you into the village, and the compounds huddled together closely.

Today the footprint of the settlement has multiplied fivefold, as can be seen from Figure 1.6. It is as though the tight fabric of mud-walled dwellings has unravelled into a looser weave of houses stretched out over what had been the fields closest to home. The villagers have lost their fear of raiding parties seeking plunder, and they want room to expand, to stake out their animals, and make a home to be proud of. This skein of new houses and compounds also symbolizes a shift from the tight structure of the Bambara household to a more fragmented scattering of the larger family, which is no longer contained by a single compound wall.

---

[5] DBG is similar to fortified settlements surveyed by Professor Kevin MacDonald and colleagues in the Ségou region. MacDonald, K.C. (2012).

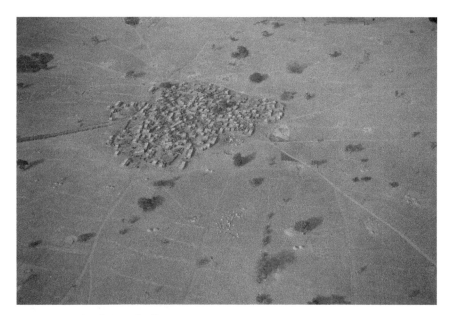

Figure 1.5. The clustered village in 1981

The settlement is surrounded by a wide ring of permanently cultivated land, known as the *soforo*,[6] stretching nearly a kilometre from the village, which receives whatever household waste and animal manure are available. On the edge of the settlement and scattered across the village fields are more than fifty wells, dug by individual households. Unlike many neighbouring villages, DBG is fortunate in having reliable ground water, some 20–30 m below the surface. To the west of the village, a group of mud buildings and plantation of neem trees, used for shade, make up the primary school, established in 2004. The maternity clinic built in 2008 lies to the north. A skeleton of posts and mats stands to accommodate traders who come for the market day each Wednesday. In the farming season, the village is surrounded by a thick wall of millet stalks, which hides the settlement until you are almost upon it. But in the dry season, the village is visible from afar, across a sandy-grey landscape, a few valued trees, such as shea, balanzan, tamarind, and baobab, providing splashes of green. Paths stretch out in all directions, leading to neighbouring villages, more distant bush fields, and the cattle camp. Originally walked on foot and horseback, they have become heavily rutted by bicycles and motorbikes, donkey-carts, and occasional lorries.

DBG is one of sixteen settlements in the commune of N'Koumandougou, the lowest level of government administration, which has its *Mairie* at Doura, a large

---

[6] 'House fields'.

Figure 1.6. Village of DBG in 1980 and 2016

Dlonguebougou in 2016

Village settlement in 1980

Roads and paths

Minor paths

Tree

Building with compound wall

Vegetable gardens

① Maternity clinic

② School rooms and shaded playground

③ Village square for dancing and festivals

④ Market stalls

⑤ Dasiri sacred grove

⑥ Euphorbia-lined track to channel sheep and goats out to graze village at the eastern edge of the commune.[7] With a total area of 2,040 km^2 and population of 16,000, this large, lightly settled commune forms part of the *cercle* and *région* of Ségou. Decentralized government was set up in 1999, when the first local elections for mayor and commune council were held, and development plans put in place, bringing tangible benefits to the villagers of DBG, such as a four-class primary school, a weekly market, and support for the maternity clinic. While initially sceptical of this new form of authority, villagers have engaged with local politics, and two men have been appointed to the commune council. Within the commune, the current *Maire* is a respected figure who is seen to act on behalf of the people in his charge, though people also recognize he has little power and even fewer resources. For safety's sake, he currently shuttles between Ségou and his office in Doura, because of threats made by jihadist groups to all government officials in this area. The Forest Agent was shot dead at his desk, in April 2016, by two masked men with an automatic weapon who sped through town on a motorbike; the *Maire's* brother was killed early one morning as he was guarding his field from cattle herds which might damage his crop, and his eldest son was attacked and injured, so he has justification for his anxiety.

The people

The founding of DBG

DBG was probably founded in the late seventeenth century. Three families claim to be first settlers of the village, the Dembélé, Toungara, and Traoré, the descendants of whom together make up 66 per cent of the village population today. They share a more-or-less common story of how they came to settle in this place. All three families had been living nearby, in a series of neighbouring hamlets. The Traoré family noticed that their big billy goat never needed to drink, despite being out all day, grazing with the herd. Puzzled by this, one day they attached a small sack to its neck, filled with ash and sand, and made a little hole from which the trail of cinders could leak. This showed them the way to a thicket of trees and bushes, in the middle of which they found a well brimming with water. Clearly, there had been a settlement there in former times. All three families agreed it would be a good place to move to, and they should work together to dig out the well. According to the Traoré and Toungara, the Dembélé, having a larger family, started work on redigging the well before the others were ready, and then claimed it as theirs. Some say this was a betrayal of their agreement as equals. But the

---

[7] Mali has ten regions, each of which is divided into four or five *cercles*, which are themselves divided into communes, of which there are more than 700 in Mali, averaging 20–25,000 people.

Box 1.1 The Dembélé clan: chiefs of DBG

Villagers can recount the names of all the village chiefs of DBG going back more than 150 years, but they cannot remember as far back as Dlonké. The earliest known chief was Boh Dembélé, who may have been chief when Mungo Park sought food and shelter in 1796 (see Box 2.1). After Boh came Murukuru, Negekoro, Dodugu, and Nene Dembélé who were chiefs during the nineteenth century. Babo Dembélé was chief of the village in the late nineteenth century when the French conquered Ségou and arrived in DBG to carry out the census, as described in Chapter 2. He was followed by BaSantigi; Binaba did 40 years; Sirke did only 3 years; Burama did 20 years; Baba did 13 years; and Dafé was chief for 9 years (from 1976 to 1984). Dafé was in post as *dugutigi* when I first visited the village in 1980, but he had become blind and never ventured from his courtyard. He was followed by Babo, who was chief for 16 years from 1984 to 1999, and then by Danson, the current titleholder, who has been village chief since 1999. His successor has been identified as Sirke Dembélé, who is the next-oldest man in the Dembélé clan (see Figure 1.7, and in the colour plates section).

Figure 1.7. Danson Dembélé, the village chief, and his deputy, Sirke Dembélé, 2014

Dembélé say it was obvious that they should be chief because their family was more numerous, so the other two families had to accept them taking the chief-tainship.[8] However, a sense of resentment occasionally surfaces amongst the Traoré and Toungara founding families that the Dembélé clan triumphed over them. Dlonké was head of the Dembélé family at that time, so the village was named after him.

The Dembélé are Bambara, part of the wider Mandé people, who came from further south, in the seventeenth century, and settled in the region of Ségou. The first famous Bambara king of Ségou was Biton Coulibaly, who came to power around 1710, and established a state based on warfare, trade, and farming (described further in Chapter 2). Traditionally, the Bambara followed a set of religious practices, built on recognizing the power of spirits associated with the land, and life forces, and the kingdom of Ségou was organized around many associated rituals, such as sacrifice of animals, magic-making, music, hunting, and drinking parties.[9] DBG has a sacred grove, or *dasiri*, on the edge of the village, where the spirits which protect the village live, and where annual sacrifices of chickens and grain used to be made (see Figure 1.8, colour plates section). In 1980, DBG also retained a powerful fetish cult, known as the *komo*, which was a secret society involving all men and circumcised boys in regular sacrificial offerings of

Figure 1.8. The village's sacred grove, or *dasiri*, 2016

---

[8] '*Dugutigiya*, meaning *chief of the soil or land*.   [9] Dieterlen, G. (1952).

chickens and grain. One of the Dembélé families had responsibility for acting as high priest, and managing the ceremonies associated with the *komo*. When I was first in DBG, the *komo* was brought out in the darkness of moonless nights, and all initiated men gathered to perform their rituals. Women (myself included), children, and non-initiates such as visiting herders were to stay hidden, since the *komo* could exact revenge from those who transgressed the rules. The *komo* was abandoned about 20 years ago, when the villagers decided to become Moslem and build a mosque (see Figure 1.9). However, there remains some joking between more- and less-devout families about the fetish objects. Some question whether they have indeed been destroyed, or instead have been hidden to be unearthed and reinstalled in future. One elderly man who had been a central figure in the fetish cult says someone must have put strong 'medicine' into the water supply to persuade all the villagers to become Moslems and abandon their powerful *komo*.

The second founding family, the Toungara clan, claim their roots in the ancient West African kingdom of Ghana, the decline of which in the late eleventh century unleashed across the region a wave of migrants, known as Marka, or Soninké (see Chapter 2 for more details). The Marka were early converts to Islam and were known for their religious learning. It is said that two Toungara brothers came to settle the area near DBG, probably in the eighteenth century, though it is not clear where they had been in the several centuries between the fall of Ghana and their

Figure 1.9. The villagers built a mosque in 1998 and abandoned their traditional religion, 2011

arrival in this region.[10] The first Toungara brother stopped at Sagalaba some 30 km to the north of DBG, and the second came to settle close to the Dembélé and Traoré (see Figure 1.10). Their Moslem roots blended with the traditional Bambara religion, and leading members of the Toungara family were amongst the most active members of the DBG hunters' society, with its special knowledge of magic and divining, which is essential for success in tracking and killing wild animals. The Toungara are also renowned for knowing how to make a special medicine from leaves, which protects you from lightning strikes.

The third founding family, the Traoré, are Bambara, like the Dembélé, and they also came up from the south. It is said that they were given a horse to look after by one of the Kings of Ségou, and they took it to graze on the rich pastures north of the River Niger. A rival family, seeking to do harm to the Traoré, seized the horse, and took it away. Fearing the wrath of the Ségou king (*fama*), whose valuable war-horse had now disappeared, the Traoré family fled north to look for a hiding place. The Dembélé of DBG hid them in a large baobab tree, providing them with food and water, and protecting them from the royal search party. Once the danger was passed, the Traoré settled in the area. As a clan, the Traoré family is said to have special powers over the earth spirits, and they are guardians of the *dasiri*.[11]

Over the 300 years DBG has been here, other families have come to join the Dembélé, Toungara, and Traoré. The Samaké came from Misribougou some 10 km away, since they needed to find shelter when conflict and raiding were at their height in the mid-nineteenth century. Once the colonial conquest established peace at the end of the nineteenth century, most of the Samaké family returned to live in Misribougou. Another Dembélé family arrived in the 1880s, having fled from neighbouring Markabougou 15 km away, when the powerful warlord N'To Diarra conquered the village. The Tangara family also came in the late nineteenth century, and they are usually known by their epithet Kangokow, meaning people of Kango—a village 30 km to the east, which had been attacked and ruined. Several families are descendants of slaves formerly attached to the founding clans. One of these families has achieved great economic success, through the hard work of three brothers, and they now constitute one of the wealthiest households in the village. Other people have settled more recently, such as MS, who had been a domestic slave in a Maure herding camp. He abandoned his former masters in the early 1960s and settled as a farmer and petty trader in DBG. Since 1980, several more families have arrived to settle in the village, including five teachers with the opening of the school, and a couple of traders.

Everybody knows their family background much better than we do in Western society, where it is a struggle for people to name their great-grandparents. In DBG, family history matters because it defines the family's status and shapes relations

---

[10] McIntosh (1998) claims the Toungara clan likely controlled the Méma kingdom, centred 150 km north of Ségou, a small successor state to the Ghana Empire, as described in Chapter 2.

[11] Bazin, J. (1975, 1988).

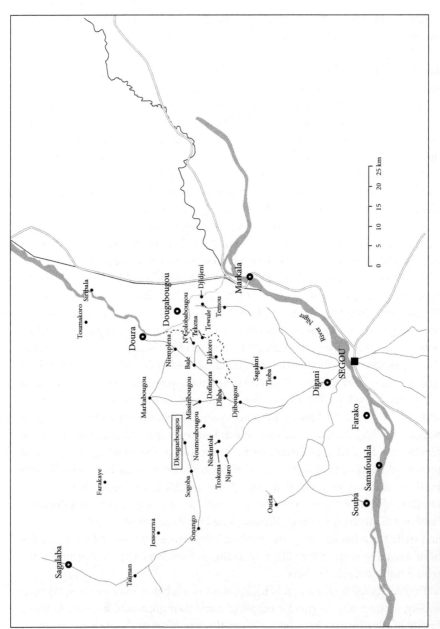

Figure 1.10. DBG in its wider landscape

with others in this and neighbouring villages. The first settlers of the village continue to have greater power in village decision-making. Bambara society operates a combination of both hierarchy and egalitarian mechanisms, which vie with each other, according to context.[12] Thus, for example, every household head is deemed equal in theory and should attend the regular meetings of village heads (*gwatigi wele*), but in practice, the founding households continue to exert the greatest weight when decisions must be made. Equally, each man and woman is member of a peer group (*ton*) made up of those of the same age, amongst whom there is friendship and equality, regardless of the family from which they come. But each age group still recognizes the power and authority exercised by those above them, and the respect that is their due from those below them.

Social organization, slavery, nobility, and clans

DBG is described by its population as a settlement of free, noble peoples, known as *horondugu*. But as will be seen from Mungo Park's account of travelling through this region in 1796 (in Box 2.1), slavery was widespread at that time, with *captifs* used for domestic labour and for farming.[13] In 1905, the French colonial administration, while not abolishing slavery, outlawed new enslavement throughout the Soudan, as present-day Mali was known. This led to a large outflow of *captifs* who seized the chance to claim their freedom. The 1904 census estimated the population of Ségou Cercle to be 160,000 (as compared to 700,000 today), of which 25,000 were described as *captifs* representing 15 per cent of the overall population. In the case of DBG, the census for 1904 gave a tally of 400 people, of which 135 were described as *captifs*, equivalent to 34 per cent of the population.[14] People today are unwilling to identify who came from slave origins, and what happened to the people their family used to own. In many cases, slaves moved away immediately after the decree of 1905, though often only to a neighbouring village. Others stayed behind, preferring familiar territory to setting off to find their ancestors' distant home. Today, people recognize that the time of slavery is past, and they should not be talking about slave status anymore, yet a legacy remains, as can be seen in choice of families and villages with whom marriage alliances are made. When we first came to DBG in 1980 and asked to visit each family to conduct a census and understand who was who, we were led on a sequence of visits which provided a clear social map of the power and status of different families. The first family to be visited was that of the village chief, while the last few on the list included the households of former slaves, an illegitimate man, and a very poor man who had suffered a series of misfortunes.

---

[12] Bazin, J. (1970); Lewis, J. vd (1978).   [13] Known as *jon*.
[14] Meillassoux, C. (1991) confirms that domestic slavery was widespread and pervasive in much of West Africa.

Bambara society is made up of large clans from which people take their family name, or *jamu*, which represents a very important marker of identity. There are joking relationships between certain clans, known as *senankunya*, which means that the Dembélé clan must castigate the Diarra, calling them small boys, or slaves, and complaining that they are worthless creatures who will steal away at dead of night to eat beans. The Diarra are obliged to return the compliment in good measure. The Tangara insult the Keita, and the Toungara the Diallo, Bouaré, and Fofana. It is sometimes surprising to hear a tirade of abuse as people from different clans exchange elaborate insults, especially when it involves people in very different positions in life haranguing each other. Verbal repartee and a good sense of humour are highly prized personal qualities, and taking part in this exchange of insults is an essential part of social belonging. It took some time to understand why eating beans was such an insult, but it is because though delicious and everyone wants to eat them, they generate flatulence.

Other residents and visitors

Bambara society has several casted groups—blacksmiths, leatherworkers, and potters (collectively called *nyamakalaw*)—people who have specialist knowledge about the powerful forces which sustain, as well as harm, life. They only marry within their caste, and many of the family names are specific to their profession. Iron working by blacksmiths began more than 2,000 years ago, and it has been vital for both military supplies and farming tools. Blacksmiths today remain vital to much of the rural economy, fixing ploughs and carts, hoes, and rifles (see Figure 1.11, colour plates section). While iron bars are now purchased from the market in town, in the past, blacksmiths smelted ore in large furnaces, the remains of which can be found scattered in the landscape. This large-scale collective firing of iron-ore must have consumed large amounts of charcoal, and would have led to significant deforestation.[15] In 1981, I listened to an elderly blacksmith Niangoro Coulibaly from Dlaba describe how, as a young boy in the 1920s, he had taken part, with dozens of other blacksmiths, in one of the last great iron-smelting parties. This must have represented a huge collective effort, drawing in blacksmiths and their families from across a wide stretch of countryside.

Other people living in and around DBG are the Peul, who used to be hired by the villagers to look after their livestock.[16] There have been Peul living in and around the village for many generations, and more than 100 Peul are registered as resident in DBG for tax purposes. Known as *foroba flaw*, these long-standing residents were settled in this region by the Kings of Ségou to look after the royal cattle herds. However, relations between the Bambara villagers and Peul have

---

[15] Haaland, R. (1980).

[16] More commonly known as *Fulani* in English, they name themselves the *Pulaar*, or *FulBe*.

Figure 1.11. Blacksmiths retain great importance for making and mending farm machinery, 2009

deteriorated since 1980, and now only two of the village households employ them as herders because they are suspected of over-milking the cows and selling animals secretly, while claiming they have been lost in the bush. There are very few marriages between Peul and Bambara, with only two apparent in the DBG record, both more than eighty years ago. Visiting Peul herders also come for several months of the dry season, seeking grazing and water, having often trekked their animals more than 100 km. Some herds are accompanied by a herder and his family, while increasing numbers are in the care of a hired herder, usually a young man in the pay of a military man, public official, or trader who owns a large herd.[17] Problems between Bambara and Peul are mainly with these visiting trans-humant herds and the damage they can cause to fields before harvest, if cattle are carelessly managed. In a recent dispute, the villagers of DBG were accused of stealing six cattle and selling them in Touba market, and the Tribunal at Markala demanded the presence of someone from the village to answer the charges. The villagers denied any knowledge of the animals, and the charges were subsequently dropped. To justify the poor relations between them, the Bambara often refer to a saying that 'if you let a Peul settle in your village, sooner or later he will become chief'.

In 1980, there were three Maure families who regularly visited DBG for several months of the dry season, pitching their elegant black goat-hair tents on the village

---

[17]   Turner, M. (2009).

Figure 1.12. Tents of visiting Maure herders camp on the village fields, dry season, 1981

fields of the well owner, exchanging the manure of their cattle, sheep, and goats for water. They were *haratin* Maures, of African origin, who had been captured by the Maures in the distant past, but escaped captivity in the early twentieth century. The colonial administration reported their presence on the North Bank of the River Niger from 1909 onwards, cutting down trees and getting into conflict with the Bambara (see Figure 1.12). However, in general, the Bambara of DBG welcomed the Maures as regular visitors, bringing plenty of dung from their flocks of sheep and goats, willing to sell a young ox for ploughing, often to be found in the village shops buying tea and sugar, and purchasing grain to ship back further north. Each year in June, they would pack up their tents, load their camels, and go further north to farm in the rainy season, returning to DBG once the harvest was finished. Very few Maures come now to DBG for the dry season because they have found a place to dig a well and settle 40 km to the north. They no longer need to water their herds in DBG, and can therefore use their flocks to manure their own millet fields instead.

My first visit to DBG

I first came to DBG in late April 1980, with Duncan Fulton, an anthropologist, to look for a good site for us to settle for 2 years of fieldwork. We had taken advice from the *Pères blancs* missionaries in Niono, who knew many of the villages in the region, but had long ago given up on the idea of leading the population to Jesus.

They recommended three possible sites—Markabougou, Dofinena, and DBG. First, we passed by the canton headquarters at Doura,[18] a large village on the edge of the canal, which had acquired a few administrative buildings. We paid our respects to the *chef d'Arrondissement*, who received us in the shade of his house, and he pointed to the courtyard in which several dejected old men were sitting on the ground in the blazing sun. 'I called all the village chiefs to come, to remind them they need to pay their taxes and fulfil their grain quota.' They had been there for 5 days, sitting in the heat of the sun, a most discourteous way to behave towards old men, who would normally be given a chair and a drink of water in the coolth of a shady tree. This way of demonstrating power and getting taxes paid mirrored the colonial approach.[19] Having told him of our mission, he allowed us to liberate the village chiefs so they could return home, and we could deliver them by car, one by one on our route. Travelling first to Dofinena, we found a warm welcome, but high levels of guinea worm and very serious shortages of water. In Markabougou, by the late dry season, people were drawing drinking water from a murky pond at the edge of the village. By contrast, DBG had more than twenty wells still operating in late April, and the chief and his council said they would be happy to build us a house. So, in May 1980, we settled there for 2 years with three research assistants: Sidiki Diarra, Karounga Coulibaly, and Baba Konaté. Sidiki's wife Bintu Coulibaly did the cooking for our household.

Our study of DBG was one of several carried out across the Sahel, led by Jeremy Swift for the Centre International Pour l'Elevage en Afrique (CIPEA).[20] The purpose was to describe the range of crop-livestock systems, societies, economies, and relationships between herding and farming peoples in this wide belt of semi-arid land which lies between the desert and savannah. Other studies were carried out by Ced Hesse and Adam Thiam on the Peul in the Gourma region of Eastern Mali, and by Cindy White amongst the WodaaBe nomads of Central Niger.[21] DBG was at the sedentary end of the spectrum from settled crop farmers to nomadic herders. Carrying out research for a full 2 years and covering two complete cropping cycles allowed us to capture a degree of variability in rainfall from year to year, and the associated variation in patterns of farming, and crop yields. Fortunately, for the study, there was indeed a significant difference in rainfall amounts and timing between 1980 and 1981, which allowed us to describe this interannual variability in the performance of different crops.[22] Two years of household data, rather than one, also gave a deeper understanding of how people organize themselves, though it was obviously not possible to pick up on significant trends over such a short period.

---

[18] *Chef-lieu d'Arrondissement*.   [19] Described so well by Amadou Hampaté Bâ (1994).
[20] Jeremy Swift was based at the Institute of Development Studies (IDS), University of Sussex, and he worked for the Centre International Pour l'Elevage en Afrique (CIPEA), now merged with ILRAD to form the International Livestock Research Institute (ILRI), based in Nairobi, Kenya.
[21] Swift, J.J. (Ed.) (1984).   [22] Fulton, D. and Toulmin, C. (1982).

Figure 1.13. The author with car in 1981

Operating under the aegis of CIPEA meant we had a car, and four research assistants, three of whom lived in DBG, with a fourth in the village of Dofinena, 20 km to the south (see Figure 1.13). Several CIPEA colleagues made occasional visits: ecologists Mohammed Cissé and Pierre Hiernaux to explore fallows and regeneration of trees and shrubs, animal scientist Trevor Wilson to survey the structure and productivity of livestock herds, Adama Traoré and Samba Soumaré to study work-oxen performance, and agronomist Pierre Gossèye to test out new varieties of cowpea and millet.[23] Mark Haywood's aerial survey in 1978 of the area to the north and east provided an assessment of how vegetation and soils had degraded since the wetter years of the 1950s and 60s.[24]

Sara Randall from the London School of Hygiene and Tropical Medicine undertook a large-scale demographic survey in 1981, which included DBG and Dofinena, and which provided a valuable baseline for many villages in the neighbourhood.[25] Including a history of births for all married women, it showed very high levels of infant mortality, with more than 40 per cent of children dying before the age of 5 years. Mary Martin, from the London School of Hygiene and Tropical Medicine, was resident in DBG in 1983 and carried out a nutritional study to compare access to food between different households in DBG and between DBG and Dofinena.[26]

---

[23] Summary results published in Wilson, R.T. et al (Eds.) (1983); Traoré, A. and Soumaré, S. (1984).
[24] Haywood, M. (1981).   [25] Randall, C. (1984).   [26] Martin, M. (1984).

Our 2 years of fieldwork in 1980–1982 fell between the big Sahel droughts of 1973–1974 and 1984–1985. The first of these two droughts had caught people unprepared, after 2 decades of wetter conditions, and they led to an estimated 100,000 human deaths and loss of a quarter of the Sahel's livestock. In the 1980s, people were better prepared; governments and aid agencies made emergency supplies available; and pastoral nomads moved south earlier to seek grazing, hence limiting animal losses. After these two major droughts, a number of agencies drew-up plans for large-scale resettlement of people from the Sahel to better-watered lands further south, given the prospect of the Sahel becoming less and less able to support its population. Millions of Sahelians did not wait for these plans to be carried out, and moved themselves. By the end of the 1990s, it is estimated that 5 million people had left their homes in Burkina Faso and Mali, settling in Côte d'Ivoire, often setting-up as sharecroppers in the coastal forest-lands to grow coffee and cocoa. Following civil war in Côte d'Ivoire and rising xenophobia, some have returned to Burkina Faso and Mali, but many have stayed there. While a number of men from DBG have spent time on migration to Côte d'Ivoire, only one has settled there definitively.

Subsequent visits to DBG

I have made many visits to DBG since we left in 1982. I came on a short visit in October 1984, when it was clear that the harvest had failed. Old Bina said, 'I never thought to see a time when a man who wants to harvest his crop must walk about the field in search of a single millet spear worth gathering.' I found many people had already left the village and were seeking their fortune in neighbouring settlements where the harvest had been better, or had left for town. Curiously, even in such a dry year, the village of Djibougou 15 km to the south of DBG had been inundated with rain, and I found many people from DBG there helping with the harvest. There had been so much rain in Djibougou, our vehicle got stuck in the mud, and we needed a lot of help to dig it out.

When I came back again in 1988, it had rained heavily across the region. In an article for the *New Scientist*, I wrote:

the villagers are out in the bush looking for grass to weave the granaries they will need to store this year's spectacular millet harvest. It is many years since they had to build granaries of such size. But they work joyfully as the crop ripens in the field, a thick green forest of millet stalks, golden heads heavy with grain nodding as you pass.[27]

[27] Toulmin, C. (1988).

The rain had been so heavy—more than 100 mm in 48 hours—that it had led to the collapse of houses and a couple of mosques in neighbouring towns. On this visit, I was 7-months pregnant with my third child, and everyone in DBG was pleased to see this fruitfulness and that I had understood, at last, that for women the bearing of children is the serious business of life.

In 1997, I managed to get a research project in DBG, with Karen Brock based there, working with my former research assistant Sidiki Diarra.[28] Karen studied how livelihood opportunities differed by household depending on access to resources, and a range of factors, such as age, gender, ethnicity, and wealth. I visited DBG twice while Karen was there, to provide support and help gather data. Her findings confirmed the continuing importance of community structures in pooling risk, mobilizing resources, and managing access to land and water. She also showed the great significance of migration revenues in enabling farm households to invest in assets and increase farm productivity.[29]

In 2006, I returned with my younger son, then 17 years old, to spend a few days in Mali and introduce him to DBG. He was a huge hit, particularly with the village children, who followed him everywhere. A day's visit in June 2008 coincided with building of the maternity clinic, which we had helped fund (see Figure 1.14, colour plates section). And in October 2009, I came back again with my daughter,

Figure 1.14. Construction of the maternity clinic, June 2008

---

[28] Led by the Institute of Development Studies (IDS) University of Sussex and funded by the UK's DFID. Sustainable Rural Livelihoods in Ethiopia, Mali, and Zimbabwe.
[29] Brock, K. and Coulibaly, N. (1999).

Figure 1.15. A group of young boys recently circumcised, February 2011

a trained blacksmith. We spent a busy day in the local blacksmiths' village Noumoubougou, where they demonstrated their skills, from making axes and hoes, to sharpening blades, and fixing carts. The highlight of the afternoon was production of a miniature plough, with yoke. They said, 'it's too small for oxen, donkeys, or goats but perfect for rabbits.' A visit in February 2011 coincided by chance with the first big circumcision ceremony for some years, involving 125 boys, and gathering hundreds of DBG's friends and neighbours from across the country (see Figure 1.15). And in June 2014, I passed a few days in the village at the start of the rains, encountering a turbulent dust storm.

These short visits allowed me to keep in touch with the people of DBG and get a sense of how things had been changing. But they also created a sense of frustration because I never had long enough to understand and document the changes underway. In 2015, having stood down from my job as Director of the International Institute for Environment and Development (IIED), I won a research fellowship from the Open Society Foundation to allow me to return to DBG and do a more systematic study of changes since 1980–1982. Supplementary funding from the Binks Family Trust, Edinburgh, made it possible to carry out the full study for 2 years from April 2016, and to work with my former research assistant Sidiki Diarra.

Each time I come back to DBG, I look forward to seeing friends and finding out the latest news, but this anticipation is always mixed with unease because I know that there will be fewer of my old neighbours alive, even if the ranks of younger folk will have hugely increased. As you near the village and get onto the track which cuts through the bush fields, you catch sight of figures in the distance bent over a hoe or with axe in hand chopping away at the bushes and shrubs. When you reach the edge of the village fields, you can see the village nestling in the curve of the land, surrounded by fields shaded by trees. A line of palms stands on the skyline. Vehicles being still infrequent today, by the time the car has reached the first houses, a welcoming party of small children will have gathered, accompanied by a noisy phalanx of barking dogs.

On arrival, it is essential to go and visit the village chief. Today, Danson Dembélé is a sprightly old man who makes a bit of money from trading in kola nuts. His hands have been crippled since birth, so he was never a great hunter or farmer. As a boy, he was sent away to the school for the sons of chiefs set up in Markala, 50 km away. His family chose him to go because they could afford to lose his labour, as he was never going to be much use in the fields. But despite this infirmity, he has managed to maintain a measure of authority as both village chief and head of the largest household in the village, which is now 185-people strong. When I arrive, he will be sitting in his *blon*, the cool shady hallway to his compound, twisting strips of plastic unravelled from an old sack to make a rope, with two or three other men at close call. He is not at all happy about the way that village life has evolved (see Box 1.2). He tells me:

> There used to be 5 or 6 big wooden platforms around the village under the shade of the fig trees, where men would pass long hours in the dry season talking about the big and small things of life. But now they have all fallen into disrepair. No-one goes there anymore. People sit at home, and whenever people talk its only about shops, and arguments, there's no serious talk left. Everyone is disagreeing and talking behind other people's backs. Young people don't respect their elders—*u te fa don, u te ba don*.[30]

Box 1.2 Clothing: what do people wear and how has it changed?

In 1980, homespun cotton cloth (*fini-mugu*) was prevalent, although some second-hand clothing had crept in. Women wore brightly coloured machine-made cotton or an indigo blue cloth worn as a wrapper or skirt, known as *taafi-fin*. Newly married women and those with a newborn would wear this dark-coloured cloth, and were often naked above the waist, especially when feeding an infant. A new wrapper would call forth benedictions from family and neighbours—*k'i kene ka fara*—meaning 'may you be healthy when it wears out'. A short blouse and a headscarf completed the outfit. Young boys wore

---

[30] 'They don't know their father, they don't know their mother', meaning they are without any bearings.

homespun cotton shorts midthigh, with a drawstring, whereas young men graduated to a longer pair of shorts down to the knee or pair of trousers, once they had gone through the circumcision ceremony. During the day, men wore knee-length shorts and a long shirt, the latter with a pocket in the front to hold money, keys, and a snuff barrel. A great variety of bonnets was worn by men, usually of different colours and patterns. When I looked inside these woolly hats, I saw they were described as ski-bonnets, manufactured in Europe, but serving here to protect the head from hot sun and wind. When we first came to DBG, and before I had begun to recognize many people, I would distinguish who was who by the particular bonnet they wore. On washing day, however, confusion crept in, as men would appear in unfamiliar headgear. In the evening, having washed, men wore a long white cotton gown to walk about the village, and engage in conversation. Plastic shoes and flip-flops made out of old tyres were and still are the commonest footwear. People wear metal bracelets, leather amulets, and beads round the neck.

Today, homespun cotton is much less common. Some older men still wear it for the evening and for festivals, but most have abandoned it. 'It's too hot, we want something which is much lighter and less expensive,' they explain. And no one is spinning and weaving cotton in the village anymore. Women have several wrappers of brightly coloured cloth, and married women from the same household are often seen with matching outfits for marriages and festivals. Girls and women wear a variety of blouses, and it is very rare to see any woman bare-breasted. Women have adopted long dresses to below the knee for evening-wear, shrouded by a multitude of scarves and shawls. Their hair is now plaited elaborately, with beads and coloured thread. Men have also abandoned *fini-mugu* in favour of coloured cotton fabrics, there are now twenty-six sewing machines in the village, and new outfits can be run-up quickly. Second-hand clothing is widespread, bought in the market and from traders visiting the village. Kids run around in T-shirts with improbable slogans, celebrating Obama or Bob Marley. For smart occasions, young men don baggy low-cut jeans, and look just like their counterparts on a street in Brooklyn, Beijing, Berlin, or Buenos Aires. Hunters have maintained the traditional cotton for their outfits, which are dyed a deep ochre, and hung with traditional talismans for protection.

Danson's view of how life has changed in the village is not just an old man's complaint, but is echoed by many others, who regret the loss of collective activity and commitment. The growth in individual interests, while celebrated by some, has had big impacts on how people organize themselves within the village and in their own households, as will be described in more detail in Chapters 4, 5, and 6.[31]

---

[31] Such growth in individualism is not only found in farming societies, but also amongst Peul herding society, such as described by Turner, M. (2009).

This research study

Thirty-five years is a long time. As one old man in DBG said '*Bi te*', literally 'today not', and meaning 'that was then and this is now'. Things have changed a lot since 1980. All the women and men who were elders in 1980 are now dead, and today, my generation are white-haired, a bit stooped, and knee-deep in grandchildren. And there are a vast number of young women, and youths who were born long after we had left in 1982.

I have been interested to document the changes that have affected people's daily life, the farming system, rainfall, ideas, and well-being, describing 'the continuities between present and past which shape the character and possibilities of people's lives'.[32] In my doctoral thesis, I looked at how people cope with high levels of uncertainty linked to rainfall, disease, and demography.[33] I recorded that most villagers lived in large domestic groups, with households made up of thirty, forty, and sometimes more than fifty people led by a single household head, and sharing a common field and granary. I argued that these large groups represented a valuable means to spread risks and ensure the survival of individuals and the group. So I was keen to see how well different households had performed over the 35-year period. Who had done well, or badly, since 1982 and why? Have there been some remarkable reversals of fortune, and what might we learn from this? I was also keen to understand how broader global trends have affected DBG and the surrounding area. Have there been major shifts in ideas and aspirations? In terms of farming, it was clear in 1982 that the boom in well digging could lead them into trouble, given limits on grazing around the settlement.[34] And I wondered how the villagers could exercise control over their large land reserve, given growing pressures on this increasingly scarce resource.

I had intended at the start of my fellowship in 2016 to spend significant amounts of time in DBG, walking the fields and bush and having many opportunities to sit, listen, discuss, and question people in the village and surrounding area. I was much looking forward to this and had been brushing up my Bambara language skills. However, following the political crisis in Mali—the coup d'état of 2012, and subsequent invasion of the north by Tuareg rebels, French military intervention in 2013, and growing conflict—the security situation deteriorated in the centre of the country, with much of the country painted red by the UK and other Western governments. The entire North Bank region has been considered unsafe; hence, DBG has been out of bounds for the last 3 years. During this time, I have made a few visits to the village, but each of short duration. Instead, I have relied on my

---

[32] Moore, H. (2018).

[33] Toulmin, C. *Changing patterns of investment in a Sahelian community*. DPhil thesis (1987) Faculty of Social Studies, University of Oxford. Published by OUP as 'Cattle, women and wells: managing household survival in the Sahel' (1992).

[34] Toulmin, C. (1992) p. 280.

Figure 1.16. My research assistant Sidiki Diarra, 2014

long-standing research assistant, Sidiki Diarra, who has provided great continuity and commitment to understanding life in this small mud village (see Figure 1.16). Makono Dembélé, one of the DBG villagers, has also been a major contributor to the study, by collecting data, plotting who is farming which field, managing the survey of people and households, keeping me up to date with sales of sesame, and monitoring the rain gauge. During my visits to Mali, if I could not get to the village because of insecurity, Makono has come down to Ségou, in order to spend a few days with Sidiki and myself.

I have asked myself in what way my own regular connection with DBG has affected the village. Is it a different place because Duncan Fulton and I spent 2 years there in 1980–1982, and in what way? Living there, it was impossible not to step in when people needed help, such as providing medicine to a sick child, or rushing a woman to hospital. My husband, Mark, helped fund the maternity clinic built in 2008, which has helped reduce infant deaths, and during her time living in DBG, Karen Brock encouraged them to register their Village Association. My nephew Myles Macinnes supported the process of drafting a local management agreement over the land and natural resources in the commune (known as a *Convention Locale*). All of these small interventions have brought some benefits to the village. Being an assertive village, with a lot going on, maybe the greatest impact I have had is in affirming their confidence in themselves. Having their very own *tubabumuso* (white woman) who comes to visit makes no difference in terms of how households make ends meet, but it gives them a certain status vis-à-vis their neighbours and the *Maire*.

Longitudinal studies: methods and reflections

In planning my research and shaping the findings, I have benefitted greatly from the insights generated by a number of research studies which document long-term social and economic change. These longitudinal studies share a common interest in mapping out how life has treated a particular place and people, and they recognize the limits to one-off surveys, which can only provide a snapshot of the complex, interwoven fabric of life. Coming from varied disciplines, they ask how internal and external factors have shaped the lives of people today, who has prospered, and who has done badly? Some seek to challenge received wisdom about environmental degradation, and they demonstrate a more positive picture of agricultural growth and intensification than those who see local farmers as responsible for large-scale land degradation and 'desertification'.[35] These longitudinal studies range from the very detailed socioeconomic surveys undertaken over 7 decades in Palanpur, India, to social and geographical histories of West Africa.[36] The innovative approach taken by Tiffen, Mortimore, and Gichuki provides many lessons for interpreting environmental, economic, and social change through use of aerial photos and other sources of data, whereas Fairhead and Leach confirm the centrality of local knowledge and practice in interpreting landscape change.[37] Anthropological work studying intergenerational change by Moser in urban Ecuador, Whitehead in northern Ghana, and Mushongah and Scoones in Zimbabwe all point to the central role played by family structures in helping people prosper and cope with high levels of uncertainty.[38] Brockington's recent studies have brought a new set of insights about who is doing well in rural Tanzania, and they show the appetite of smallholder farmers to gain access to markets and try new crops and activities, even in settlements far away from major roads.[39] Hudson's simple narrative of his relationship with people in a Southern Mauritanian village shows the strength of friendships over time and distance, whereas Jackson uses his revisit to Sierra Leone to ask searching questions about what constitutes well-being for people with few material assets.[40] Guyer's longitudinal study of Yoruba farming communities around Ibadan in Southwest Nigeria demonstrates the big increase in population, urbanization, and market growth and the vibrancy of livelihood diversification in much of West Africa.[41] All of these and other studies show the importance of mixing methods, crosschecking

---

[35] Mortimore, M. et al (2001); Leach, M. and Mearns, R. (1996).
[36] Tiffen, M. (1976); Bliss, C. and Stern, N. (1982); Lanjouw, P. and Stern, N. (1998); Himanshu, Lanjouw, P. and Stern, N. (2018). Hill, P. (1972, 1977); Berry, S. (1993); Mortimore, M. (1989, 2009); Batterbury S. (2001); Mushongah, J. and Scoones, I. (2012); Hudson, P. (2015).
[37] Tiffen, M. et al (1994); Fairhead, J. and Leach, M. (1998).
[38] Moser, C (2009); Whitehead, A. (2006).
[39] Brockington, D. and Noe, C. (OUP forthcoming).   [40] Jackson, M. (2011)
[41] Guyer, J. (1997).

assumptions, and being open to new interpretations. In addition, these longitudinal studies all demonstrate clearly the power and agency of 'ordinary farmers' in often uncertain, risky conditions, yet taking advantage of new opportunities and seeking multiple ways to improve their lives.

In the case of DBG, the original fieldwork in 1980–1982 involved 2 years' continuous residence in the village and support from three research assistants, who visited each household and field every 2 to 3 days. Living in the village meant we could pursue inconsistencies and sensitive topics more easily. During her research on sustainable livelihoods, Karen Brock was resident for much of the time and able to collect data on agricultural and income for selected households over 18 months. When I began my study in April 2016, I had to limit myself to short visits to the village and adapt my data collection to tasks which my assistant Sidiki Diarra could complete with help from Makono Dembélé and several of the schoolteachers. We therefore focused on a survey of people in all households (as described in Chapter 5), measurement of millet harvests (Chapter 3), identifying field areas by cultivating group (Chapter 4), a survey of assets held at the household and individual level (Chapter 6), and interpretation of aerial photos and satellite images, to understand patterns of land use change (Chapter 4). We recorded and transcribed a series of interviews in 2011, 2014, and 2016–2019 in the village of DBG, in neighbouring settlements, and in Bamako.[42] And I passed several days in the colonial archives in Bamako, leafing through the many folders of political, economic, and military reports for the Ségou region and *cercle*.

This combination of methods and materials tells the story of a village which is proud of its past as a strong, respected traditional Bambara settlement, and of its recent success in growing crops, investing in new technology, and becoming one of the largest villages in the commune. However, many of the factors which enabled DBG to prosper in the past are now running into difficulty, as will be described in the following chapters.

Structure of the book

Having introduced the village and its people in Chapter 1, I have structured the rest of the book as follows. Chapter 2 presents a history of the region from early times, as well as how shifts in climate have shaped patterns of settlement and empire. Chapter 3 describes the ecology, rainfall, crops, and farming system. Chapter 4 examines how the people of DBG have moved from a position of land abundance to scarcity in the space of 25 years because of a combination of population growth and, above all, the installation of a large sugar cane plantation

---

[42] Apart from Makono Dembélé and the village chief Danson Dembélé, I have not referred to people by name, to assure a degree of anonymity in discussions which occasionally touch on sensitive topics.

30 km away, which has evicted hundreds of farming families. Chapter 5 presents demographic data which show the tripling of the village population over the last 35 years, and the continued growth and strength of very large domestic groups. Chapter 6 examines the range of different investments made by households in DBG, the timing of these booms, and how such assets are distributed between domestic groups. Migration away from the village is the subject of Chapter 7, covering both the regular seasonal pattern of time spent earning money to bring back, and those who have definitively left the village behind. Finally, Chapter 8 considers major challenges which face DBG today, such as further extension of the irrigation zone, the Daouna pastoral project, the implications of the new Land Law (*Loi Foncier Agricole*), and how the establishment of decentralized government is affecting the rights and powers of villages like DBG. This chapter also reflects on the broader effects of development aid, and what if any impacts the 'development business' has had on the life and economic growth of a village like DBG.

2

History of Dlonguébougou
and the wider region

Ka fajiri jirana, kan kelen kelen wuli.[1]

Introduction

The rolling landscape around Dlonguébougou (DBG) is made up of sandy hollows
and plains, derived from dunes laid down during the last Ice Age, when the
Sahara Desert was much larger than it is today. This long dry period lasted until
around 12,000 years ago and was followed by much wetter conditions with retreat
of the Ice Age, and a transformation of the West African landscape. Heavy rainfall
created a green Sahara, with forest and grasslands offering fertile territory to
the many people and animals settling in the area. Cave paintings in the Hoggar
mountains in the central Sahara of hunters pursuing antelope testify to the wealth
of wildlife—giraffe, rhino, and elephant.[2] The marks of a much wetter period are
very evident when you fly over the Sahara, as an extensive skein of old river
valleys and huge lake basins are clearly visible from the sky. An abrupt change to
the climate 5,000 years ago brought in more unstable conditions which have led
sometimes to wetter intervals but mainly to long drier periods. People retreated
southwards bit by bit, from what is now the Sahara, as the lakes and rivers which
had supported them dried up.

Archaeological finds from 3,000 to 5,000 years ago include the remains of wild
animals, fish bones, and domesticated livestock at settlement sites found on the
banks of old lakes and rivers, which cut across what is now the southern Sahara
and Sahel.[3] As conditions became yet drier, and the great lakes shrank to nothing,
patterns of agriculture started to develop; fonio and millet grains were harvested
and cooked; and the beginnings of iron working become visible. The pattern of
settlement on this southern Saharan fringe presents a mosaic of peoples and
livelihoods, with fisherfolk, pastoral herders, and cereal farmers each finding

---

[1] The benedictions at the end of the evening, when people go off to sleep: 'May dawn be shown to
us, may we rise one by one.' The second of these refers to the hope that there will be no sudden alarm,
such as a raiding attack, which brings everyone out of bed in an instant.

[2] Hugot, H.-J. (1974).   [3] McIntosh, R.J. (1998); Raimbault, M. and Sanogo, K. (1991).

Land, Investment and Migration. Camilla Toulmin, Oxford University Press (2020). © Camilla Toulmin.
DOI: 10.1093/oso/9780198852766.001.0001

their ecological niche, and mirroring the specialisms found today.[4] Major swings in rainfall patterns have led to big shifts in people and polities across the region. The period 300 BC to 300 AD was particularly dry, but was followed by conditions that were more humid, until around 1100 AD. There was then a period of highly unpredictable climate before relatively wetter and more stable conditions set in from the midsixteenth to midseventeenth centuries, after which climatic conditions have been generally dry, with a few wetter phases such as from 1950 to the late 1960s.[5] Although many of the large lakes in the central Saharan basins dried up 3,000–4,000 years ago, the network of river channels closer to the River Niger and fed by the annual flood may still have had significant seasonal flows until much more recently.[6]

Ghana, Mali, and Songhai

The first written accounts of West Africa come from early Islamic travellers. They describe a series of great Empires which held sway in the Sahel (as shown in Figure 2.1), each one expanding and contracting over time as the central state gained from or lost influence to its neighbours. In 1068, El-Bakhri documented the findings of travellers to the Empire of Ghana, also known as Wagadu, which exercised power over much of the Western Sahel from the third to the eleventh century.[7] Its wealth was based on control of gold mines in Bambuk (in today's Eastern Senegal) and Kangaba (in what is now Guinea). By the fourth century CE, Ghana's capital at Kumbi-Saleh on the present-day border between Mali and Mauretania was a significant trading centre, linking the savannah regions to the south with traders from North Africa. El-Bakri notes that although the king of Ghana was animist, Arab and Berber traders lived in the Moslem quarter, which boasted a dozen mosques, and was surrounded by wells and gardens. During the late eleventh century, the empire weakened, probably owing to years of persistent drought.[8] The legend of Wagadu recounts its fall as attributable to the slaying of the serpent, which lived in the city's great well, by a brave but foolhardy young man. He was seeking to rescue his beloved from being sacrificed to the beast, but his rash act led to the well drying up, and the scattering of Wagadu's people.

After Ghana's decline, there were many decades of turmoil as smaller polities contested power, such as the Méma region to the east of ancient Ghana, where archaeological work has found a large number of furnaces and slag heaps, which imply iron smelting on an industrial scale.[9] Some 100 km north of DBG, the

---

[4] McIntosh, R.J. (1998); Togola, T. (2008).   [5] McIntosh, R.J. (1998) pp. 72–3.

[6] Villagers in Dofinena recounted a big flood in the early 1960s, which even brought fish into a shallow channel next to their settlement, some 15 km from the River Niger.

[7] Levtzion, N. and Hopkins, J.F.P. (Eds.) (2000) pp. 79–81. Fauvelle, F.-X. (2018) pp. 56–63.

[8] Conrad, D.C. and Fisher, H.J. (1982).   [9] Togola, T. (2008).

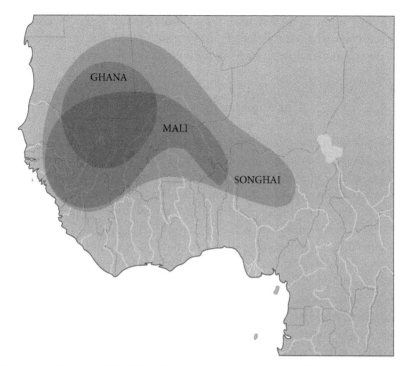

Figure 2.1. Empires of the West African Sahel: Ghana, Mali, and Songhai

Méma is said to have been ruled by the Toungara clan, one of DBG's founding lineages, before falling to the Songhai king Sonni Souleymane around 1450.[10] The Méma had offered an early refuge to Sunjata Keita, who went on to found the Mali Empire, around 1230. This empire is best known for one of its kings, Mansa Musa, who travelled to Egypt in 1324 on his way to Mecca to perform the Hajj pilgrimage. He brought with him such fabulous wealth in gold and slaves that the Egyptian currency suffered a major fall in value. The Catalan Atlas, dated 1375, provides an image of Mali's ruler, and describes him as 'the lord of the Blacks, the richest and most noble lord of the whole region because of the abundance of gold that is collected in his land'.[11] Recent archaeological work has found a large city some 25 km west of Ségou, at Sorotomo, to the south of the River Niger, which dates from the period of the Mali Empire.[12] It is argued that, rather than a single capital city, the Mali Empire may have relied on a number of political centres, of which this was one.[13] By the 1600s, the northerly parts of the Mali Empire fell under the power of the Songhai Askia kings based in Gao, 900 km to the northeast of Ségou. But the Songhai had only partial control over more distant territory.

[10] Pageard, R. (1961b).   [11] Fauvelle, F.-X. (2018) p. 192.
[12] MacDonald, K.C. et al (2011).   [13] Gestrich, personal communication.

Much of the Ségou region was under the authority of smaller-scale rulers, such as the Traoré clans, who were subdued by the Bambara in the late seventeenth century, when they moved into the Niger River region from further south.[14]

The Bambara Kingdom at Ségou

The story of the foundation of the Ségou kingdom in around 1710 tells of a young hunter, Mamari Coulibaly, who as leader of the youth association (or *ton*) contested and wrested power from the traditional Bambara families at Ségou.[15] Mamari Coulibaly was able to transform the *ton* from its focus on farming to create a military unit which expanded in size and power by incorporating young men taken as captives into the *ton* itself.[16] Under his rule, the Ségou state depended on continual warfare to ensure a supply of booty for redistribution amongst the warriors, and the king (*faama*) could only maintain his authority for so long as his warriors felt satisfied. The Coulibaly dynasty was overthrown after Mamari's death in the 1760s by N'Golo Diarra, a powerful military slave, who then established his own dynasty. It was his son Monzon who Mungo Park found on the throne in Ségou when he came to visit in 1796. From Ségou, the Bambara expanded their kingdom in the eighteenth and nineteenth centuries, until at its height, it stretched to Tombuctou in the east and beyond Bamako in the west. As with previous kingdoms across the savannah and Sahel, their power was based on warfare, and trade in gold, salt, and slaves, relying on a close and uneasy alliance with Maurish powers to the north, who controlled the desert-side trade.[17]

In the early eighteenth century, the Bambara kings of Ségou set up a series of fortified villages on the North Bank of the River Niger to protect the northern flank of their kingdom. Royal cattle herds, in the care of *foroba fulaw*,[18] grazed the pastureland protected by these villages and soldiers (known as *tonjon*[19]) were stationed there. DBG is described by its inhabitants as a *horondugu*—that is to say a settlement of noble people, who were already established in the area before the arrival of the *tonjon*. All villages needed to be fortified, the gates were barred at dusk, and entry denied to strangers. Villages without adequate defences were attacked and destroyed, and their occupants seized and sold into slavery. On his travels in 1795–1797, the Scottish explorer Mungo Park (see Box 2.1) found many such ruined villages along his route, and widespread use of slave labour both for the domestic tasks of farming, livestock herding, and housework, and for military

---

[14] Pageard, R. (1961a); Bazin, J. (1970); Lovejoy, P. (1986).

[15] Associations, *ton*, made up of age-mates have a continued presence today in Bambara farming settlements.

[16] Roberts, R.L. (1987) p. 34.   [17] Lovejoy, P. (1986); Roberts, R.L. (1987).

[18] Herders owned by the Segou state, managing cattle herds belonging to the king.

[19] *Tonjon* means slave belonging to the *ton* or 'youth association'—effectively military slaves.

Box 2.1 Mungo Park passes the night at DBG, 19 July 1796

Mungo Park was a Scottish explorer, hired by the Royal African Society to discover the source of the River Niger, and to assess the trade potential of the West African interior. On the first of his two voyages, it took him more than a year from the mouth of the River Gambia to reach the River Niger. He had been captured and held prisoner for 3 months by Maurish Arabs on the edge of the desert, but finally was released to continue his journey to the River Niger at Ségou. By this time, his horse was barely able to carry him; so much of his journey southwards from the desert was spent on foot, driving his horse before him. Judging by his treatment, he offered a pitiful spectacle, which excited both suspicion and sympathy.

On 18 July, 1796, the day before he reached DBG, he noted in his journal, 'the towns were now more numerous, and the land that is not employed in cultivation affords excellent pasturage for large herds of cattle; but owing to the great concourse of people daily going to and returning from Sego, the inhabitants are less hospitable to strangers'.[20] As a consequence, he found it difficult to get food and it was only through begging that he and his companions were fed at Geosorro.[21] At daybreak, on 19 July, he resumed his journey. 'I was walking barefoot, driving my horse, when I was met by a coffle of slaves, about seventy in number, coming from Sego. They were tied together by their necks with thongs of a bullock's hide, twisted like a rope; seven slaves upon a thong, and a man with a musket between every seven. Many of the slaves were ill-conditioned, and a great number of them were women. In the rear came Sidi Mahomed's servant, whom I remembered to have seen at the camp of Benowm; he presently knew me, and told me that these slaves were going to Morocco, by the way of Ludamar and the Great Desert. In the afternoon, as I approached Doolinkeaboo, I met about twenty Moors on horseback, the owners of the slaves I had seen in the morning; they were well-armed with muskets…When I arrived at Doolinkeaboo, I was informed that my fellow-travellers had gone on, but my horse was so much fatigued that I could not possibly proceed after them. The Dooty[22] of the town, at my request, gave me a draught of water, which is generally looked upon as an earnest of greater hospitality; and I had no doubt of making up for the toils of the day by a good supper and a sound sleep; unfortunately I had neither one nor the other. The night was rainy and tempestuous, and the Dooty limited his hospitality to the draught of water.'

(continued)

[20] Park, M. (2003) p. 155.
[21] Known as Jessourna today, 15 km to the northwest of DBG.
[22] A shortening of the Bambara term *dugutigi*, owner or chief *(tigi)* of the town or land *(dugu)*.

Box 2.1 Continued

'July 20th: In the morning I endeavoured, both by entreaties and threats, to procure some victuals from the Dooty, but in vain. I even begged some corn from one of his female slaves, as she was washing it at the well, and had the mortification to be refused. However, when the Dooty was gone to the fields, his wife sent me a handful of meal, which I mixed with water, and drank for breakfast. About eight o'clock I departed from Doolinkeaboo, and at noon stopped a few minutes at a large korree, where I had some milk given me by the Foulahs...[23] (Then the following day) Looking forwards, I saw with infinite pleasure the great object of my mission—the long sought for majestic Niger, glittering to the morning sun, as broad as the Thames at Westminster, and flowing slowly to the eastwards...'[24]

Mungo Park, having reached the river bank, requested permission from the King of Ségou to cross the river and enter the city. But the Maures had captured the king's attention and warned him against this stranger from an unknown land. Having waited on the North Bank for some days, he went exploring further to the east, reaching Sylla, on the edge of the great Inner Niger Delta. He then set off to return home, by a more southerly route and did not revisit DBG. On his second visit to West Africa, he travelled by boat along the River Niger from Bamako and, hence, did not pass through DBG again.

---

purposes, as foot soldiers. Around DBG, small settlements like Misribougou and Jessourna were ruined by warfare during the nineteenth century, and their people had to seek shelter in DBG, which was better fortified.

The character of the Ségou kingdom is expressed in the exuberant poems recounted by traditional storytellers (*griots*) which make up the *Epopée de Ségou*.[25] This narrative poem follows the conquests and disasters of the great Ségou kings, as they fight their enemies and battle against each other. Their personalities show a combination of courage, bravery in battle, ability to command, and cleverness in designing ruses to catch out their rivals. Honour and pride play central roles in the stories. In the poems, women are faithless, captivated by gold, and willing to betray their husbands for spoil. Vassal chiefs and kingdoms were pillaged, and captives sold as slaves in the big markets on the western edge of the empire in

---

[23] These are the cattle keeping Peul or Fulani people.

[24] In fact, the River Niger is more than three times wider than the Thames at Westminster. Park, M. (2003) p. 158.

[25] Ba, A.K. (1987). Also described in *Ségou: Les murailles de terres*. A novel by Maryse Condé (1984).

Kangaba. Other key resources were salt from the mines north of Timbuktu and gold from Bourem. In addition, craftsmen made cotton textiles, leather goods, iron for knives and rifles, and lead shot. The river provided a major route for transport, managed by the Somono fishing clans, who exercised mastery of the long black canoes, which today continue to ply their way along the River Niger.

The Ségou kings relied on powerful occult forces tied to fetish shrines, and they paid for fortune-tellers to divine their future. They refused to follow Islam themselves, but were tolerant of Moslem traders, and holy men such as the Maraka, who claimed their ancestry from the Empire of Ghana. At its height, stretching more than 1,000 km from west to east and 500 km north to south, the Ségou Empire was said to be able to mobilize 60,000 horsemen and 100,000 foot soldiers. Soldier-slaves led attacks on neighbouring areas, which brought in further slaves to add both to the kingdom's military strength and to the growing of crops for filling its grain reserves. Settlements paid tax to the Bambara king, in the form of honey (for making the alcoholic drink *diji* much loved by the King, his generals and followers), and manpower. Close to Ségou city, there was greater peace and security, but distant villages were at risk of attack from neighbouring people, including the Maures. It was common for people to go to the fields with rifles and spears, to protect themselves in case of attack. Mungo Park describes several villages where farmworkers were accompanied by armed men, who both protected them from raiders and stopped slaves from fleeing. Being on the northern edge of the Ségou kingdom, DBG needed to protect its people, with a thick mud wall enclosing the settlement, with few entry points. Its hunters were renowned for their strength and bushcraft, and even in 1980, the hunters' society remained a powerful and vibrant association, concerned as much with protection of the community as with killing wild animals.

The village of DBG was well-established by the time Mungo Park arrived in 1796, as was Jessourna, its neighbour 15 km to the northwest. No one knows anything of the earlier inhabitants of the place, although the story of the village's foundation—told in Chapter 1—makes clear that there was a well already dug. There are many old settlement sites scattered across this region, with baobab groves, pottery shards and iron ore waste in mounds, indicating these open grassy plains, with light sandy soils, have been inhabited for many centuries (see Figure 2.2).[26] Archaeological work has been done in several sites north of DBG, but many old settlement mounds remain unexplored. However, people know that they contain material from former times, and, in a few cases, they have robbed sites of jewellery and other objects. In one case, it is said that someone found gold bracelets worth many millions of francs, enough to buy two houses in Bamako.

[26] McIntosh, R. (1998); Togola, T. (2008).

Figure 2.2. Massive baobab trees dot the landscape, indicating old settlement sites, 2016

The Bambara kings held power in Ségou until 1861, when they were conquered by El Hajj Umar Tall, the Toucouleur Peul leader who came from the mountains of the Fouta Jallon further west, the source of the River Niger. He established an Islamic theocracy across his dominions, declaring a jihad in 1852 against all pagans, lapsed Muslims, and the European invaders. However, having failed to triumph over the French, he made a treaty with them in 1860, allowing him to turn east to conquer Ségou in 1861, and establish his rule over the middle Niger River from Masina to Timbuktu.

He left his son Ahmadou Tall to rule Ségou, while he set off eastwards, dying in combat in 1864. Following Umar's death, the polity fragmented amongst his sons and nephews, and there were many years of turmoil with pillage and predation ubiquitous.[27] Umarian fighters went on their own razzias to ensure continued booty, and seized assets from merchants and grain from markets, generating great damage to trade and the regional economy. Under siege from competing kin, Ahmadou Tall was unable to maintain firm control over the Ségou region, and many Bambara warlords and former Ségou *tonjons* set

[27] Roberts, R. (1987).

themselves up as local tyrants.[28] Ahmadou reigned until he in his turn was conquered by the French in 1890.

The years of French colonial administration

Conquest and control

Following the conquest of Ségou in 1890, the French set about establishing control over the territory. Their first plan was to maintain order through indirect rule, by installing Bodian Diarra as king at Ségou, and Mademba Sèye at Sansanding on the North Bank. Both had proved themselves loyal to the French in fighting the Toucouleur, and it was hoped they could establish peace over the territories they had been granted. However, in neither case did these rulers come from the Ségou region, nor have legitimacy and authority over the people and lands they were meant to control. Consequently, they were plagued by continuous revolts, and by 1893, the French decided to rule the middle Niger directly, through a Commandant de Cercle at Ségou.[29]

The North Bank was described as having suffered permanent warfare, the result of 30 years of turmoil: 'the result is the total de-population of this rich country, where you find no more than ruins, and migration towards yet more hostile lands further north, or in the few big fortified villages'.[30] The region was divided up between several canton chiefs, each responsible for a number of villages. A head tax and forced labour were instituted, following a census of the entire population, with the French demanding that taxes be paid in cash, not the traditional cowries (see Box 2.2 for a description of Lieutenant Morize's visit to conduct the first census in DBG, 1895). Poor villages had to pay 1.50 f per head, while better off villages paid 2.50 f or 3.00 f/head.[31] Taxes in 1894 were largely paid in kind—millet, cattle, blankets, cowries, sheep, rice, cotton, and wood—but by 1899, most tax was paid in coin. The village chief had to exchange cowries for francs often at exorbitant rates.

In the case of the North Bank, the French recognized the power of N'To Diarra, a military leader who had fought alongside the French against the Toucouleur. He and his forefathers had been warriors for Ségou and gained special favour from the faama for their loyalty to the Diarra dynasty. N'To had

---

[28] Roberts, R. (1987); Galliéni, J.-S. (1885).
[29] Roberts, R. (forthcoming).   [30] Rapport Politique Cercle de Ségou 1893, Archives ID55.
[31] In a good year, millet sold at 0.15 f/kg, so the head tax was approximately 10 kg, remarkably similar to the millet equivalent of the head tax today.

Box 2.2 Lieutenant Morize demonstrates French authority in DBG in 1895

In 1895, 100 years after Mungo Park's visit, Lieutenant Morize set off from Ségou to undertake the census on the North Bank of the River Niger. The French army had beaten the Toucouleur leader Ahmadou Tall, son of the great El Hadj Oumar, 5 years earlier, established their military and administrative base at Ségou, and were keen to stamp their authority on this large territory. The monthly report of political and military affairs for May 1895 notes, 'it would be unwise to take the apparent calm as evidence of submission by the population, since the case of DBG demonstrated that revolt was only just below the surface, waiting for its moment to explode.'

Lieutenant Morize reached DBG in the morning of 15 May, with a detachment of six soldiers and a corporal. He described how from the first moment of their arrival, the brother of the chief displayed an arrogant and hostile manner. Mr Morize settled himself in the vestibule (or *blon*) of the chief's compound and told the chief not to let people pass through. Soungho Dembélé, the chief's brother, refused to obey him, stating that since this was his usual route into his own home, he would continue to pass as he liked. After heated words, Lieutenant Morize felt the need to demonstrate his authority and had Soungho arrested and kept under guard, while continuing the census. In the middle of the night, a crowd of armed men gathered outside the hut, shouting for Soungho to be set free. Morize withdrew from the village with his soldiers and baggage to camp some distance away. But Soungho took advantage of a moment's inattention to escape and join the crowd. The following morning the village chief brought presents to him, to demonstrate the village's submission to the French, but Morize demanded that the chief find and bring him Soungho, setting a deadline for the end of the day. Morize also sent off a messenger to Ségou for reinforcements. By dusk Soungho had still not been delivered, so Morize then had the chief seized by his men. A large number of armed men then appeared, shots were fired, including by Morize, who wounded the chief. With his troops, they beat a retreat and passed another night some distance from the settlement. An additional twenty soldiers arrived next morning, and when they entered the village, they found it abandoned. The troops burnt the granaries and rounded up the 200 sheep and goats left behind. The Lieutenant then continued the census, arriving back in Ségou on 21 May.

Following his return to Ségou, the colonial administration demanded that the newly designated *chef de canton* at neighbouring Niempiena find and bring four brothers and two sons of DBG's chief for imprisonment in Ségou.

They were duly delivered, and the chief himself, having been wounded, was forced to give himself up. These seven members of the Dembélé chiefly family were sent into exile to Bissandougou, in today's Guinée. No one ever heard of them again.

In the meantime, the villagers of DBG had been told they must disperse to neighbouring settlements in the canton, as the village was not allowed to be re-established. In 1980, an old woman in her nineties told me she remembered as a young girl being picked up and rushed away to live in a different place, at the time of the French conquest. After Morize's visit, the villagers of DBG sent a regular petition to the *Commandant* at Ségou, pledging their complete submission, and asking to be allowed to resettle the village, and, after 3 years, this was agreed. Subsequent political reports for the Ségou region note that the firmness with which the revolt at DBG had been dealt with provided a salutary message for other villages in the region.

Source: Rapport Politique Ségou June 1895.

become an independent warlord, based at Markabougou some 15 km to the northeast of DBG. The French were confident that « *Le pays de Markabougou sera tranquille et devoué, tant que N'To sera à sa tête* ».[32] However, DBG and a number of other villages refused to be under his authority and consequently had to be administered directly by Ségou.[33] The French relied on the traditional chiefs to carry out local administrative duties and collect taxes, but they found them unimpressive, because they tended to be elderly and infirm. The political reports from the *cercle* describe many as 'not very intelligent but willing,... a blind chief without any influence,... a worn-out chief but greatly esteemed by his people'. They note the need to increase chiefly power somewhat, but not enough to constitute a threat to their authority.[34]

Today, if you ask the village elders about the events outlined in Box 2.2, they have a different version. They insist that the French were encouraged by N'To Diarra, the warlord of the neighbouring village Markabougou to deal roughly with DBG, given the fierce enmity between the two villages. In the 1880s, N'To Diarra had camped outside DBG and asked for his large band of men to be

[32] Rapports politiques Cercle Ségou 1E-71 1892. 'The territory of Markabougou will be peaceful for so long as N'To Diarra is at its head.'

[33] As long-standing settlements, which had provided protection to Ségou's northern flank, villages such as DBG, Sonango, Toumakoro, Sagalaba, Tiemandeli, and Ouetta paid yearly tribute to the Ségou king or *fama*, but described themselves as people of Kala (*Kalankaw*). One hundred and fifty km north of Ségou, Sokolo was the capital of Kala. Pageard, R. (1961a).

[34] *Il nous faudrait trouver un moyen de la grandir sans que pour cela alla devenir trop considérable.* Rapport Politique cercle de Ségou 1898.

watered and fed, but the people of DBG had judged him too dangerous and had barred the door. N'To then travelled on to the next-door village of Markabougou. Despite the village chief being warned by his brother on no account to let them come in to feed and sleep, he ignored this advice. N'To and his men were let in and, having been fed and watered, they killed the village chief and scattered the villagers, including one family, which then sought shelter in DBG. According to the people of DBG, N'To coveted the beautiful horse which belonged to the chiefly Dembélé clan of DBG, and used the French to ruin his neighbours.

The Dembélé family of DBG and the Diarras of Markabougou have never intermarried despite being neighbours. The Dembélé call the Diarra nothing but *tonjon*, meaning soldier-slaves and, therefore, people of no nobility and deserving no respect. However, in April 2016, 121 years after the incident with Lt Morize, a delegation of Diarra men from Markabougou arrived at DBG to ask for this enmity to be put aside. In pledge of their seriousness, they offered a fine bullock, to be killed for a big collective feast. After deliberation, the thirteen Dembélé households agreed that the dispute could be formally put behind them. No one, however, has yet organized a marriage between the two clans.

The early years of the French colonial administration focused on mobilizing labour and getting the taxes paid. The North Bank was seen as so impoverished that several administrators argued they should pay lower taxes because of low rainfall, poor water supplies, lack of transport, recurrent drought, and locust attacks. It was suggested that a coin worth 20 cowries be made available, since this was the average consumption requirement per day. The Sahel region was not obviously a rich agricultural territory, unlike forested Côte d'Ivoire, and its assets were mainly in the form of manpower. Slaves had formerly been a significant export from the region, both northwards to the Maghreb and southwards for the trans-Atlantic trade. While the French administration did not abolish slavery, per se, the revision of the legal code in 1903 outlawed the presentation of 'status' in the newly created native courts, and the December 1905 decree outlawed new enslavement. Together these weakened the legal underpinnings of slavery and contributed to the massive slaves' exodus of 1905–1912.[35] They had set up *villages de liberté* as early as the 1880s, where former slaves could be recruited as labourers into the multiple projects needed by the colonial authorities.[36] Former slaves also signed up to the army, although they were obliged to part with a share of their first pay in favour of their former masters. In 1907, the Segou Commandant noted that every day he received hundreds of former *captifs* who declared that they did not want to work for their master anymore, but there was also growing discontent

---

[35] Richard Roberts, personal communication.
[36] The labour held in *villages de liberté* were widely referred to as the 'Commandant's slaves'.

Figure 2.3. Young West African soldiers in Europe (*tirailleurs sénégalais*) from 1918

amongst the former masters.[37] Colonial labour recruitment was managed by village and canton chiefs, with men being selected into two categories: 'portion 1' who were destined for the army and 'portion 2' who were drafted into forced labour works.[38] Women were also required to contribute their labour, principally for fetching water and providing food for the workforce.

During the First World War, 192,000 *tirailleurs sénégalais* were recruited from French West Africa, many of whom came from what is now Mali, and many of these were recently freed *captifs* (see Figure 2.3).[39] The sacrifice made by each portion was referred to as the blood-tax and the sweat tax.[40]

French colonial works

The principal colonial works on which the villagers of DBG provided forced labour comprised digging the *Office du Niger* irrigation scheme, building the dam at Markala, and construction of the administrative buildings in Ségou. Elderly men in 1980 could recall the combination of very tough work and camaraderie associated with these big public works projects. One old man from DBG, so small

---

[37] Rapport Politique, Cercle de Ségou, 1907.   [38] Magasa, A. (1978).
[39] Mann, G. (2006); Mbajum, S. (2013). Though increasing resistance to large-scale recruitment led to revolts in 1915–1917. Richard Roberts, personal communication.
[40] *Taxes en sang, taxes en sueur.*

to have been useless for physical labour, nicknamed *Toto* or rat, was given the job of singing and dancing to keep the work group motivated. Whips and beatings were in regular use, to keep order and get people to work harder, and the food by all accounts was disgusting.[41] In 1980, three old men from DBG reminiscing about their experience with forced labour, told how they would set off in the evening, after a long day's work, to look for other things to cook, to make up for the terrible food provided.

The French administration also needed to find families to settle the irrigation scheme, once constructed. There was no flood of willing settlers from the dryland villages nearby, so they resorted to moving entire villages from the Mossi Plateau in the neighbouring colonial territory of Upper Volta. In the absence of volunteers, villages close to the irrigation works, like DBG, were obliged in the 1940s to select one family to go and settle the scheme. The Tangara family was chosen for this obligation, possibly because they were not one of the founding families, having arrived during the turmoil of the late nineteenth century. They were told by the French they must do 7 years on the scheme, after which they could return home, it being thought very unlikely that people would willingly give up an irrigated plot to return to their dryland fields. But they did indeed return, much preferring the millet fields and pastures of DBG, with its greater spaces and freedoms, than being in a regimented irrigation scheme growing cotton for the French.

The 1930s were a harsh decade for the North Bank, with poor harvests, cattle disease, and locust attacks. The colonial administration agreed to reduce the taxes paid per head, but despite this, they note very large amounts of gold were being brought for sale so that people could pay the tax due. The Political Report for 1934 notes that villagers had exhausted their reserves, and the combination of forced labour and continued taxation made the role of the French increasingly odious to the population.[42] And an old man in DBG is reported as saying 'it is so much more difficult to survive hard times today; at least in the old days if your harvest failed you could go off raiding.'[43]

When Geoffrey Gorer travelled through French and British West Africa in 1934, he observed there were many people moving from lands under French administration into the British territories further south, partly because of higher rainfall, and partly because of heavy levels of taxation, recruitment into the army, and forced labour demands. He paints a sorry picture of France's *mission civilisatrice*.

> It is to escape conscription that thousands of families cross the English frontiers every year…There is no doubt that the negroes of French West Africa are a dispirited, miserable and resentful people, who can now only be ruled by fear. It is not merely the colonial policy…, but the brutal and abusive manner in

---

[41] Magasa, A. (1978).   [42] Rapport Politique 1934, Cercle de Ségou.
[43] Rapport Politique 1932 Cercle de Ségou.

which the French treat them on nearly every occasion, and the systematic way in which they are cheated in every transaction.[44]

From his position as a highly respected *noir-blanc*[45] in the French colonial administration in the 1920s and 30s, Bâ presents a similar picture as Gorer of how power was exercised. Each *Commandant de Cercle* was a little king in the area he controlled, and few took the trouble to learn the local language, which gave great power to the official translator.

In the 1930s, during this time of drought and repeated swarms of crickets, people turned to underground crops like groundnuts, and manioc, which could survive the winged hordes. The economic situation was so bad, many trading houses in Ségou shut down, as no one had the cash to buy their goods. Many young men were recruited into the army (as described in Box 2.3) or set off to the Gambia to work in the groundnut fields.[46] The *Société de Prévoyance* required that each village in the French Soudan establish a collective grain store, ostensibly to help provide food in case of famines. But these stores duplicated each household's own grain stores. By 1941, word was given that all reserve-granaries must be transported to Ségou and onwards to Dakar to feed the West African troops, a demanding feat of logistics in which thousands of days were spent transporting grain from hundreds of villages to be shipped upriver by canoe.

After the Second World War, France abolished forced labour in its colonies, and attempts were made to encourage economic development and spread technology, such as oxen-drawn ploughs, to increase agricultural productivity, with groundnuts and cotton as the main cash crops. A school for chiefs' sons was set up at Markala, to educate a few children from the North Bank. When a boy, the current village chief of DBG was sent to this school, but little remains of his education. Military recruitment continued, with several men from DBG fighting for France in Madagascar and Indo-China. As Mali prepared for Independence, alongside France's other West African territories, political parties were largely dominated by educated, urban elites, with few people from areas like Ségou's North Bank gaining a voice.

Although the colonial administration only lasted 70 years, from 1890 to Independence in 1960, France has had a profound and long-lasting impact on present-day Mali. Indeed, old Ma Toungara, who died in 1981, could remember both the arrival of the French and the visit of Lieutenant Morize, as well as their subsequent departure from the territory they called the French Soudan. The colonial legacy remains strong, with use of the French language, many aspects of the French legal system, including asserting the state's domanial rights over all land

---

[44] Gorer, G. (1945) p. 83. Also described by Hart (1982).
[45] 'Black whiteman' as the indigenous colonial administrators were called. Bâ, A.H. (1994).
[46] Known as *navetanes*, taken from the local Wolof word for *seasonal migrant*.

Box 2.3 Babo Dembélé comes back from World War II

Babo Dembélé, a son of the chiefly family, was taken off to fight in the Second World War in 1939, and did not come back until 1946, having been held as a prisoner of war in German-occupied France. He had been recruited into the French West African army, as a *tirailleur sénégalais*, taken by ship to Europe and put into the front line. Along with 50,000 fellow *tirailleurs*, he was captured in June 1940, and taken to the German prisoner of war camps (known as Stalags), set up in Northeast France. Given German hostility to the black French troops, derived from being part of the occupying force after the First World War, West African prisoners were held in occupied France. They received very different treatment from their white French fellow prisoners, who were transferred to camps in Germany.[47] Life in the prison camps was very tough; it was very cold; the food was minimal; and African prisoners were put to work in the fields. Babo remembers cultivating sugar beet, often working in the fields at night. He considered the German guards brutal, often taking African prisoners out for target practice. At least half of all African prisoners of war died from pneumonia or were shot by the Germans.[48] But Babo was one of the survivors.

Once the war was won, he could not wait to get back to his village. He was eager also to know whether the girl who had been promised him as a wife was still waiting, or had been given to another. His heart was full of uncertainty and hope as he saw again the familiar settlement lying before him. Fifty years later, his voice still shook with feeling, and his eyes filled with tears remembering and describing that day.

Babo had struggled to get home from France as quickly as possible, waiting many months for the boats to take former prisoners of war from Marseilles back to Dakar, Senegal. Once landed in Dakar, he had to travel eastwards the 1,500 km to his home city of Ségou. But there, he had been told he must first travel to Niono, another 100 km away, which had recently been made the administrative centre for the area in which DBG fell. Babo had to get officially demobilized if he was to secure his pension as a registered *ancien combattant*. At this point, it felt cruel to be so close and yet be obliged to go a further step before reaching home. Having been away so long, he and his fellow returnees had wanted to go on strike and insist they be allowed to get home by the shortest route. But they remembered the terrible punishment meted out by the French in Thiaroye, Senegal, in 1944.[49] Some of their *tirailleur* brethren, who

---

[47] Mbajum, S. (2013).   [48] de Gobineau, H. (1953).
[49] Echenberg, M. (1985); Mbajum, S. (2013).

had also suffered years of German captivity, had demanded proper pensions and back-pay and had seized a French officer as hostage. The French declared this a mutiny, shot seventy *tirailleurs*, and wounded many more. So Babo exercised further patience, got up to Niono and back, and then took a long black canoe across the River Niger and set off home. His feet spurred on by his desire, he was very pleased to find that his wife-to-be, though impatient for his return, had not yet been married off to someone else.

Babo went on to live into old age, becoming village chief for 15 years, from 1984 to 1999. Though he is now dead, his eldest son is proud to recount his military history. And while he was the only one to have survived years in a prisoner of war camp, a handful of other old men had their own horror stories from serving in the French Army in North Africa and Indo-China.

and natural resources, and maintenance of a highly centralized state. Relations between the governments of France and Mali are close, as was seen in the rapid military support provided by President Hollande to push back the jihadist insurgency of 2013. Many middle-class Malian families hold dual nationality, send their children to university in France, and have relatives and property there.

Following Independence in 1960

Mali's first president, Modibo Keita, sought to establish a socialist state, and nationalized key sectors of the economy, including all trade. Relations with France, as the colonial power, deteriorated, and Mali left the franc zone. Instead, as a strong member of the Non-Aligned Movement, Keita strengthened ties to the USSR and China, with the latter building a textile factory, and the Sukala sugar plantation and mill north of Ségou. Attempts to socialize farming and control trade were not popular, and the economy did not prosper. In 1968, a coup d'état brought General Moussa Traoré to power. He re-established connections with the former colonial power and re-entered the common monetary system, which Mali remains within today.[50] The West African Economic and Monetary Union (UEMOA), uses the West African franc (FCFA), which is supported by the French Treasury at a stable fixed rate against first the French franc, and since 1999 against the Euro.[51] A major devaluation, which halved the value of the CFA franc, was

[50] In 1962, on leaving the CFA zone, the Malian government established the Malian Franc. In 1984, the Malian franc was abandoned, and the shift made to the CFA franc, at a rate of 2 Malian francs = 1 CFA franc.

[51] The Union Economique et Monétaire de l'Afrique de l'Ouest (UEMOA) includes eight West African countries: Benin, Burkina Faso, Cote d'Ivoire, Guinea-Bissau, Mali, Niger, Senegal, and Togo. Central Banks are required to deposit 50 per cent of their foreign reserves at the Banque de France.

pushed through in 1994 by the French government and the International Monetary Fund on the grounds that it would help these countries become more competitive globally. Critics of the CFA franc argue that it remains significantly overvalued, which benefits elites wishing to transfer money from the region to Europe, but unfairly penalizes domestic industries seeking to compete with cheap imports. Countries using the CFA franc do not have independent control of their monetary policy, and being tied to the Euro reflects the priorities of the European monetary system, not those of West Africa.[52]

The Government of Mali was obliged to pursue an extensive set of structural adjustment measures in the 1980s, including big cutbacks to state budgets, layoff of government employees, privatization of parastatal enterprises, and freeing up of markets. For a village like DBG, many of these changes had limited impact because, unlike villages farther south in the cotton zone, its farmers saw few if any government services and did not rely on purchased inputs. But the abolition of cereal quotas brought greater freedom to villagers to trade in grains. Each village had been obliged to sell a certain quota of millet to the state's grain marketing board, OPAM, at a fixed price usually substantially below market levels.[53] In some ways, DBG has had the good fortune of being fairly distant from major cities and towns and hence ignored by government officials. Places nearer to town found themselves visited more regularly, including by the hated Forest Guards of the *Eaux et Forêts*, seeking fines and bribes.

Establishing democratic government

The Revolution of 1991, against the corrupt and authoritarian rule of Moussa Traoré, brought thousands of students and market women on to the street, and led to a coup, succeeded by the installation of a transitional government. Elections in 1992 led to two terms of office by President Alpha Konaré at the head of the ADEMA party. The arrival of democracy generated great energy and excitement after 23 years of autocracy. Decentralized government, in the form of urban and rural communes was set up in 1999, and the mood was optimistic.[54] Mali became a favourite for many donor agencies, and development assistance flooded in for projects and budget support. A smooth political transition was achieved with the election of President Ahmadou Toumani Touré (ATT) in 2002, a popular former general who had led the coup of 1991 against Moussa Traoré. He established a broad governing coalition of political parties, but under the surface of an apparently peaceful consensus, increasing tensions grew. With a highly centralized state, all benefits from aid and development had accrued to Bamako, and there

[52] Nubukpo, K. (2015).   [53] Office des Produits Agricoles du Mali.
[54] Sy, O. (2009).

was growing evidence of corruption, with powerful people in government able to siphon off significant aid flows, and a burgeoning group of rich traders and property developers growing fat on import quotas and land speculation. A huge gap existed between the urban elite and the mass of the population, generating growing resentment, exemplified by protests against large-scale land acquisitions in 2010–2011.[55] President ATT was overthrown in a coup in March 2012, shortly before the planned presidential elections, and following the loss of the north of Mali to an alliance of Tuareg and jihadist forces.

The Northern conflict

The Tuareg who live across a significant area of Northern Mali and Niger, Eastern Mauritania, and Southern Algeria and Libya, had never been happy with the French handover of power to newly independent countries, since they would shift from being dominant within the Saharan region to being a small minority within each new state. A series of rebellions against rule from Bamako took place in the north of the country in the 1960s, followed by brutal repression and exactions by the army. The droughts of the 1970s and 80s hit the north particularly hard, and many destitute Tuareg went northwards to live and work in Libya. Further civil strife in the 1990s, demands for autonomy and a fair share of aid budgets for the north, led to negotiation of a Peace Agreement in 1995, which aimed to grant special status to the north, resettle refugees, incorporate Tuareg fighters into the Malian army, and promote greater economic and political development in this neglected drought-stricken region. But little was done to ensure its implementation, and the government in Bamako ignored the growing lawlessness in the north of the country. In this huge ungoverned space, it was easy for dissident Tuareg groups to grow, alongside Salafist fighters who had been pushed south by the Algerian security forces. They could make an income based on age-old knowledge and control of trading routes, dealing in narcotics, kidnapped hostages, and arms.[56]

The fall of Gadhafi in Libya in late 2011 unleashed several thousand well-trained fighters from his body-guard, many of Tuareg origin, and a large cache of weapons and trucks. Seizing the opportunity to achieve independence for Northern Mali, which they called Azawad, they advanced quickly southwards, meeting little effective opposition. With the ill-equipped and demoralized Malian army unable to hold back this advance, a coup d'état was launched in Bamako in March 2012, in protest at the military losses in the north. In the struggle between

---

[55] See for example the Kolongo Charter, outlining concerns about 'the flagrant violation of citizens' rights...brutal occupation of agricultural lands by investors, and risks to family farmers', issued following the Kolongo Farmers' Forum November 2010. http://pubs.iied.org/pdfs/G03055.pdf. Oakland Institute (2011).

[56] Scheele, J. (2012); Thiam, A. (2017).

former allies, the secular Tuareg rebel group, the MNLA,[57] lost out to a range of Islamist groups seeking to install Sharia law. French troops were scrambled to hold back the advance of jihadist forces, who, by January 2013, had reached as far south as Boni, near Mopti in Central Mali.

French and Chadian troops were able to push the rebels back and retake the main cities in the north of Mali. However, the vast surrounding desert lands have been much less easy to control, and an uneasy stalemate exists in the north of the country. After the French intervention, Western donors pushed hard to re-establish constitutional government, and elections were held in July 2013, despite well-founded fears that voting was not going to be possible in many areas. Ibrahim Boubacar Keita (known as IBK) was elected president, a familiar political figure from earlier governments, and was considered a safe pair of hands. However, his first 5 years in power have disappointed many Malians and outsiders, being dogged by inability to make progress with securing the peace and accusations of cronyism and corruption. Re-elected in September 2018, President Keita made tackling conflict and insecurity his number-one priority, but many observers doubt his ability to make serious progress, given that the situation by 2019 is much more dangerous and insecure than it was 5 years ago.

From North to Central Mali

The conflict has spread from the lightly populated desert area of Northern Mali into the central region, home to many millions of people making a living from the land. Many parts of Central Mali are now out of government control, following the spread of jihadist groups and local militias. Government officials, school-teachers, and health workers have fled from rural areas and small towns, given fears for their safety. Army patrols now criss-cross the wider region, but local people fear the army as much as they do the jihadists, given their reputation for killing innocent people who fall into their hands. Jihadist groups have drawn successfully on the strong resentment felt by marginalized groups, especially the Peul, towards the government and their officials, who they see as having done nothing but fill their pockets at the expense of local people. At the same time, past disputes over land and water have reopened with neighbouring Bambara and Dogon farming groups, leading to armed attacks by both sides.[58] As described in Chapter 8, the economy of the Mopti and Ségou regions has been badly impacted by insecurity. While the village of DBG has not been directly targeted by either jihadists or the army, the entire North Bank is considered to be in the red zone. Mali's economic progress has stalled, and there is little investment and few new

---

[57] Mouvement National pour la Libération de l'Azawad.
[58] Benjaminsen, T.A. and Ba, B. (2018).

jobs emerging, as people wait to see how the politics and conflict play out. There are no foreign aid programmes or nongovernmental organizations active on the North Bank, Ségou is empty of expatriates, and the tourist trade is nonexistent. The government continues to offer large-scale land allocations to local elites and foreign investors, and it sends in the police and army to repress demonstrations by those made landless.[59] Overall, there is deep cynicism towards the government, its high level of centralization, and focus on military solutions rather than winning hearts and minds.[60] Many of the young migrants setting off across the Sahara Desert to try their luck in crossing the Mediterranean to Europe come from Mali, because they feel they have no future if they stay at home. Chapter 8 considers these issues in more detail.

[59] CMAT (2018).   [60] Mara, M. (2019).

3

The farming landscape

Soils, rainfall, and crops

An ye senekalaw ye, an te foy ke seneko.[1]

The Bambara of Dlonguébougou (DBG) describe themselves, first and foremost, as tillers of the land: 'We farm the land, we do nothing but cultivate.' While the statement is not strictly accurate, as they engage in a wide variety of other activities, tilling the soil does provide them with the principal purpose around which family, society, and village landscape are organized.[2] Millet grain provides the base of their diet, and they are proud of their farming heritage, and the fact that they can curve their back over the hoe, in a weeding gang, working swiftly as a team, for hours at a time. Despite describing themselves as 'nothing but cultivators', ownership of livestock—large and small—is a central element in people's livelihoods and wealth. Livestock are also critical elements of the farming system; cattle, sheep, and goats provide dung for the fields; oxen are used for plough teams; and the ubiquitous donkey is the main form of transport for people, water, and goods across the landscape, and from village to market.

This chapter describes the farming system of DBG, how it fits within the wider landscape and the soils on which it is based and how rainfall patterns have shifted since 1980. Farmers in DBG grow a range of different crops, and this chapter recounts their changing importance, and the fields, labour, timing, equipment and other inputs required for their cultivation. The role of livestock in the farming system is outlined, alongside the difficulties of maintaining a balance between land for crops and for grazing, and the labour requirements of maintaining a healthy herd. Finally, this chapter will show what has happened to millet yields and the overall size of harvests, demonstrating the significant fall in millet harvested per person, the reasons for these changes, and the consequences for food security.

Understanding the landscape and farming system

When Mungo Park passed through the region in July 1796, he noted that 'cultivation is carried on here on a very extensive scale; and, as the natives themselves express

---

[1] 'We are cultivators. We do nothing other than cultivate.'
[2] Meillassoux, C. (1975); Wooten, S. (2009).

Land, Investment and Migration. Camilla Toulmin, Oxford University Press (2020). © Camilla Toulmin.
DOI: 10.1093/oso/9780198852766.001.0001

it "hunger is never known". In cultivating the soil, men and women work together'
using a sharp hoe. After heavy rain, he writes, 'the roads were wet and slippery;
but the country was very beautiful...As corn is very plentiful, the inhabitants are
very liberal to strangers.' Approaching DBG, from the northwest, he notes that
'the towns were now more numerous, and the land that is not employed in
cultivation, affords excellent pasturage for large herds of cattle.'[3] If Mungo Park
were to return, he would see familiar crops of millet, stands of majestic baobab
trees, and men and women farming together with short, sharp, hand-held hoes.
But he would probably be surprised to see teams of oxen ploughing the land, and
the widespread manuring of land, which he had noted was a rare sight throughout his voyage.

Soils and vegetation

The landscape on the North Bank of the River Niger is mainly flat and sandy,
criss-crossed by former river valleys, which left behind deposits of clay and gravel.
Farmers name the different soil types and recognize their qualities for different
crops and rainfall patterns. Clay soils (*bwa*) and gravelly land (*bélé*) to the south
and east of DBG were of greater value in the wetter period 50 years ago, which
many old people today can remember from their first days of farming. But for the
last 4 decades, the villagers have preferred the light sands (*cencen*) to the north
and west of the village, which provide a greater chance of a harvest, even in years
of low rainfall. Consequently, as will be described in Chapter 4, villagers have
tried to contain the fields of incoming farmers to the south and east of the village,
while retaining control over the land to the north and west.

Clay soils had also been identified in the 1920s by the planners of the large
French colonial project, the *Office du Niger*, as appropriate for irrigated agriculture
as noted in Chapter 2, and, in the 1930s, they used forced labour to construct a
network of canals, north of the large dam built over the River Niger at Markala, to
reach these soils. As a consequence, today villages on clay soils close to the irrigation canals are vulnerable to losing their land to agricultural investors because the
government of Mali is keen to allocate this land for irrigated farming.[4]

DBG lies on slightly higher sandy ground, 30 km to the west of the *Office du
Niger* (see Figure 3.1). Since the land is generally flat, there is limited runoff and
erosion. In the occasional depression, rainfall gathers in the wet season to form
ponds where livestock drink, and from which people draw water when farming
a long way from the village. Several of these ponds have been dug out and

[3] Park, M. (2003) pp. 154–155.
[4] As will be described in Chapter 4, under the 1932 legislation, the *Office du Niger* has total control
over 2 million hectares which fall within the 'irrigable zone' linked to the canal system.

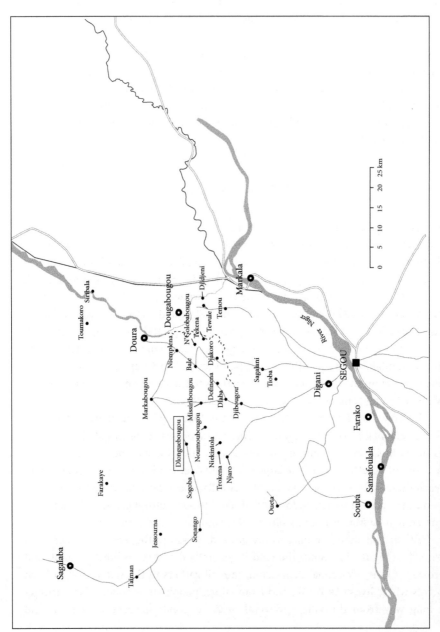

Figure 3.1. Location of DBG village in its wider landscape

developed by villagers for fish farming during the rainy season.[5] To the north and west of DBG, settlement is sparse because the water table is very deep and supplies are scarce. A few favoured villages, such as DBG, find water fairly easily at 25–30 m but, in many places, even with a borehole of 50 m, it is hard to reach a steady supply of water. This northerly zone has therefore had little permanent settlement, and has provided excellent seasonal grazing for visiting transhumant herds coming southwards from Mauritania, and westwards from the inner Niger Delta. There are also many cattle herds owned by traders from Ségou and farmers from the *Office du Niger*, which compete for pasture in this area, alongside the resident livestock belonging to Peul settlements and Bambara villagers.

The North Bank is lightly wooded, with species typical of the Sahel, such as baobab (*Adansonia digitaria*), kapok (*Bombax costatum*), *dugura* (*Cordyla pinnata*), and *gwele* (*Prosopis africana*).[6] Each tree is valued for its products. The baobab's fruits are collected and powdered into a refreshing drink; its leaves are dried and used to make the staple daily sauce to eat with millet porridge (*tô*); and its bark gives fibres that are twisted into ropes for tying up sheep and goats, pulling water from the well, and a hundred other tasks (see Figures 3.2 and 3.3) Baobab trees stand as magnificent markers within the flat landscape, each one portraying a singular personality because of its particular profile and pattern of growth. Beehives are strung in the branches; people gather under the shade to rest during the heat of the day; and its hollow trunk can both store water and offer a hiding place in times of trouble, as the Traoré family history recounted in Chapter 1. Seedpods from the kapok tree are collected for their fibres, and its soft wood is turned by blacksmiths into stools. *Dugura* provide a sour fruit, and the *gwele*'s hard wood is much prized both for making mortars for the daily pounding of millet flour, and charcoal for sale in town.

Balanzan (*Faidherbia albida*), tamarind (*Tamarindus indica*), and shea (*Vitellaria paradoxa*[7]) dot the fields around the village. The first of these has the remarkable property of shedding its leaves at the start of the rainy season, hence providing no competition to crops from its shade, while putting out new leaves at the start of the dry season, giving welcome shade to livestock waiting their turn at the well. As a consequence, land around Faidherbia trees is always black with manure.[8] A parkland of Faidherbia trees can be found around many old settlements on the North Bank, as well as in the farmlands surrounding the city of Ségou. Its leaves are often cut as fodder for livestock towards the end of the dry season, and its deep taproot allows it to survive long periods of drought. Tamarind and shea

[5] The villagers took up this activity following a visit we made together in 2011 to the neighbouring commune of Bellen, where the German Technical Agency GIZ had successfully introduced fish farms.

[6] Maydell, H.-J. von, (1986).

[7] Formerly known as *Butyrospermum parkii*, named after Mungo Park, who brought back the first specimens of this tree in 1790s.

[8] Garritty, D. et al (2010).

Figure 3.2. The giant baobab tree provides leaves, fruit, and bark fibre, DBG, 2014

trees around DBG were formerly much more productive, but now rarely produce much fruit because of lower rainfall since the 1960s. Consequently, the tree population today is the relict of a wetter time, with little regeneration of the most valuable trees, the old and dying being taken by blacksmiths for charcoal and carpentry. The fig tree (*dugule, Ficus gnaphalorcarpa*) is planted within the village, and it casts deep shade, thereby offering a canopy above the wooden platforms where people used to pass the afternoon when the hot season was at its height, now abandoned, as described in Chapter 1.

Villagers look for leaves from a number of bushes and shrubs to provide fodder to animals in the dry season, for dyeing cloth, and as local medicines. *Changara* (*Combretum glutinosum*) provides remedies for influenza, rheumatism, gastric disorders, and malaria, while its bark, leaves, and roots produce a yellow-brown dye used to colour a hunter's outfit. *Gala* (*Pterocarpus lucens*) puts out leaves in the dry season, which are highly valued for feeding livestock when pastureland is bare. The *béré* shrub (*Boscia senegalensis*) provides berries used as a famine food in years of harvest failure. Wild yams are dug up, and wild rice found on the margins of some ponds used to be harvested, but women say the work is too hard for them to do this anymore.

Figure 3.3. Breaking open baobab fruit to harvest its white flesh for food, DBG, 2014

The pattern of bush-field cultivation followed by long-term fallowing of land makes for a particular mix of trees, shrubs, and grasses over time. After 5 years of cropping, bush-field land is usually abandoned and left to recover for 20–30 years. Shrubs and grasses regrow on this fallow land, providing grazing to village and visiting herds.[9] Women pick *wuluku* (*Schoenefeldia gracilis*, or 'dog's tail' in Bambara), to make a brush for sweeping the sandy floor of the house and compound. Cramcram (*Cenchrus biflorus*), known in Bambara as *zamara*, was once a famine food, despite its seeds being hidden in a prickly carapace. Old women remember collecting the grass known as *ncin* (*Panicum laetum*), which gives a small grain also eaten in times of shortage. Every October, men search for the perennial *wa* (*Andropogon gayanus*) which grows to 3 m and provides essential material for thatching and weaving of granaries. It is also collected by young men to fabricate the rustling skirts of the masked *sogo* creatures, which are brought out to dance in the village square, to celebrate the forthcoming harvest. The young green *wa* shoots also offer excellent grazing in April and May as the dry season nears its end and animals search desperately for any fresh fodder.

[9] Cissé, M. and Hiernaux, P. (1984).

Rainfall and climate

The Sahel region is a zone of low rainfall with a short rainy season from June to September, followed by 8 months with little or no rain. Even within the wet season, rainfall is highly variable, both from place to place and from year to year. Over recent decades the rainfall has become very patchy, with a heavy downpour in one place while a field 5 km away might remain dry. Figure 3.4 presents rainfall for the Sahel from 1901 to 2017. This shows a cyclical pattern of wet and dry years, such as the drought years of the 1910s, and the exceptionally wet period in the 1950s and 60s. The latter period was the time when farmers in DBG did well from farming groundnuts and investing profits in oxen plough teams. At the end of the 1960s, a sharp decline in rainfall occurred, which lasted until the 1990s. No other region of the world has experienced such a magnitude of rainfall change in the twentieth century.[10] At the time of these intense droughts across the Sahel, some scientists considered the cause to lie in destructive patterns of land use, deforestation, and baring of soils in the Sahel and wider West African region. Governments, therefore, needed to curb local farming and grazing practices to stop 'desert advance'.[11] Recent work has been able to model more carefully the way that land–atmosphere interactions connect with global climate processes. These show that patterns of Sahelian rainfall are driven largely by global climate change and differences in sea surface temperatures in the North and South Atlantic oceans. High levels of sulphate pollution in northern Europe from the 1960s onwards partially blocked the sun's energy and led to a cooling of the North relative to the South Atlantic, and this inhibited the northward movement of the West African monsoon

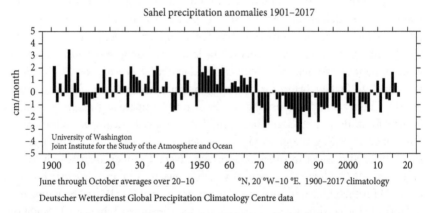

Figure 3.4. Sahel precipitation anomalies: a century of rainfall fluctuation

[10] Giannini, A. et al (2013).
[11] Behnke, R. and Mortimore, M. (2016); Toulmin, C. and Brock, K. (2016).

across the Sahel. European legislation from the 1980s to stop 'acid rain' led to big cuts in sulphate pollution, and a consequent rise in sea surface temperatures in the North relative to the South Atlantic. This shift in relative sea surface temperatures seems to have brought about a partial recovery of rainfall levels in the Sahel.[12] However, while the average amount of rainfall received in the Sahel has risen, it has become increasingly volatile, arriving in a few large, heavy storms rather than continuous lighter rainfall. Thus 'the character of precipitation during the recent recovery appears to have had a distinctly different flavour if compared to the wet period around the middle of the 20th century: fewer rainy days, as during persistent drought, made up for in the seasonal totals by an increase in median intensity of daily rainfall.'[13] This is the expected result of a warmer global atmosphere absorbing greater moisture, and being driven by a more intense water cycle.

Climate scientists are not able to predict rainfall trends and patterns for the West African region as a whole with great confidence because of the complexity of forces at work. Sahelian rainfall is brought by warm winds coming up from the southwest, having picked up their moisture as they travel over the Atlantic Ocean and Gulf of Guinea. These winds meet a powerful counterforce from hotter, very dry northeasterly winds pushing down from the Sahara Desert. The relative strength of these winds at different times of year helps account for the timing of the start of the wet season, the volume of rainfall, and how quickly the rains stop after the wettest months of July and August. Some climate models show the possibility of significant increases in the volume of rainfall, while others predict a significant fall in expected rainfall. A likely increase in rainy season temperatures had been predicted for the Sahel, but this seems not to have occurred because of higher rainfall bringing moister conditions in the wet season and, hence, greater evaporation. By contrast, temperatures at the end of the hot dry season have risen by more than 1°C.[14] There has been increased variability in rainfall totals and distribution, with heightened intensity of storms, and increased risks of soil erosion and flooding. Research drawing on 35 years of satellite observations, shows that compared to 1982 there has been a three- to fourfold increase in the number of intense convective weather systems, which lead to the large storms responsible for 90 per cent of the Sahel's rainfall.[15] Researchers consider this is likely due to an increase in the temperature gradient between the Sahel and the Sahara, with the desert region warming much faster than the Sahel.

[12] Giannini, A. (2016).

[13] Giannini, A. et al (2013). This greater concentration and intensity are clearly visible in Figure 3.6.

[14] Normally during the wet season, much of the energy received by the land from sunlight is used to evaporate soil moisture. This keeps things cool, like a natural air-conditioner. If there is a drought, that energy is instead used to increase the temperature. As seasonal rainfall in the Sahel has increased since the 1980s, this cooling effect has counterbalanced the warming from increased carbon dioxide in the atmosphere, to give almost no warming during the monsoon months (in contrast to the premonsoon period) (Chris Taylor, personal communication).

[15] Taylor, C. et al (2017).

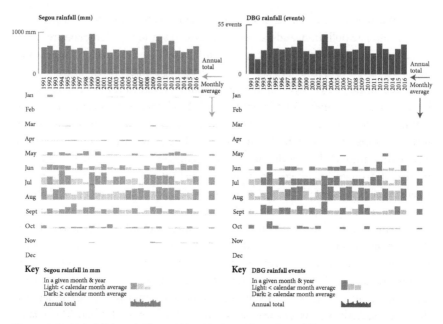

Figure 3.5. Rainfall (mm) Ségou, 1991–2016; number of rainfall events DBG, 1991–2016

The left-hand side of Figure 3.5 shows annual rainfall totals for Ségou for the period 1990–2016. While the average is 646 mm a year, there is marked variability from year to year, and no clear trend over the period covered. Going north from Ségou, there is a rapid drop in both rainfall volume and reliability. For DBG, 40 km north of the river as the crow flies, for those years when we have actual rainfall (in mms) received for both Ségou and DBG, the annual average is 200 mm lower in DBG, demonstrating a rapid fall-off in expected annual rainfall of 50 mm for every 10 km you travel north.

The right-hand side of Figure 3.5 portrays the number and distribution of rainfall events in DBG over the last 30 years. These data collected by villager MD make clear the high level of variability in rainfall patterns from year to year, and the varying distribution within the season. August is the month with the greatest number and reliability of rainfall events, followed by July. It is more patchy in June, with very occasional rainfall in May. From mid-September, rainfall is particularly important for filling out the millet grain, but it has become increasingly uncertain and volatile.

MD says:

I started measuring the number of rainfall events in 1988. I observe that some years there is a lot more rain than others. Take the year 2000, there were 22 rains during that season here in DBG, and the millet we got was so good we hadn't seen it's like for a long time. Other years, you can have 40 or 45 rains during the season, and we don't get much of a harvest at all. Some years a big rainfall comes and some do so well that everyone hears of it. It's all to do with the way the rain comes. Last Saturday, the rain came and lasted all through the night till the morning. Following that if we were to get no more rain for a week, and you went out to look at the millet, you'd find it doing well in our soils. But if we were to get lots of rain in the daytime and then at night, our soils would lose their strength. The millet wouldn't be able to sprout and grow. It needs the heat of the sun. The way in which rain comes (*sanji na cogo*) now has really changed…We've changed the way we farm, that's the result of rainfall changes. The old varieties of millet had more force, now we plant shorter cycle varieties—but you don't get the same strength from them.[16]

Figure 3.6 below illustrates rainfall received at DBG for the years 1980–1984 and 2016–2018, these being the years when we had a rainfall gauge installed at DBG. It shows the very poor rainfall of 1984 (a year of widespread drought throughout the Sahel). In 2016, there was exceptionally high rainfall, totalling 720 mm but, though it started well, the rains stopped early in September. In mid-August, a huge downpour of 105 mm, falling in 6 hours, flooded parts of the village, causing several houses to collapse, but fortunately no loss of life. Several areas of the fields surrounding the settlement had standing water which caused significant crop losses. In the following year 2017, DBG received only 470 mm. The rains started very late—with no millet sown until mid-July—and then it stopped in mid-September. In late 2017, farmers said that they expected the 2017 harvest to be even worse than in 2016.[17] By contrast, in 2018, the total rainfall received was 557 mm in thirty-five events, the largest of which was 82 mm in early August. The overall quantity combined with reasonable spacing of showers should have delivered a better harvest for DBG, but (as can be seen in Figure 3.23) the 2018 harvest was lower than in 2017, and was especially poor for the bush-field millet *sanyo*.

Figure 3.6 shows that the volume of rainfall is greater today than in the 1980s, but its distribution has changed. It comes in bigger more intense storms, often preceded by a giant dust storm (as shown in Figure 3.7) within a shorter rainy season. Villagers confirm this shift in rainfall patterns and trends from the 1960s onwards. Old women and men remember from their childhood that rainfall used to come in a gentle mist, often every day, in the height of the wet season. Now it is all much more uncertain.

Everyone agrees with MD that the pattern of rainfall is more important than the total amount. Older farmers also recall crops which have now largely disappeared,

---

[16] Interview, June 2014.
[17] Measurement of the village-field millet harvest for the 2017 season gave a total harvest of 42 tons, with an average yield of 100 kg/ha, which villagers recognized as devastatingly poor.

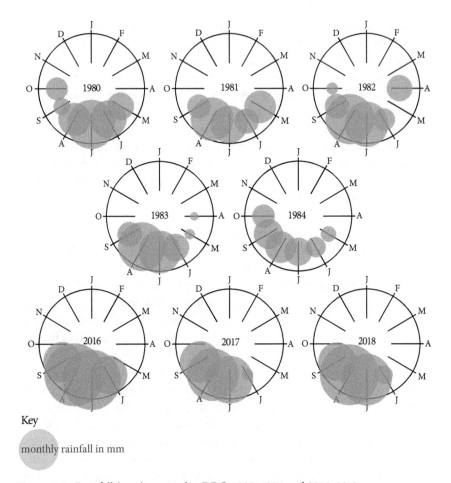

Key

monthly rainfall in mm

Figure 3.6. Rainfall (mm) received at DBG, 1980–1984 and 2016–2018

such as guinea-corn or sorghum (*Sorghum bicolor*), and groundnuts (*Arachis hypogaea*). 'Rainfall used to come in a fine, misty drizzle', says 90-year-old OS:

> through the day, and all night for a week or more. The big black clouds would come, and whatever the place, you'd know they had got rainfall. But its different today. A little rain hits one side of your field but not the other. The rain which came in the old days was a lot more useful to the crops. When the rain fell, the moisture would last for a week, but now after a couple of days, the soil is dry. It's the way the rainfall comes which is really different, rather than the total amount. We used to have a longer-cycle millet that did very well. Now we're looking for a shorter cycle millet.[18]

---

[18] Interview June 2014.

Figure 3.7. A dust storm presages a heavy downpour, June 2014

Coping with rainfall variability

Traditionally, farmers have responded to this uncertain rainfall pattern by combining crops of different cycle length, so that they hope that at least one of their fields will do well.[19] The mixing of short-cycle *sunan* millet planted on the village fields, and longer-cycle *sanyo* millet on the bush fields represents a long-standing strategy, which continues today. Farmers are now seeking millet varieties with an even shorter cycle to maturity, given the early cut-off of rains in recent years. One such variety, known as 'iniadi', a short-stemmed millet with a distinctive whitish-grey seed, could reach maturity in 60 days, and it was much appreciated in the 1980s.[20] But now, none of the villagers have the seed anymore.

Farmers have no explanation for the decline in rainfall since the 1950s–1960s, and they attribute it to God's will. When faced with a dry period in the middle of the growing season in August 1981, farmers in DBG became desperate about their wilting millet fields. The village chief sent an envoy to visit us and asked that we drive a delegation to visit the Islamic holy man at Ouetta, some 35 km away, who was considered one of the most powerful spiritual figures available in the neighbourhood. On our arrival, the holy man pronounced blessings, heard the villagers' petition and received their gifts, and told us firmly we must go straight

---

[19] Toulmin, C. (2009).   [20] Distributed by the international research centre ICRISAT.

back home, without stopping on the way. In one of the villages we passed through on the return journey, we were forced to make a short stop, so that one of the villagers in the car could greet a kinsman. Was this the reason why there was no great downpour following the imam's intercessions? After another 10 days of drought, the rains finally came, but by then, much of the village-field millet was brittle to the touch.

Being pragmatic, farmers are willing to try any source of divine inspiration which might bring success. In 1984, a year of severe drought and harvest failure, a delegation of villagers from neighbouring Misribougou went down to Ségou, to visit the Catholic Mission to ask for their help. According to the 'white fathers', after having prayers together in the church in Ségou, and giving lunch to their visitors, the missionaries offered to drive the villagers home. On the long road home, a bank of big black clouds could be seen gathering in the distance, and thunder began to rumble. Some 5 miles short of the village, the storm broke and the rain came down in such torrents, the missionaries' car could continue no further. The villagers had to make the rest of their way back home on foot, but they were glad at heart that their visit had been a success, and were quite impressed by the spiritual powers held by the missionaries.[21] That same terrible drought year, when I came on a visit to DBG in October, I found their fields empty and dried to a crisp. But the village of Djibougou, only 20 km away from DBG, had had exceptional rainfall and was harvesting a bumper crop, with the help of many visitors from the surrounding villages who could earn a little grain to take home to their families in return for their labour.

Once the first rains begin, villagers consider whether it is time to start sowing, and there are animated discussions about which month has arrived, and whether this accords with the position of certain constellations in the heavens. They now mix the traditional Bambara calendar—*jomine, sunkalomakono, sunkalo*—with Western months, so there are fewer doubts about timing than in 1980. For example, everyone will ignore an early rain in May, as it is unlikely to be followed by anything substantial, so millet seed sown then would be wasted. By mid-June, a heavy rain usually provides sufficient confidence for most farmers to get out into the bush fields to sow the longer-cycle *sanyo* millet, but they will wait until July before sowing the short-cycle *sunan*.

Crops and patterns of land use

The farming system revolves around cultivation of millet, and a variety of other crops. Bullrush millet (*Pennisetum glaucum*) is the dominant cereal crop, and it

---

[21] There were, however, no conversions to Christianity as a consequence.

forms the basis of people's diet.[22] Millet's centre of diversity is in the West African Sahel, where it is thought to have been domesticated 4,000–5,000 years ago. It is a remarkable plant, being able to grow from a tiny seed in late June to a 10-foot plant by mid-September, having flowered and set seed in 3 months of rapid growth (see Figures 3.8–3.10) There are two main varieties of millet grown in DBG: *Sanyo* a longer-cycle millet, which takes 4–5 months to maturity, grown on shifting bush fields without use of manure. Its grain is pale greyish-white, and the seedhead long and slim. It grows to 10 feet or more, and it develops a broad root system, which means it is more resistant to drought than the shorter-cycle *sunan* is. It can also be stored for longer. In the village fields around the settlement, farmers grow *sunan*, which grows to 6–8 feet, and takes only 2–3 months to mature. The grain is yellower in colour; the seed head shorter and fatter. But to do well, and achieve its potential during the short growing season, the plant needs well-manured soils. It does not store as well as *sanyo* does, and it usually needs to be eaten within 2 years of harvest. Combining the two types of millet with

Figure 3.8. *Sanyo* (bush-field millet) seedlings, 8 days after sowing, June 2014

[22] Also known as pearl millet, each stem bearing a single head of grain, in contrast to finger millet (*Eleusine coracana*), which is more common in South Asia and has a number of narrow seed heads.

Figure 3.9. Bush-field millet, *sanyo*, is tall and thin

different cycle length and differing requirements is a central means by which farmers seek to hedge their bets, given the uncertain pattern of rainfall.

Sesame (*bene, Sesamum indicum*) has become the second-most-important crop in DBG. No one grew it in DBG in the 1980s, but by 1997–1988, it was becoming widespread, cultivated in small plots by individuals as a source of cash.[23] Today it represents a major crop, especially for individuals wanting to earn some cash, and it is grown on private fields cut in the space between the village and bush fields (described in Chapter 4; see Figure 3.14 in the colour plates section). The seed is sown on lightly tilled soil, with no fertilizer added, and the crop is weeded by hand. Sesame is not eaten in the village, the entire harvest being threshed, bagged, and sold to traders who visit in December.

Cowpeas (*sho, Vigna unguiculata*) are intersown with both varieties of millet. People love the taste of cowpeas, which ripen before the millet harvest and help fill the hunger gap. Cowpea is much valued because, as a leguminous crop, it fixes nitrogen in the soil. The trailing vine of cowpea leaves is collected up, dried, stored for several months, and then fed to donkeys and oxen at the end of the dry

---

[23] Brock, K. and Coulibaly, N. (1999).

Figure 3.10.   Spears of village-field millet, *sunan*

Box 3.1 What can I make from millet?

Each morning, the household head goes to the granary, measures out the day's grain ration, and hands it to the woman responsible for food preparation that day. She will divide it between other women and girls to make the task of pounding it into flour less burdensome. First it needs to be poured from one bowl to another several times to blow away the last of the chaff. Then the grain is washed so that sand and stones collect at the bottom of the basin, and can be discarded. The clean damp grain is put into the mortar and pounded gently to remove bran from the seed, before being shaken across a coarse-mesh sieve, through which the bran falls. Finally, the grain is put back into the mortar and pounded hard into flour.

(continued)

Box 3.1 Continued

Figure 3.11. *Môni* porridge for breakfast

Figure 3.12. A dish of millet porridge, *tô*, for lunch with meat sauce

Traditional Bambara dishes include: *môni* gruel for breakfast (see Figure 3.11), flavoured with tamarind, milk and sugar; *dégé*, a refreshing afternoon dish, with soured milk and baobab fruit flour; *tô*, the main staple dish when the family is working hard in the fields, a porridge stiff enough to tear off with your fingers and then dip into a spicy sauce (see Figure 3.12); and steamed millet couscous, known as *baasi*, for special occasions, like weddings, served with meat and groundnut sauce. Rice is also offered for festive meals (see Figure 3.13).

Figure 3.13. A festive dish of rice and goat stew

season, when they need fattening up. Roselle (*dah*, *Hibiscus sabdariffa*) is planted around the edge of bush fields to demarcate the border of newly cut land, and it provides condiments to spice up the millet porridge.

Maize is grown in small plots on the village fields, and, though not significant overall, it plays a vital role in offering food in the hungry season, before millet is

Figure 3.14. Farmer with his sesame crop after harvest, 2010

ready to cut. In September, fresh maize cobs are being grilled and chewed by everyone in the village. The Bambara earthnut (*tiga nkuru*, *Vigna subterranea*) also provides an early maturing crop, being ready to harvest in 6–8 weeks, and it thrives even on poor soils and erratic rainfall (see Figure 3.15). It is much appreciated in late September, while people are waiting for the main millet harvest to start. This underground crop looks similar to the more familiar groundnuts, which were widely grown in the 1950s and 60s, but have largely disappeared because today people rarely harvest as much seed as they sow.

Fonio (*fini*, *Digitaria exilis*) is the Sahel's oldest native crop, with archaeo-botanical evidence showing it having first been cultivated 7,000 years ago.[24] Barely more than a grass, it was sown as a household crop in DBG until the 1970s, and then became a women's crop. However, they now say it involves too much hard work, and they cannot get their menfolk to help with the harvesting and threshing. The emergence of a significant market for fonio in Ségou might encourage women to restart production, if the prices were good enough. Tobacco and a range of irrigated vegetables are grown on small plots close to the village, where water can be brought to irrigate the crops in the dry season. Some vegetables—onions, tomatoes, spinach, aubergine, and okra—are also grown in the wet season, relying on rainfall, produce which varies the diet and enables women to earn a little money from sales within the village.

[24] McIntosh, R.J. (1998).

Figure 3.15.   Bambara earthnuts, *tiga nkuru*, in their shell, DBG, 2016.

Field systems

The landscape around DBG is typical of many West African farming systems.[25] As can be seen from Figure 3.16, the centre is a cluster of houses, surrounded by a ring of permanently cultivated village fields that receive whatever manure and household waste are available. A set of large, shifting bush fields are cultivated some 5 km or more from the settlement. In the intermediate zone, made up of old fallows, people farm individual plots of sesame. Herds of cattle, sheep, and goats graze across the landscape, creating concentrations of soil fertility, in places where animals are kraaled overnight. This extensive agro-pastoral system works for so long as there is a substantial land reserve, so that bush fields can be fallowed for 30–50 years, to allow the soil's fertility to recover before land is ploughed again. A large pasture area provides cattle, sheep, and goats with enough grazing around the settlement for herds to find the fodder they need in both wet and dry seasons. And at nightfall, the livestock return to the village, bringing nutrients in the form of dung to the village-field soils. However, as will be seen, this system of crop-livestock integration has now broken down because of a growing imbalance between grazing and cropland, as discussed in this chapter and in Chapter 4.

---

[25]   Raynaut, C. (1997); Hart, K. (1982); Ruthenberg, H. (1980).

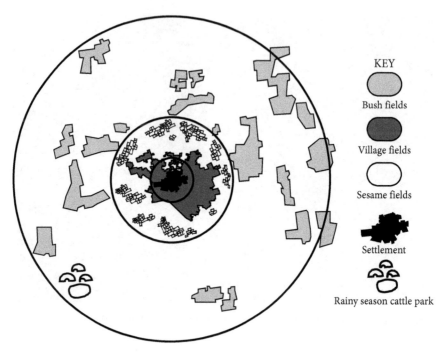

Figure 3.16. Land use around DBG, 2016

Bush fields

The bush fields of DBG are large areas of lightly cleared land, with many trees and bushes left in place. They are unfenced and have no obvious field boundaries, although their edges are visible on the aerial images because of cultivated land looking paler in colour compared with neighbouring bush fallow. The largest of these fields today is 115 ha, and it is cultivated by the household of the village chief, up from 67 ha in 1981. While this field is exceptionally large for the households in DBG, many others cover 30–50 ha. These are enormous areas, explained partly by the very large size of the Bambara households concerned and partly by the extensive farming methods practised. The average field area per adult person in the farming team is 3–4 ha. These large fields are also the result of the widespread use of oxen-drawn ploughs, which allow for rapid ridging and weeding of the light sandy soils, to take maximum advantage of the short rainy season. There are 121 ploughs in the village, with all households having at least one piece of equipment, though several families have to borrow a second ox to complete their team. The family of the chief has ten ploughs, and it is very impressive to see them all at work at the start of the farming season. Introduced to DBG in the 1950s for groundnut cultivation, these light ploughs are used for preparing land by creating a ridge along which the millet is sown, and for weeding once it has sprouted. Ploughs are made and repaired locally by the blacksmiths of Noumoubougou, 8 km away. It is interesting to note that the chief's field, while it has nearly doubled in size over the last 35 years, has not increased in line with the size of the household, which grew more than threefold from fifty-six people in 1980, to 184 in 2016. This illustrates a trend by which labour has shifted from work on the household millet field to channelling effort into private plots of sesame, described in more detail below.

Placed side-by-side, bush fields move slowly over time, away from the village, adding a piece of new land onto the front, and leaving behind the oldest land. Each field is a patchwork of pieces of land cleared in successive years, as shown in Figure 3.17. Before the widespread ownership of ploughs, it was common practice to sow rapidly the old bush-field surface without having ploughed it first. This aimed to get the millet seed into the soil as quickly as possible following the first serious rainfall, using a long-handled hoe to scoop out little planting pits, a technique known as *paki*. Most households are now choosing to plough and ridge the entire bush field before sowing millet, to generate more breathing space for the workforce and allow them to get the village field ploughed and sown, before returning to weed the bush field. However, ploughing the entire bush field before

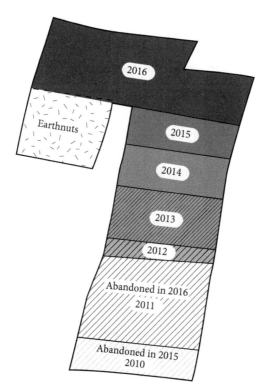

Figure 3.17. Bush-field composition: a patchwork of plots (age/date when land cleared and abandoned)

sowing takes longer than the rapid *paki* method, and thus risks jeopardizing the harvest if the rains end early.

New land at the front edge of the bush field is often put under crops like Bambara earthnuts, which benefit from the better fertility, and leave a welcome legacy of nitrogen in the soil for next year's crop of millet. Field boundaries are planted with *dah*, which makes an attractive border, as well as clearly demarcating the new field. Since it is harvested late, after the millet, it also demonstrates to herd owners the continued occupation of the field space. Soil fertility declines after 4-5 years of growing millet, so the strip of land abandoned each year is usually 5 years' old. By this stage, it has become pretty tired, and it hosts a number of plants which indicate its exhaustion—especially *fogo-fogo* and *zamara*.[26]

Village fields

Village fields form the circle of permanently farmed land around settlements like DBG, receive some level of manure and household waste to boost fertility, and host stands of *balanzan*, tamarind, and shea trees. The village fields are usually sown with the short-cycle *sunan* millet variety, and there are small patches of maize and earthnuts. Today, a couple of households facing shortages of labour and manure have sown *sanyo* on their village fields. You can expect some harvest from *sanyo*, even if the soil is poor, whereas *sunan* needs manure if it is to mature in the short time available for its growth, flowering, and setting seed. Village-field land is always ploughed before sowing because it will be covered with sprouting weeds by the time the family leaves the sowing of the bush field and gets onto sowing the shorter-cycle millet. *Sunan* millet is usually intercropped with cowpea, which adds a bit of nitrogen to the soil, but the widespread pink patches of a parasitic weed (*ségé*, Striga, or witchweed) indicate that many of the village fields are exhausted by decades of cropping without enough nutrients being put back into the soil. No one enjoys the tiring and smelly job of carting rubbish and dung, so it is only the more energetic young men of the household who devote serious time to this. It was much easier to keep your fields manured when cattle herds were regularly shifted from field to field over the dry season, their overnight kraal being set up on each plot in turn. There has also been an increasing problem attributable to infestation by a shrubby plant, *Sesbania*, which has seeded itself across much of the village-field land and needs early uprooting to stop it suffocating the millet.

Most wells are dug on plots of land around the village so that the field owner benefits from the dung deposited by livestock being watered at his well (see Figure 3.18, colour plates section). In the long dry season, you used to find many Fulani and Maure herders camped, in huts, tents, and shelters on the fields belonging to the well owner, but far fewer are present today (see Chapter 6). The shortage of grazing within easy reach of the village means that herd owners want

---

[26] *Calotropis procera* and *Cenchrus biflorus*.

Figure 3.18. Cattle waiting to be watered at the well in the dry season; in the
background the shade trees of the schoolyard can be seen, 2011

to keep their animals out grazing for as long as possible, often taking 2–3 days
between each watering, so they can access more distant pastures.

Grazing lands

The landscape around DBG is the product of many decades of settlement and
cultivation, so that the mix of trees and bushes shows clearly when land has been
farmed and fallowed. Of the broader area around DBG, about a quarter of the
landscape is not suitable for farming, has been left uncultivated, and is used as
grazing land. Land which has been cultivated but is now in fallow gradually re-
establishes a layer of bushes and grass, which provide feed for cattle, sheep, and
goats, which forage by themselves for those months of the year there are no crops
in the ground.[27] Boys are sent out to the bush to collect hay for the large number
of donkeys on which so many transport operations now rely. Four households
have a horse, but this is considered a luxury, which only older men are tempted
to acquire, remembering the olden days. Herders cut branches from several shrubs
and small trees to provide forage for animals in the hot dry season, before the
annual regreening of pastures takes place. During the farming season, village cattle
are kept in a camp on the southwest edge of the village fields, close to a large pond,
and they are left free to wander in the dry season, returning to the village wells
when they need water.[28] Well-established livestock routes run north–south

[27] Cissé, M. I. and Hiernaux, P. (1984).
[28] Livestock assets and their management are described more fully in Chapter 6.

across the landscape, allowing for the seasonal movement of large herds. These routes are meant to be protected from cultivation, but increasingly fields are encroaching on them, generating conflicts with herders as they trek their animals south next to ripening fields at the end of the rains.

Water

In a dryland region like the Sahel, access to a good water supply is critical to humans and livestock, and controlling access to water provides a source of power over others. Villages with poor water supply not only suffer ill health from reliance on small quantities of often-dirty water, but they must also beg for help from neighbouring villages. This puts them in a situation of dependence; it slows the number of people wanting to settle there and discourages young women from marrying into the settlement because they know their household duties will be extra hard. DBG's neighbours Misribougou and Jessourna both have faced difficulty in getting a reliable source of water, and have struggled to provide supplies for people and animals through the long dry season. In the case of Misribougou, a brother of the chief has been living in Senegal's capital, Dakar, and sending money back to help his natal village find water. But despite his generosity, they have still not succeeded in getting a reliable supply because of the depth and unpredictability of the water table. They may now try to pipe water from a neighbouring village instead. For Jessourna, a new well in 2010 has greatly improved access to water, but it has not been enough to support the villagers' livestock in the dry season, which continue to trek to the wells of neighbouring Taiman.

In the case of DBG, digging a well has been a key strategy in getting better millet yields. As described in more detail in Chapter 6, this is because they have been a means to gain access to dung with which to manure farmers' fields. Manure is valued more highly than chemical fertilizer, because the latter is considered too strong, and it risks 'burning' the millet plant. In addition, people say that once your soil gets used to chemical fertilizer, you have to buy it each and every year, or be faced with total crop failure. By contrast, the positive effects of manure can last for 2–3 years before needing renewal. If used, fertilizer is mixed into the seed so that a few grains of urea or ammonium sulphate are added to the planting hole.

The farming cycle

The farming system rotates around an annual calendar of activities, as shown in Figure 3.19. The rainy season is short and uncertain in terms of the distribution of rainfall in both time and space. Hence, to ensure a full granary of millet at the end of the harvest, the household needs to be prepared to make the best of whatever

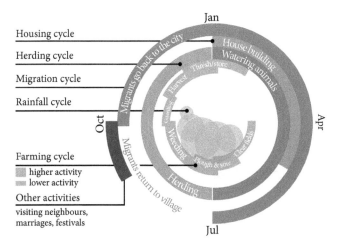

Figure 3.19. The annual household farming cycle at DBG

the rains may bring. In May, before the rains begin, people go out to their more distant fields to clear them of bushy growth. Many trees are left standing in the fields, so much of this work involves collecting up and burning old stubble, uprooting smaller shrubs, and hacking away at branches that will shade the millet crop too much. The farm workforce will also clear a new piece of land to add to the bush field, leaving a stretch of older land behind to regain its strength through fallowing. A few valued trees may be felled, such as *gwele*, and *kapok*, but most farmers prefer a large, partially cleared field to a smaller immaculate plot. Once the rains come, the fields will need to be ready for sowing as rapidly as possible because getting the millet sown early makes a big difference to the final harvest, especially when rain stops early in September.

By mid-June, a heavy rain usually provides sufficient confidence for most farmers to get out into the bush fields to sow the longer-cycle *sanyo* millet, but they will wait until July before sowing the short-cycle *sunan*. Weeding is the main task, and young men return from migration to help their families with this, if for nothing else. The 2 months of July and August offer long days of hard work, with teams of oxen-drawn ploughs loosening the soil and uprooting many weeds, followed by a team of hoers who clear away the remains. Keeping weeds down gives the millet the best chance of gaining whatever moisture and nutrients are available . If the bush field is a long way from the village, for much of July and August, part of the workforce stays out in huts on the edge of the field, so no time is lost on the long walk to and from home (see Figure 3.20). By mid-September, the weeding is finished, and there is little to do but guard the field against live-stock and birds while waiting for the crop to mature.

The *sunan* village-field millet is harvested first, from late October, although by then, those families short of grain will already have started cutting millet for

Figure 3.20. Straw huts for the weeding team to sleep in at the height of the farming season, June 2014

their immediate food needs. The millet is threshed and winnowed before being transported back to the village, and stored in a new granary. Threshing and winnowing takes place on hardened soil on the edge of the village fields, the millet spears having been transported by donkey cart from the fields. In 1980, hand threshing was done by a team of young men wielding sticks, which passed systematically to and fro, over the bed of millet heads (see Figures 3.21 and 3.22). However, in 1981, the villagers hired a *nyo goshi mashin* or threshing machine, which took the form of an old tractor, which was driven in circles over the crop laid out on the ground. The truck driver came from Ségou, and passed several months out in the villages, earning millet in exchange for the threshing work. Women winnow the millet, once the threshing is done, separating the chaff, straw, and sand from the grain. They say it has become much easier to winnow, thanks to the mechanized threshing, and it means they can work more quickly. The winnowing work is an exclusively female domain, with women from neighbouring households helping each other out with the work. It is a hot, dusty, and exhausting task, and women make their way back to the village at the end of each winnowing day covered in *nyenye*—the itchy husks in which the millet grain nestles. Women award themselves wages paid in millet for their work, the scale of generosity to themselves and other helpers depending on the success of the harvest. Once the millet is winnowed clean and standing in a shining pile on the threshing floor, the men and boys are allowed to fetch it in their carts to take back to the village. The *sanyo* bush-field millet, harvested from December, follows a similar process to that of *sunan*, and usually, it is safely stored by mid-January.

Figure 3.21. In 1980, young men threshed millet by hand

Figure 3.22. 'Threshing machine' at work, 1981

Figure 3.19 presented an orderly sequence of the work to be done in the household fields. In practice, each rainy season is different in terms of the amount and distribution of rainfall, and farmers do not know in advance what is going to be the best strategy.[29] After the first rains, they ask themselves should we start sowing the bush field, even though there maybe a couple of weeks without a follow-up storm? When should we shift from bush to village-field work, especially if the rains have started late, and activities are tightly squeezed together? In the past, farmers agreed a common strategy to start work at the same time when sowing their bush or village fields. But now each household tends to decide for itself what it is best to do. The cycle of activities presented in Figure 3.19 related to the household, rather than individual farming. For the latter, the main activity today, in which almost everyone is involved, is cultivation of a sesame field. As this is a private crop, people are meant to limit their time to Mondays (when, by tradition, millet should not be cultivated), and to early mornings or late afternoons, once work on the family's field has finished for the day. When possible, people hire a plough team to prepare the land, and labour to weed the crop. However, many people are spending more time and energy on their private sesame plots, arriving tired and late to weed the household millet, which damages the household's harvest.

Livestock system

Every household in DBG owns some livestock because they provide essential services both to farming and to the broader economy, but their needs must be accommodated within the farming landscape, and labour must be found to herd the animals away from crops. In the rainy season, most cattle are kept in a camp away from the village and taken to pasture by a young man or boy, but work oxen will be led out to the fields each day and tethered in the compound at night. Sheep and goats are also kept in the compound, and they are taken out to pasture during the farming season by a hired herder during the day. Donkeys and horses are tethered in the compound, and fodder is brought to them. Watering of animals is a major task for all households with cattle, which must be done from November when the pools in the bush have dried up, until the start of the rains in June or July. Herding of cattle used to be carried out by hired Peul labour, but most families have now sacked their herders and prefer to get one of their young men to take on the task, despite this removing labour from the family field.

Table 3.1 shows a consistent increase in the number of work oxen over the period 1980–2016, which illustrates the importance of ploughing in the farming system.

---

[29] Richards, P. (1989).

Table 3.1. Bambara livestock holdings
1980 and 2016

	1980	2016
Cattle	602	685
Oxen	120	189
Sheep + goats	698	1051
Donkeys	45	352

Cattle numbers have only seen a small increase, which may be partly accounted for by the pressure on grazing today, which reduces cattle productivity, and partly, from significant sales over recent years because of poor harvests. By contrast, there has been an eightfold increase in the number of donkeys, which reflects their central importance for transport of water, wood, and people to the fields and to market. Women say their burdens have been significantly reduced thanks to this big increase in the donkey population. The value of a donkey and cart can be seen by their popularity as a key item in the 'trousseau' a girl takes on her marriage. Sheep and goats are important assets for many individuals, though their total number has risen more slowly than the human population has. A more detailed description of livestock ownership and its distribution by household, along with the risks and returns from these assets, is presented in Chapter 6.

Harvests and crop yields

Table 3.2 presents data on the total size of the villagers' annual millet harvest, from the period of my first fieldwork in 1980–1982, compared with harvests from the last three seasons.[30] This shows the continued growth in the overall harvest of bush-field millet, while the village-field millet harvest has fallen to a third of its former size. The total millet harvest has barely changed between 1980–1982 and 2016, because of a mediocre bush-field harvest. The total harvest in 2017 at 330,417 kg was somewhat better, because of a significantly better bush-field harvest, but it fell back in 2018. Given the growth in population, the harvest of millet in kilograms per person has tumbled to less than half its former value. In none of the years 2016–2018 was enough millet harvested to feed an adult over the year (estimated at 1 kg/day), let alone provide for other essentials, such as purchase of farm equipment or a new ox or payment of taxes.

---

[30] In 1980–1982, and 2016–2018, the millet harvest for each household was estimated by measuring the circumference of each granary, which is broadly cylindrical, at top, middle, and base, their height, and the depth of millet within them. An adjustment was made for the thickness of the mud and straw wall, and the volume of millet in cubic metres then converted into weight. This method, while rough and ready, has the merit of consistency across the different periods of research.

Table 3.2. Comparing the millet harvest for Dlonguébougou, 1980–1982 and 2016–2018

	Average 1980–1982	2016	2017	2018	Average 2016–2018
Total harvest BFM	132,000	222,228	290,167	225,973	246,122
Yield per ha BF	212	72	94	73	80
Total harvest VFM	136,000	44,482	40,250	65,260	49,997
Yield per ha VF	1002	99	90	146	112
Total millet harvest	268,000	266,710	330,417	291,232	296120
Kg millet per person	502	168	206	176	183

Abbreviations: BF, bush field; BFM, bush-field millet; VF, village field; VFM, village-field millet.

Figure 3.23 presents the data on millet harvests in visual form. The collapse in the harvest of the *sunan* millet grown on village-field land is particularly striking. In the period 1980–1982, this represented half of the millet harvest, whereas in 2016, it was less than 20 per cent of the total. Data for the farming seasons of 2017 and 2018 tell a similar story, although the village-field *sunan* performed somewhat better in 2018, whereas the bush-field *sanyo* harvest was more substantial in 2017.

Why have millet yields fallen so low?

There are three principal reasons for the fall in millet yields.

First, there is increased pressure on grazing land and loss of soil fertility in the village fields. The large-scale application of dung by herds of cattle, sheep, and goats, which we observed in 1980–1982, produced average yields of 1,000 kg of grain per hectare from the village fields. But today, farmers say yields have plummeted, despite rainfall being at similar levels. Harvest measurements for 2016–2018 show that yields have fallen by more than 80 per cent to less than 100 kg/ha. There is much less grazing available for village cattle and visiting herds because of the large expansion in cultivated area.[31] Animals must go further to forage, and they are less able to get back every night to sleep and manure the village soils. As will be described in Chapter 6, some visiting herders still come to DBG in the dry season to water their stock at the village's wells, but they prefer to pay with cash to access water, so they do not have to bring the herd back to be kraaled on the well owner's field every night, and can therefore reach better pasture. Pressure on

---

[31] Ruthenberg (1980) argues that long-cycle bush fallow systems, in which livestock transfer nutrients from grazing to village fields, can operate effectively as long as the proportion of cultivated to total land remains below 5 per cent. As will be seen in Chapter 4, land pressures today mean that more than 25 per cent of land is under cultivation, which helps explain the erosion of soil fertility.

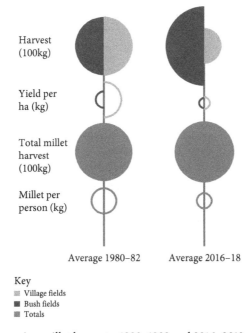

Key
▨ Village fields
■ Bush fields
■ Totals

Figure 3.23. Comparing millet harvests, 1980–1982 and 2016–2018

scarce grazing has also increased with the arrival of herds from villages further south next to the new sugar cane plantation, which must avoid the risk of animals getting into the cane fields, or risk their confiscation and fines.

Second, the increase in cultivated area has reduced the land reserve available to DBG farmers, as will be described in Chapter 4, especially in the northwest, where farmers prefer the lighter sandy soils found there. The bush-field fallow cycle is shortening, and it will likely bring about a further fall in productivity for the long-cycle *sanyo* millet. Some farmers are adding a little inorganic fertilizer to their bush fields, mixed in with seed at sowing time, but large-scale use of inorganic fertilizer has not yet been taken up.

Third, people are spending much more time on their private fields, rather than the household's millet field. Given the shortness of the rainy season, early weeding of millet is essential to getting a reasonable yield, if the plants are not to be overcome by competition from weeds. This is particularly true for *sunan* millet in the village fields. Thus, as one man commented, the collective millet granary is shrinking in size, while private pockets are filling, and he observed, 'if people are getting up in the morning at dawn to go and spend a few hours on their private plot, before turning up for work in the household's field, and leaving by about 3pm, it's not surprising that the millet granary suffers.'[32] The scale of the increase

---

[32] Interview, June 2014.

in private fields is discussed further in Chapter 4, and Chapter 5 provides more detail on the shift in the balance of people's responsibilities away from the collective household estate and towards their private interests.

Conclusion

The seasonal cycle of activity linked to the cropping system is at the heart of DBG life at the household and village level, and the centrality of farming and livestock keeping is made evident by the pattern of land use around the settlement. While many young people go away on migration each year, the majority come back for 2 or 3 months to help their families at the height of the cultivation season, when weeding labour is most in demand. Rainfall is becoming more unpredictable and intense, with the distribution of rainfall within the season more important than total volume, as was clear from 2016 when yields were very low despite a large total of rainfall received. Increased pressure on land because of the spread of cultivation and large number of livestock grazing the area around DBG have led to falling millet yields from the large extension of bush fields, and much scarcer quantities of manure for maintaining village-field soil fertility. The fall in millet yields is also due to a shift in the amount of labour from collective household activities to private farming of sesame. A further factor constraint on the farming system is the large inflow of migrant farmers seeking land to cultivate around this and neighbouring villages. Both the reasons for this inflow and its scale will be explored in Chapter 4.

4

From abundance to land scarcity

Kongo ka bo, a tese ka ban.[1]

Introduction

In 1980, when I first visited Dlonguébougou (DBG), the village lay on the edge of the farming zone, and going north from the village, there seemed a never-ending supply of land to farm. 'The bush is so big', said the villagers 'it can never finish'. But when I went on a visit to DBG in 2006, the villagers said sadly 'the bush is finished, it's ruined'.[2] And since then, even more people have arrived to farm the village's land, generating multiple consequences for the viability of this agro-pastoral system. How could this great land abundance turn to scarcity in the space of 25 years? With the help of fieldwork and satellite images, it has been possible to answer this question, by tracking changes in land use around the village, and exploring the origins of and reasons for the large increase in people coming into this area in search of farmland.

Institutions, politics, and land tenure

What are DBG's customary boundaries and tenure?

DBG's history as a long-established settlement is the basis for the traditional rights its inhabitants claim over land and other resources in its territory. Villagers consider their 'customary rights' to extend over the surrounding territory, with their boundaries set at the halfway point between DBG and the next-door settlement of any historical significance. They can point, for example, on the road between DBG and Markabougou in a northeasterly direction, to a grove of baobab trees that marks the midpoint between the two villages, which everyone knows as the frontier marker, as shown in Figure 4.1. However, these are unwritten rights, which are not formally recognized by government. The new land law, described below requires that the village lands be mapped, ownership rights attested, and a certificate issued before they acquire legal recognition.

---

[1] 'The bush is so big, it can never finish.' [2] *Kongo banna, a tiena, pew!*

Land, Investment and Migration. Camilla Toulmin, Oxford University Press (2020). © Camilla Toulmin.
DOI: 10.1093/oso/9780198852766.001.0001

Figure 4.1. Baobab trees on the road to Markabougou show the boundary of DBG's customary lands, 2014

Figure 4.2 shows the rough boundaries of DBG's customary land. It is most extensive towards the north, where it stretches 25–30 km to include Farakaye, and Jessourna, and over to the west to meet Sonango's lands halfway. Jessourna, Noumoubougou, Misribougou, and Sogoba are all offspring villages, settled on DBG's traditional lands, as are Niaro, Trokena, and Nienkindola. While they used to be dependent on DBG for collection and payment of taxes, more recently they have become villages recognized in their own right, which means that they now pay their taxes directly to the commune. Noumoubougou, where blacksmiths settled in the 1970s, is still registered through Dlaba, the village 15 km to the south from which the smiths originated. The boundaries of the commune, established in 1999, cut through DBG's customary territory, and fragment its integrity. As a result, the village council no longer feels in control of their lands, and they have seen several incursions into what they consider their customary territory.

Until the mid-1980s, there was relatively little pressure on land, and DBG could control its boundaries. There was still much game to be had, and, during our 2 years at DBG, hunters brought back an ostrich, an aardvark, a pangolin, and lots of antelope, partridge, and guinea fowl. The hunters' society was very active, and a big festival was held in honour of its oldest and most eminent members in 1982. Until the mosque was built in 1998, the *dasiri* sacred wood and the strong *komo* animist society were maintained, both linking the first settlers to the spirits of the place, and providing a powerful means to control strangers and other non-initiates, such as women and children. But now, most of the land to the east and

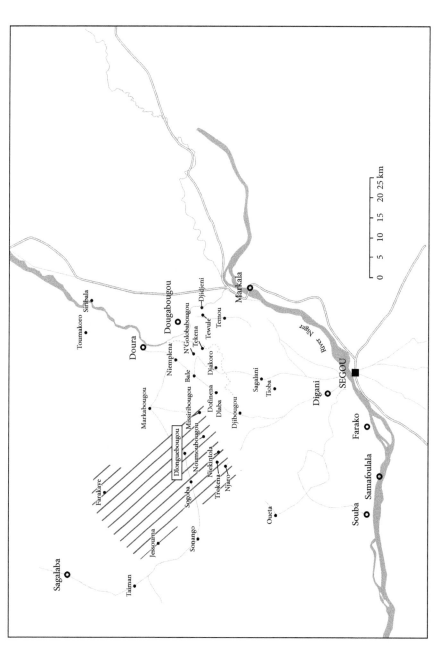

Figure 4.2. DBG customary territory: a rough guide

south of the village is farmed by families from villages badly hit by their proximity to the irrigated *Office du Niger*. As noted in Chapter 3, the villagers of DBG have aimed to preserve the sandy soils of land to the north and west of their village for their own use, so far as possible. They prefer these lands in large part because they have sandy soils, which give better harvests in years of low rainfall, rather than the harder clays and gravelly soils to the south and east of the village. In the 1990s, they say they made the mistake of handing out large amounts of land to the north of the village to migrant farmers, which they subsequently closed off to newcomers.

The strength and geographic extent of the customary rights which DBG claims have yet to be tested in law. Currently, someone seeking land in DBG comes to visit a family with whom he or she has some kind of social relationship, typically through marriage. The family head becomes the host, or *jaatigi*, of the incoming 'stranger', acting as the intermediary between the 'stranger', the village council, and other people in DBG.[3] The villagers insist that no money changes hands in exchange for this land, but that the common humanity which binds them to their wider kin obliges them to give access to land to those in need. *Jaatigiya* is a very long-standing institution found throughout West Africa, and it provides a means for people to establish themselves in a new location and community. Using a similar relationship, many Sahelian families settling in Côte d'Ivoire have worked through a local *jaatigi* in the forest zone, to gain access to land for growing cocoa and coffee.[4]

A complex legal position

While the villagers of DBG are keen to assert their de facto ownership of customary land, from a legal point of view, the actual status and extent of their land are more uncertain. In the colonial period, the French administration claimed for the State the rights of eminent domain over all land and resources, above and below ground.[5] On Independence, the government of Mali adopted this legislation and the associated powers, which allowed the state to take land from customary rights holders without needing to pay compensation. In 1991, when the overthrow of Moussa Traoré's regime heralded the establishment of democracy, new laws— such as the 2000 *Code Domaniale et Foncier*—recognized customary land tenure and provided some level of protection to these rights.[6] They also confirmed

---

[3] Strangers are known as *dunan*.

[4] Chauveau, J.-P. (2001); Brock, K. and Coulibaly, N. (1999).

[5] The few exceptions concerned the rare cases of land that had acquired some form of legal title, mainly in the capital Bamako, and the extensive title allocated to the *Office du Niger* irrigation scheme.

[6] Rochegude, A. and Plançon, C. (2009).

that in the event of state acquisition of land, compensation to customary rights holders would be paid for loss of a house, fruit trees, standing crops, and so on. However, in practice, the state retained pre-eminent rights over all land, even where long-standing customary occupation and use could be clearly established. There has been a fuzzy understanding of the boundary between the very large proportion of land in Mali which is untitled and held under customary tenure systems, and land which falls within the private domain of the state, a fuzziness which has provided considerable discretion to government officials.[7]

The new Agricultural Tenure Law (*Loi Foncier Agricole*), promulgated in April 2017, sets out to resolve this confusion, and it states clearly that the government only has rights over land either for which it has its own property title or where land truly has no clear customary owner.[8] Those lands which have not been titled but over which there are recognized customary rights have been taken out of the state domain (*domaine privé de l'etat*) and can be owned by a village or herders' camp. Both cultivating and herding communities that can demonstrate their long-term occupation and use of an area of land, without contest, can then seek to have such claims formally certified through attestation by a recognized government body. The implementation of the *Loi Foncier Agricole* is being planned, and pilot areas are being chosen for testing out the new structures and procedures. Recent decrees outline the composition and functions of land tenure committees at the level of villages and herders' camps, the procedure for registering land transactions, and the establishment of a national observatory on land rights, but progress with implementation is slow.[9]

The establishment of local government in 1999 has created room for doubt over who determines land rights because it raises the question of how village rights, represented by the chief and his village council, relate to those of the commune, as represented by the *maire* and communal council. The *maire* is not authorized to allocate land within the commune to particular individuals, though they can authorize the reclassification of farmland into building plots. Whatever the law says, however, *maires* have been known to play a more active role in land markets.[10] The *maire* of a neighbouring commune has made such a land allocation at the northern end of DBG's territory, in the Farakaye area, which the villagers consider very firmly as belonging to them. Land has been given to an influential person seeking grazing for his cattle herd; he has constructed a water tower filled from a borehole, and is enclosing a large tract of land. The villagers consider this land allocation to be illegitimate because it is on their customary land and they were not consulted. Equally, it was done by the *maire* of a neighbouring

---

[7] Professor Moussa Djiré, interview on the new *Loi Foncier Agricole*, August 2017. https://www.iied.org/qa-how-new-law-mali-securing-villagers-rights-land.
[8] *Loi 2017 001 11 avril 2017 portant sur le Foncier Agricole.*
[9] Décret no. 2018 0333/P-RM du 4 avril, 2018. Décret no. 2018 0334/P-RM du 4 avril, 2018.
[10] Djiré, M. (2004, 2007); Bertrand, M. and Djiré, M. (2016).

commune, who does not have any authority outside his commune's boundaries. However, regardless of the formal situation, the villagers of DBG recognize they are powerless to act, and are fearful of what this new arrival might do, if they contest his land claim. Perhaps he has rich and powerful allies in government. DBG villagers describe themselves as powerless (*fantan*) pawns in a game being played by the more powerful people associated with government (*faama*), who know the rules and how to make them work in their favour.

In DBG as elsewhere, everyone recognizes the need for a document or *papier*, which confirms their rights over land.[11] They are not sure of the form this should take, but they agree that any paper is better than no paper. In the case of DBG, there is a body representing the village and associated settlements around it, the *Association Villageoise de Dlonguebougou et Hameaux Voisins* (established in 1997), although its status and legal recognition are unclear. There is also the draft *Convention Locale* drawn up in 2013 at *Commune* level, which copies the *Convention Locale* developed by the neighbouring Commune of Bellen with German support (see Figure 4.3).[12] The purpose of the latter has been to gain recognition by the *Préfet* of the Cercle de Ségou, of the Commune's right to organize and manage land and natural resource use in its territory, specifically common grazing and

Figure 4.3. Grazing management scheme in neighbouring commune of Bellen, supported by Germany, 2011

---

[11]   Mathieu, P. et al (2002).   [12]   GTZ (Ed.) (2000).

woodlands.[13] The *Préfet* has not yet signed the *Convention*, and, even were he to do so, this document would provide no real protection against land being sought by a powerful third party. Until the passage of the 2017 *Loi Foncier Agricole*, the legal basis for such Conventions to manage land and natural resources was not assured. As discussed in Chapter 8, the piloting of the new law will test how easy it will be to put new provisions, such as Local Conventions, into practice.

The *Office du Niger* and irrigated sugar cane

For DBG and the wider area, a further complication on the legal front derives from the presence of the *Office du Niger*, which exercises rights over a wide area, totalling 2 million hectares, well beyond the 120,000 ha which are currently irrigated. The eastern half of N'Koumandougou commune falls within the zone deemed as potentially 'irrigable', and hence, the *Office* has the power to allocate land within it to those seeking an irrigated plot.[14] The village of DBG lies just on the western edge of this extensive irrigable zone. The *Office du Niger*, established in 1932, planned to use the old dried-up river valleys of earlier times to channel water northwards by building a dam at Markala on the River Niger. This ambitious project was originally intended to water 1 million hectares of land for cotton, and then rice, but by 1960, just 45,000 ha had been developed.[15] Today, after major investment and reorganization, 120,000 ha are being irrigated. After Mali's return to democracy in 1992, international agencies were called on to fund the rehabilitation of canals and infrastructure to improve management of water, and increase yields and returns to farmers. Significant improvements were made in the 1990s and 2000s, such that rice yields have risen fivefold.[16] Since 2010, there has been a new push to expand greatly the area under irrigation, with the Government of Mali proposing to increase to 200,000 ha the area it will develop with irrigation, and pledging to make available to private investors an additional 300,000 ha of land. It is argued that irrigated agriculture is the best means to modernize the agricultural sector, ensure greater food security, and produce key commodities, such as sugar and oil seeds. However, as will be seen in Chapter 8, questions remain about the financial sustainability of irrigated agriculture, given its reliance on donor funding, and difficulties with maintenance of the system. Many of the farmers in the *Office du Niger* remain below the poverty line,

---

[13] Appointed by central government, the *Préfet* is responsible for administration of a *Cercle*, usually made up of ten to fifteen communes. DBG falls within the commune of N'Koumandougou, in the Cercle of Ségou.

[14] 1932 Ordonnance, Article 3: *La gérance de l'Office du Niger peut s'étendre aux terres non irrigables que le Gouvernement estimera utiles à la mission de l'Office du Niger.*

[15] www.on-mali.org.

[16] Ministère du Développement Rural (2015); Adamczewski Hertzog, A. (2014).

despite big improvements in yields, because of fragmentation of plots and reliance on rice. At the same time, there are doubts about whether there are sufficient water supplies in the dry season for small-scale vegetable production, which brings a higher return, alongside thirsty crops like sugar cane, given the great fluctuations in seasonal flow of water in the River Niger. However, a new dam upstream in Guinea may provide a more predictable flow of water to the *Office du Niger* in the dry season, but at serious cost to farmers, fisherfolk, and herders downstream of the Markala Dam, as discussed in Chapter 8.

Irrigated sugar cane production began in the 1960s, with development of a plantation and construction of a sugar mill at Dougabougou by the Chinese government, but in the 1970s, production fell into decline. In 1996 a joint venture company between Sinolight and the Malian government, Sukala-SA, was set up to reinvigorate and expand production. In 2009, an agreement was signed between the China Light Industrial Corporation for Foreign Economic and Technical Co-operation (CLETC) and the Malian Government allocating a further 20,000 ha of land to a new sugar scheme, called N-Sukala.[17] This combines pivot-fed plots on the eastern side of the main Canal du Sahel, and fields under furrow irrigation on the west side of the Canal (see markers for identifying the boundaries of land allocated to N-Sukala in Figure 4.4).

The land was titled in the name of the Malian State before being transferred to the company N-Sukala. Of the 20,000 ha, 857 ha have been titled for purposes of building the necessary industrial infrastructure, while the remaining 19,143 ha are in the form of a 50-year lease. The government took a 40 per cent stake in the company, using the valuation of the land being transferred as its collateral. Article 6 of the convention notes that the government of Mali will both ensure the transfers of land are carried out in conformity with the *Code Domaniale et Foncier*, and will make aware (*sensibiliser*) the local population likely to be affected by the project. Article 7 notes that China Light (CLETC) commits to financing the necessary technical and socio-environmental studies, and the costs linked to raising awareness, the eviction and the resettlement of villages and populations affected by the project.[18]

During a visit to the area made by government and N-Sukala representatives in July 2010 to inform people in the affected communes of the planned project, the government representative noted the importance of the sugar cane project for the

---

[17] Signed by the *Ministre du Logement, des Affaires Foncières et de l'Urbanisme,* 22 June 2009, Bamako. While N-Sukala was stated to be a new company and, hence, eligible for a number of tax advantages, there have been close links between Sukala and N-Sukala from the beginning, such as a common board of directors, leading some to wonder whether N-Sukala had ever been a new enterprise (Nolte and Voget-Kleschin (2014)).

[18] *Article 7: Obligations de la CLETC: La CLETC s'engage à pré-financer pour le compte de N-SUKALA : les frais des études techniques et les études socio-environnementales ; les frais liés à la sensibilisation, au déguerpissement et à la réinstallation des villages et populations affectés par le projet.*

Figure 4.4. Boundary markers used to stake out N-Sukala's land-takings, 2017

Presidents of Mali and China.[19] Estimating the total investment at 80 billion CFA Francs,[20] to be funded by a 20-year loan made to the Malian government, the project was presented as a positive factor leading to greater development for people living in the project zone, with the prospect of 10,000 seasonal and 600 full-time jobs. Social benefits were also promised, with provision of roads, schools, and health centres all envisaged. The government representative reminded his audience that in Mali all land belongs to the state, and most particularly in the zone of the *Office du Niger*, so seeking agreement of the population for this project was not necessary. But it is an option he has taken advantage of, to let them know about the project before work starts.[21] But villagers should know that the boat transporting the equipment had already left China, and, hence, it would be a matter of days before work starts. In the *Compte Rendu* of the visit, the few remarks and questions from villagers reflected concerns about the exact location

[19] *Compte Rendu d'info sur N-Sukala, juillet 2010. Office du Niger, Direction Générale.*
[20] Equivalent to US$136 million at 2018 rates.
[21] *'Il est loisible d'informer les dites populations sur les enjeux du projet avant son démarrage.'*

of the factory and cane fields, pollution of water supplies from the existing Sukala project, and problems for livestock to make their way through the area given the multiplication of fields. Several villagers said they would welcome the project if it offered employment to their young men. Officials confirmed that an Environmental and Social Impact Study was due to be conducted, which should offer an opportunity for the concerns of the population to be taken into account. The deputy director of N-Sukala noted that they would rely on local labour and, hence, would leave in place most significant villages. However, herders' camps would have to be moved.

Work on N-Sukala began shortly after the visit in July 2010, with clearing of land, building new roads, construction of a bridge over the canal at Dougabougou, and digging of canals. The speed with which the project got underway was due to pressure from the then President ATT, who wanted to show progress had been made before the elections that had been due to happen in April 2012.[22] By 2016, around 8,000 ha of land were under sugar production on the west side of the canal. Villagers from affected areas had been told they must give up their fields, grazing, and woodlands for the benefit of Mali's development. An inventory was done of all their possessions, land, trees, housing, and livestock, with the understanding that some form of compensation would be forthcoming. A Committee was set up by the Regional Governor of Ségou, to provide oversight of the compensation process, but, by 2018, many farmers had still received no form of compensation for the loss of their fields and livelihoods.[23]

From the moment the farmers realised they would lose their land, they started searching for fields to cultivate elsewhere. Interviews with people from many of the affected villages say their households are now farming land up to 100 km away, around villages such as DBG, Markabougou, and Sonango, and beyond, into the neighbouring region of Koulikoro. All able-bodied men and women leave their homes in June, with donkey carts piled high, to walk for several days to wherever they have managed to negotiate access to land. They spend the entire cultivation season away from their home village, coming back with the harvest in December and January. They usually choose to go to villages where they have some kind of connection, to make negotiations easier, each family looking to identify friends and relations in villages to the north and west.

---

[22] The elections were cancelled, following the coup d'état of March 2012.

[23] The law requires an ESIA to be carried out before any project takes place, with the *Direction Nationale de l'Assainissement, du Contrôle des Pollutions et des Nuisances (DNACPN/DRACPN)* responsible for assessing its adequacy. Compensation for loss of land and assets is meant to be agreed before work starts. It appears that there has only been one meeting of the compensation committee to provide oversight of the compensation process.

Changes in land use around DBG, 1952–2016

A combination of aerial photographs, satellite images, and ground-level inter-views have been used to document changes in patterns of land use around DBG over the last 7 decades.[24] The earliest photos are from the aerial survey done in 1952, which provided the basis for a series of 1: 100,000 maps showing villages, tracks, and geographic features.[25] The grainy black-and-white image of DBG in 1952 (Figure 4.5) shows the tiny settlement and ring of village fields surrounded by a huge expanse of open country. A former soldier (OS) remembers this moment well. He had just come back from serving in the French colonial army as a *tirailleur sénégalais* in the Indo-China war, and he cut his small field out of the fallows behind Bina Tangara's large bush field, to the west of the village. Being a former soldier, he was able to bring back home a bit of capital with which to buy a plough and a bicycle, and set up as a farmer with the promise of a military pen-sion. His purchase of a plough allowed him to cultivate a field significantly larger than might be expected for a single couple, reliant on the hand-hoe.

Enlarging the photo image, the big trees which dot fields around the settlement are clearly visible, the baobab, tamarind, and *balanzan* (Figure 4.5). The sacred grove (*daasiri*) to the south of the settlement, and the fetish thicket (*komo tu*) to the west, can be clearly seen, as can the livestock route to the southeast of the settle-ment, the tell-tale signature of DBG from the air which appears like a comma in all the aerial images. This corridor, lined with euphorbia hedges, is the route along which sheep and goats are herded out of the village in the morning and back as dusk falls. The hedges stop this noisy flood of animals from rushing into the fields neighbouring the track and destroying the crops. From the village, a network of paths can be seen radiating in all directions, taking people out to their fields, and to surrounding hamlets and villages. The photo shows how some bush fields have grouped together, to share a common boundary, which helps when the crops need guarding from wandering herds and flocks. But others lie by themselves in a sea of bush. Some families like to strike out on their own, and try a new place with fresh soils. Others may join them later and create a cluster of fields shifting out together into the distance, following a direction that may take them 20 km from the village over a decade, before coming back to the village-field boundary and starting anew.

From the photos, you can see the striped pattern of bushes and shrubs, lying in strips along the folds of the landscape where rainfall congregates.[26] In the photos for 1952 and 1965 (Figures 4.5 and 4.6), there are a few patches of bare soil around

[24] Grateful thanks to Gray Tappan at USGS, Pierre Hiernaux at ILRI, and Chris Field and his team at GEODATA, University of Southampton, for providing a wide range of satellite images, and helping in their interpretation.
[25] *Institut Geographique National*, France. Available from *Institut Géographique Malien*, Bamako, Mali.
[26] Hiernaux, P. and Gerard, B. (1999).

Dolonguebougou, Mali - 1952

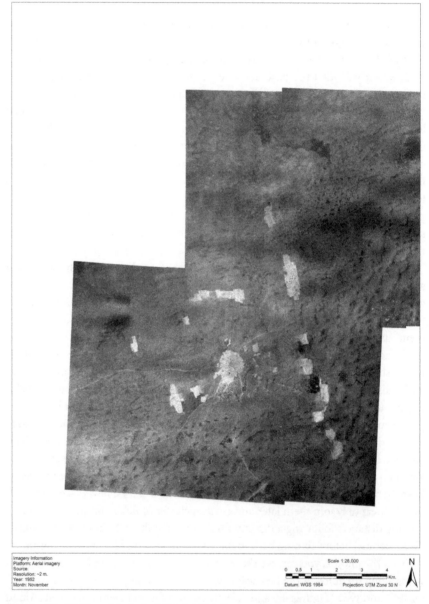

Figure 4.5. DBG aerial photo 1952. Institut Geographique National, IGN

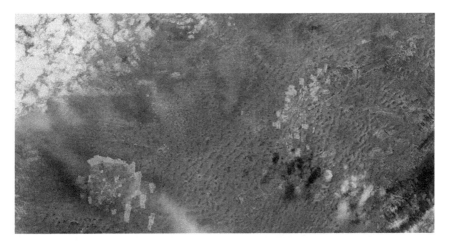

Figure 4.6. DBG 1965 Satellite image; U.S. Geological Survey

watering points, but most of all, settlements like DBG seem lost in a huge expanse of bush. Indeed, you can understand why villagers asserted firmly that the bush could never finish.

The 1965 photo in Figure 4.6 shows a similar pattern to 1952. The bush fields around DBG present a very well-organized grouping of linked fields marching out together, in contrast to neighbouring Markabougou (on the right-hand side of the image), where the bush fields are more scattered. The 1960s were a period of relatively high rainfall, and most villagers were starting to equip themselves with oxen-drawn plough teams, having seen the success of farmers like OS. Cloud has hidden the settlement of neighbouring Jessourna to the north-west.

Satellite images for 1975, 1984, 1995, and 2005, presented in Figure 4.7, show the shifts in cultivated area across the landscape over subsequent decades, and the gradual filling up of space in DBG's territory, which becomes particularly marked for 2016, 2017, and 2018, as shown in Figure 4.8. The quality for the early satellite images is not as good as the aerial photos of the 1950s, but the overall pattern is clear.

Patterns of land use today

Looking at the satellite image of DBG's land in 2016, 2017, and 2018 (Figure 4.8), there are fields in all directions, and almost all the land to the south and east has been filled up by fields. The orderly progression of bush fields, marching out together, is much less clear than in the 1970s and 1980s, when there were two major bush-field blocks, whereas today many are not contiguous. Many of them

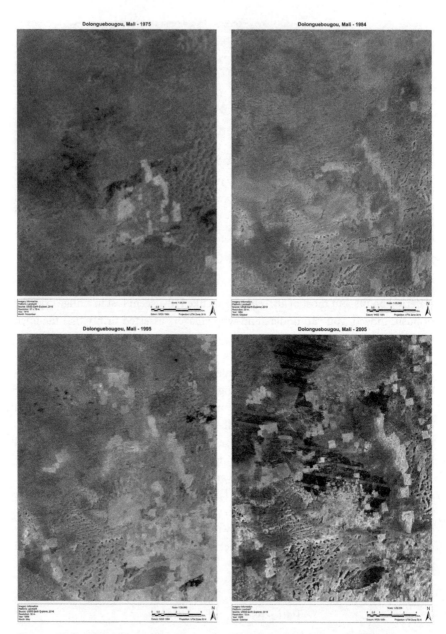

Figure 4.7 (i, ii, iii, iv). Satellite images for DBG, 1975, 1984, 1995, and 2005; U.S. Geological Survey

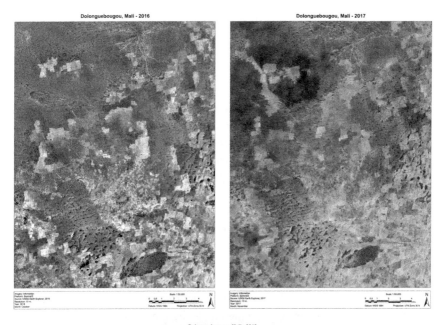

Figure 4.8 (i, ii, iii).   Satellite images of DBG, 2016, 2017, and 2018; Copernicus Sentinel data 2019

are a long way out, with the furthest more than 12 km away from the village. Several fields have been established on the northwest edge of the village's territory, as an explicit statement to outsiders about where DBG considers its boundaries to be. In two cases, the families farming these fields are also digging wells there as a further means to demonstrate occupation and ownership. As of 2018, they had not yet reached water, but they hope with further digging to get a decent supply, so they do not have to transport water daily all the way from the village. It is the larger families with an extensive workforce which tend to be on the outer margins of the village territory, and are able to make best use of the more fertile land that has been fallowed for longer. The small, poorly equipped families are closer in, on more recently fallowed land, which is just a short distance from the village fields. They have neither the plough teams nor workforce to maintain a large bush field. However, they will suffer the consequences of farming millet on land that has had little fallowing and, hence, is unlikely to give an excellent harvest, even if it gets good rainfall.

Table 4.1 presents the area of land under different forms of cultivation in the space around the village, and their share of the overall total land area, taking the satellite image as a rough approximation of the area under DBG's customary authority.[27]

Table 4.1 shows that the overall area under cultivation has grown steadily from 505 ha in 1952 to 7,503 ha in 2016, a fifteenfold increase over 65 years, and an eightfold increase from the 888 ha under cultivation in 1980–1982.The area of land cultivated by the actual inhabitants of DBG has grown from 840 ha in 1980–1982 to 4,356 ha, a fivefold increase, which compares with a threefold increase in village population over the same period. This implies that the farming system has become more extensive over the last 35 years. The data also show the rapid filling up of DBG's land since 1995, as a consequence of large numbers of incoming farmers seeking land. In 2017, there was a further increase in cultivated area, especially in the northwest of the village territory, bringing an additional 1,292 ha under the plough. This brings the total area cultivated for 2017 to 8,995 ha, equivalent to 26 per cent of the area around the village. And, in 2018, the total area under cultivation around DBG grew by a further 350 ha, made up of bush fields cut by incoming farmers, bringing the cultivated area to 27 per cent of total area.

Figure 4.9 shows these data visually for the different forms of land use. Bush fields have always been the largest element of the village land-use system, representing more than 70 per cent of land under cultivation for most years until 1995. Today, they represent 71 per cent of land area cultivated by the villagers of DBG. Average field size is 50 ha, the largest being more than 100 ha. Village fields grew by a factor of 3.4 between 1980–1982 and 1995, because there was a large increase

---

[27] Equivalent to 16.5 km by 21 km (346.5 km^2, or 34,650 ha).

Table 4.1. Changes in cultivated areas by field type, Dlonguébougou (DBG) territory: 1952–2016

Date of image	Bush-field area (ha) and per cent of all cultivated land	Village-field area (ha) and per cent of all cultivated land	Private fields (ha) and per cent of all cultivated land	Strangers' fields (ha) and per cent of all cultivated land	Total area cultivated (ha)	Area cultivated as per cent of total DBG lands
1952	384 (76 %)	94 (19 %)	27 (5 %)	0	505	1.5 %
1965	412 (67 %)	93 (15 %)	60 (10 %)	46 (8 %)	611	1.8 %
1975	701 (75 %)	161 (17 %)	70 (8 %)	0	932	2.7 %
1980–2*	631 (71 %)	164 (18 %)	45 (5 %)	48 (6 %)	888	2.6 %
1995	1,000 (47 %)	554 (26 %)	323 (15 %)	263 (12 %)	2140	6.2 %
2016	3103 (41 %)	447 (6 %)	806 (11 %)	3147 (42 %)	7503	21.7 %

*Note: for the years 1980–1982, areas cultivated were calculated from field measurements, not from aerial photos or satellite images.

Source: Calculations based on aerial photos and satellite images, confirmed through interviews in DBG.

Abbreviation: ha, hectares.

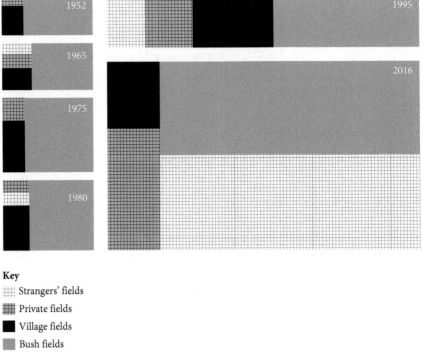

Key

▦ Strangers' fields

▦ Private fields

■ Village fields

▨ Bush fields

Figure 4.9. Changing distribution of agricultural land use, DBG, 1952–2016

in well digging by farm households in the 1970s and 1980s to secure dung from visiting transhumant herds.[28] Thus, by 1995, 26 per cent of all land being cultivated was made up of village fields. However, as cultivated area expanded and grazing became scarcer, fewer herds have sought water at DBG, and access to manure has consequently decreased. With falling access to manure, village fields have become less important, shrinking back to 10 per cent of land being cultivated by villagers today. Despite the decline in soil fertility, chemical fertilizer is used only in very small amounts.

Table 4.1 also shows that the area of land under private cultivation has greatly expanded, and it now represents 19 per cent of DBG cultivation. This mosaic of tiny plots occupies the space between the village and bush fields, and it is cultivated by individual men, women, and girls in their spare time. There are also several larger plots farmed by the *ton villageois* (the village youth association) and a few households. Sesame is the principal crop grown on private plots by individuals, known as a *jonforo*—meaning literally a 'slave-field', because in the past, household slaves were allowed to farm a small plot of land for themselves, once their work on the master's field had been finished for the day. As noted in Chapter 3, the *jonforo* are cultivated first thing in the morning and at the end of

---

[28] Described in detail in Chapter 6.

the day. They contrast with the collective field cultivated by the whole family, which is called *foroba*, literally 'big field' but which also means 'collective' or 'joint' property. People tend to clear individual plots on abandoned village lands, and in the fallow left by their family's old bush field.

In 1980, when I first arrived in DBG, everyone said they had abandoned their *jonforo* some years before (possibly in the late 1960s), and were investing all their energies in collective *foroba* production of millet.[29] The only people with private fields were elderly men and women who had retired from the family field, and some married women. But many households did not allow married women of an age to be working in the family field to devote time to private fields because they knew it would divert time and energy from collective production. Most households do not view sesame as a *foroba* crop, and it is farmed almost entirely by individuals for their personal gain. It has generated large sums for many people in the village. Individuals with energy and ambition can make 300,000 francs from a good harvest, which beats the earnings made from many months of migration.[30] In one particularly successful year, the *ton villageois* earned more than 3 million francs thanks to a big field and high prices. It is not surprising, therefore, that some household heads are worried that the lure of easy money from private fields is sapping the energies of the farm workforce, and they fear that the millet harvest is suffering as a result. This is evident in the size of millet harvests per person for 2016–2018, when compared with harvests 35 years ago (as was shown in Figure 3.23). The village chief is particularly concerned about people's focus on individual crops and private profit rather than collective household food production.

The very large increase in land farmed by 'strangers' is also very apparent from Table 4.1. This land covers more than 3,000 ha, and now represents an area slightly larger than the DBG villagers' own bush fields. The fields of strangers are similar to the villagers' bush fields, being large lightly cleared areas of land and sown with *sanyo* millet. There is one important difference, however, since incoming farmers are meant to stay within their boundaries, and not shift the plot over time to allow for soils to rest. For this reason, they have been using small amounts of chemical fertilizer on their crops, and having their livestock kraaled on the land where possible, to boost fertility.

'Stranger' farmers—who are they and where do they come from?

In 2016, 2017, and 2018, incoming farmers occupied more than 50 per cent of the bush-field land cultivated around DBG. Villages like DBG, and neighbouring settlements in this zone—Sonango, Jessourna, Shokun, and Taiman to the

---

[29] Wooten, S. (2009) notes a similar recent shift in favour of collective activity, especially for harvesting, amongst the Bambara of Western Mali.
[30] Equivalent to US$550.

northwest—have all received many incoming Bambara farmers asking permission to cut a field in their territory. But increasingly, because of the large numbers involved, the DBG village council says they have been turning people away, telling them to go onto the next village or the one beyond that, as they want to preserve some land for DBG villagers in future.

In 2017, there were seventy-two households of incoming farmers, making up a total of 881 people, allocated land at a number of settlement sites around DBG. They arrive in June of each year and stay until the harvest is threshed and stored in January, before returning home with the millet harvest. These incomers come from sixteen villages to the southeast of DBG, the largest number stemming from Tekena (twenty-seven households), followed by Niempiena (seven), Banougou (six), Sagalani (six), Balé (four), and Tiobaa (four), as can be seen from Figure 4.10.

The village of Tekena is surrounded by the recently established N-Sukala sugar cane plantation, as shown in Figure 4.11, whereas Niempiena, Banougou, and Balé are all on the edge of the plantation, have lost much of their farmland, and are plagued by bird pests. Many of these stranger households are recent arrivals in DBG, fifty-one of them having arrived in the last 10 years, and eleven have been here for between 10–20 years. However, ten have been cultivating in the DBG area for more than 20 years, and they came originally to escape the damage caused to their millet harvest by birds nesting in the irrigation canals.

Many of these villages to the south and east of DBG are long-established settlements which have been there since precolonial times. Sadly, this long heritage has afforded no protection to their farmlands, because they have the misfortune to be on land that was classified in the 1930s as within the 'irrigable zone' of the *Office du Niger*.

Even when villages have not lost much of their farm and grazing land to irrigated agriculture, the neighbouring sugar cane estates, and irrigation canals are the perfect nesting site for quelea,[31] golden weaver, and sparrows, which have multiplied in their millions. These birds descend in a ravening cloud on fields of millet before harvest, and they are so brazen, they cannot be chased away. Consequently, from the late 1970s, farmers in villages close to the *Office du Niger* have been looking for land further west, to avoid the bird-pest problem. Villagers in Dofinena, close to the sugar cane and badly damaged by birds, complain, 'Our people are exhausted. They spend all day in the field, they sleep in the field.'[32] In October 2016, they were harvesting their millet fields several weeks' early to stop predation by hordes of birds.

In 1997, Karen Brock in her study recorded that there were 753 'strangers' from fifty-nine farming households camped in eleven hamlets around DBG, all fleeing

---

[31] *Quelea quelea*, a finch-like bird from the weaver family.
[32] *Anka mogow segenna! U be tile forola, u be si forola.*

Figure 1.1. The village nestles in a saucer-like depression, 1981

Figure 1.7. Chief of the village Danson Dembélé (left) and his deputy Sirke Dembélé (right), 2014.

Figure 1.8. The village's sacred grove, or *dasiri*, 2016

Figure 1.11. Blacksmiths retain great importance for making and mending farm machinery, 2009

Figure 1.14. Construction of the maternity clinic, June 2008

Figure 3.8. *Sanyo* (bush-field millet) seedlings, 8 days after sowing, June 2014

Figure 3.14. Farmer with his sesame crop after harvest, 2010

Figure 3.18. Cattle waiting to be watered at the well in the dry season; in the background, the shade trees of the schoolyard can be seen, 2011

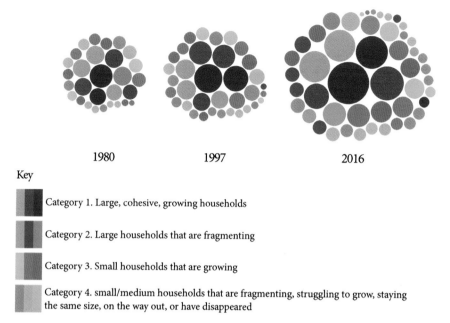

Key

Category 1. Large, cohesive, growing households

Category 2. Large households that are fragmenting

Category 3. Small households that are growing

Category 4. small/medium households that are fragmenting, struggling to grow, staying the same size, on the way out, or have disappeared

Figure 5.3. Household growth and change in DBG, 1980, 1997, and 2016

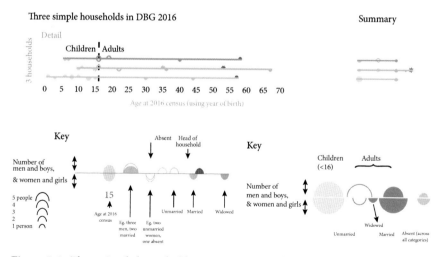

Figure 5.4. Three simple households in DBG, 2016: in detail (L) and summary (R)

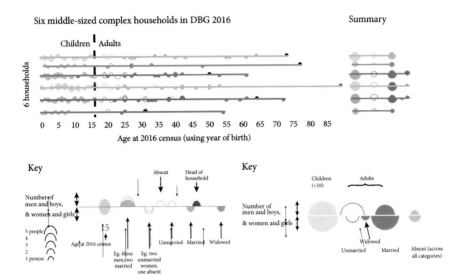

Figure 5.5. Six middle-sized complex households in DBG, 2016: in detail (L) and summary (R)

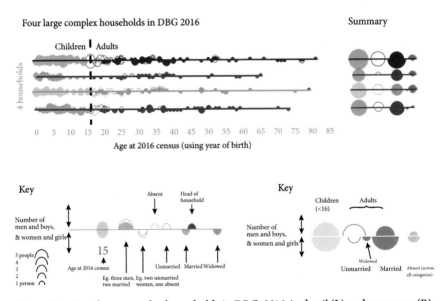

Figure 5.6. Four large complex households in DBG, 2016: in detail (L) and summary (R)

Figure 5.7. Young men from the family of the village chief come back from migration to help sow the bush field, June 2014

Figure 5.8. Drawing water from the well early in the morning, a regular daily task for women, 2014

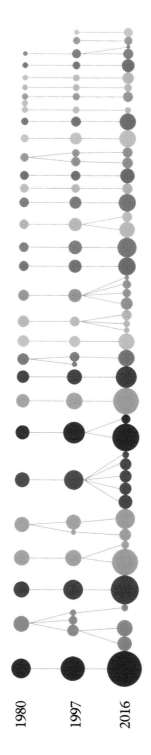

1980

1997

2016

Key

Category 1. Large, cohesive, growing households

Category 2. Large households that are fragmenting

Category 3. Small households that are growing

Category 4. small/medium households that are fragmenting, struggling to grow, staying the same size, on the way out, or have disappeared

Figure 5.9. Household fragmentation DBG, 1980–1997–2016

Figure 6.3. Women and girls earn money from hair-dressing, 2014

Figure 6.5. Village herds contain the red Maure and grey-flecked Peul cattle breeds 2011

Figure 6.6. As evening falls, calves are let off the rope and allowed to drink milk from their mothers, 2011

Figure 6.7. Donkey carts are invaluable for transporting water to the field, 2011

Figure 6.9. The first day of digging a new well, 1981

Figure 6.14. In the dry season, older men can earn some extra income in the village with their sewing machines, 2014

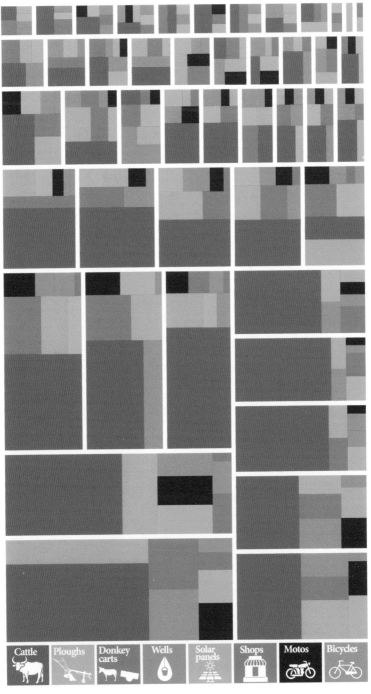

Scale: ▬ = 1 item of a particular asset

Figure 6.17. Actual wealth holdings per household, DBG, 2016

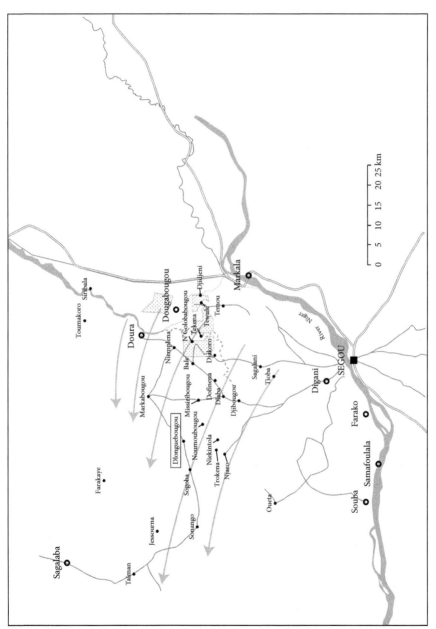

Figure 4.10. Migrant farmers next to the N-Sukala sugar-cane plantation seek land to the north-west

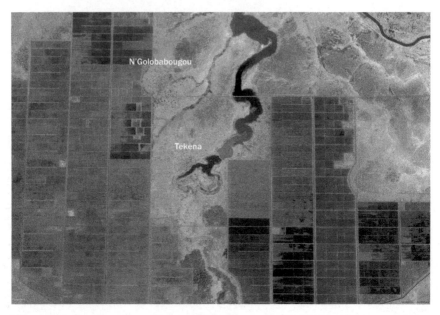

Figure 4.11. Satellite image of two villages surrounded by N-Sukala's sugar cane fields, 2018

bird damage, a number equal to the then Bambara population of DBG.[33] However, by 2000, the villagers of DBG had become fed up with having so many people coming to cultivate land around the village, spending 6 months in the area, and then taking their harvests away. They complained that there were too many strangers, and accused them of stealing cattle, cutting down trees, destroying their bush, and seducing their women. The chief said it would be different if they wanted to settle permanently in the village, but they just wanted to make use of DBG's land without any commitment to the village's long-term well-being. The village council agreed to send all the migrant farmers back home, and, as a result, they all packed up and left. But, by 2006, two families had been allowed back to farm to the south of DBG, having begged the villagers for land in the name of their common humanity, and the ties of marriage and kinship which bound them together. A trickle of returning migrants arrived each year after this, which became a flood after the newly established irrigated sugar cane scheme at N-Sukala started clearing land in 2011. Loss of land to N-Sukala and a worsening of the bird problem have generated a further wave of farmers seeking land, so there are even more migrant farmers today around DBG and neighbouring villages than in 2000.

---

[33] Brock, K. and Coulibaly, N. (1999).

Consequences of the growth in cultivated area

There are three major consequences of the increased pressure on land. First, as described in Chapter 3, there has been a sharp fall in village-field millet yields because of a big reduction in available manure, since there is now much less grazing available for village cattle and visiting herds.[34] As was seen from Figure 3.23, the size of the bush-field millet harvest persists because of a large increase in field size, but the yield per hectare has fallen by half. Village-field millet production has fared much worse, both in total volume and yield per hectare. Farmers blame this in part on the particularly poor distribution of rainfall, but they acknowledged that soil no longer has the strength it had before because of loss of soil fertility.[35]

Second, there is growing conflict between herders and farmers, especially linked to crop damage. Across the region, fights between Peul and Bambara have involved knives and rifles, leading to several deaths, and a series of larger-scale battles 60–70 km north and east of DBG. In the past, DBG was on the northern fringe of the farming area, and all land to the northwest was open grazing land. But incoming farmers have now fragmented much of this area with their fields, which constitutes a major barrier for cattle movement when crops are in the ground. Livestock herders feel increasingly hemmed in by farmers' fields, and the *burtol* livestock routes are often not recognized when villagers plough the land. The *Conventions Locales* drawn up for the two communes of N'Koumandougou and Bellen note there being six pastoral tracks which run from north to south, and from west to east. However, these are neither well-marked nor respected.

Third, the people of DBG have a strong sense that they have lost control over their village's territory and associated resources because of the large influx of people coming to farm and graze the land. They can see this is leading to a competitive rush for what valuable resources remain. This is evident in the large quantity of charcoal being exported, and the eradication of wildlife, which was formerly a good source of meat. The options open to villagers for re-establishing control over their space are very limited, given the pressure of numbers, and it is unclear as yet whether the *Loi Foncier Agricole* will strengthen the hand of villagers relative to outsiders. For example, will the village council still have the right to dismiss 'stranger farmers' as they did in 2000? As they watch more villages further south being evicted from their land in order to grow sugar cane, they wonder whether and when the same thing may happen to them. They recognize that their sandy soils are much less suitable for sugar cane than the clays further south are,

---

[34] Millet residues are on average of lower quality in terms of nutrient content than the standing herbage is. In the rainy season, the need to keep herds away from cultivated areas also significantly constrains grazing management. Fernandez-Rivera, S. et al (2005).

[35] *Anka dugukolo, fanga t'ala bilé* / 'Our soil has no strength left anymore.'

but they have heard rumours, as yet unsubstantiated, that irrigated wheat is an option being considered for their area.

Summary

At the start of this chapter, I asked how could the village of DBG, which boasted abundant land in 1980, find itself land scarce just 25 years later? The answer lies in part with a tripling of the village population, the widespread use of oxen-drawn plough teams, and continued extensive patterns of farming. However, as shown by Table 4.1, by far the largest factor explaining the rapid occupation of space has been the arrival of hundreds of incoming farmers from further south, seeking land to feed their families. The first wave of farmers came in the late 1980s, from villages badly affected by bird damage to cereal crops, given their proximity to the irrigated lands of the *Office du Niger*. The second wave of incoming farmers has been unleashed by the establishment of N-Sukala, a sugar cane plantation, 40 km to the southeast of DBG. In 2009, this company was allocated 20,000 ha of land, and, in 2010–2011, it started clearing land on both the east and west side of the Canal du Sahel, and constructing a sugar mill. Hundreds of families have lost their farmland to this irrigation scheme, and the plague of grain-eating birds has spread further. Given the government's plans to extend the irrigated zone farther, DBG and neighbouring villages along the northern farming edge are likely to receive many more close and distant cousins begging for land.

With the *Loi Foncier Agricole* signed into law in 2017, its implementation will need to deal with the complexity of land-use rights in an area such as that around DBG. There is a high level of frustration amongst villagers who have been evicted from their land, and those in the wider region now receiving large numbers of incoming farmers needing land to cultivate. Equally, the many livestock herders in the region are seriously damaged by the large inflow of farmers into former grazing lands, and the anarchic field pattern, further aggravating tensions between crop-growing and livestock-keeping peoples. Chapter 8 explores these issues further, including the proposal for a large grazing project to be established on the North Bank.

5

People and domestic organization

Foroba tô ka di, nka foroba na ka ko.[1]

Introduction

When I first went to Dlonguébougou (DBG), I was struck by the large size of the households in the village. In 1980, there were 534 people in the Bambara village, living in twenty-nine households, known in Bambara as *gwa*. This gave an average household size of eighteen people, varying from two people in the smallest household made up of a married couple, to more than fifty in the very largest. I was interested to understand what factors explained the existence of these large domestic groups—was it to do with their farming activities and significant economies of scale, or did large size help cushion people from a range of risks?[2] Maybe such large households were a relic of some former purpose and set of values, and they would gradually disappear in favour of smaller nuclear units.[3] I was astonished to find 35 years later that average household size had grown to thirty-three people. At the large end of this spectrum, there are now four households with more than one hundred people, the largest of which is 185 strong. At the same time, several households which used to have more than forty people have broken up, and some of the smaller, less successful households have splintered further.

This chapter describes how the village population has grown over the last 35 years, and it shows the pattern and evolution of household size and organization. It describes the position of women and girls in the life of the household and village. It then reviews the current rights and responsibilities of households to their members, and how these have changed since 1980, and it compares the advantages and constraints of large domestic groups, which I identified in 1980, with the situation today. The chapter then explores patterns of household growth and fragmentation.

---

[1] 'Millet porridge which comes from the collective granary tastes good, but the collective sauce tastes bad.' Meaning that you rely on the foroba for the basics, but not for the sweet things in life.

[2] Toulmin, C. (1992).

[3] As described by Hill, P. (1972) and Smith, M.G. (1955), for the decline of the *gandu* institution amongst the Hausa people of northern Nigeria, and Raynaut, C. (1997) for the Sahel more generally.

Land, Investment and Migration. Camilla Toulmin, Oxford University Press (2020). © Camilla Toulmin.
DOI: 10.1093/oso/9780198852766.001.0001

Methods

Data on household size and composition were collected in October 2016, by means of a questionnaire under the supervision of my research assistant Sidiki Diarra. He had participated in the household data collection we had undertaken in 1980–1982 and with Karen Brock in 1997–1999. The core of each household in DBG has remained sufficiently stable over time, despite some cases of fragmentation, for it to be easy to track the pattern of growth and change over the 35 years. This chapter therefore presents demographic data collected from the forty-seven *gwa* present today which have a continuous link to those present in 1980, and it includes those *gwa* which had arrived by 1997. We have not included in the analysis the eight *gwa* which have recently set up in DBG (the matron at the clinic, several teachers, and a couple of traders), because we have no prior data for them. The data collected cover: first name, family name, year of birth, marital state, gender, tax status, present or absent, relation to the household head, whether a private field is cultivated, and any other observations. I am confident of the good quality of the information generated by this survey, which was checked for consistency against the earlier household surveys, and other forms of information. We reviewed the data with Makono Dembélé, household by household, to check inconsistencies and fill in missing data. This was particularly important in ensuring inclusion of people who might otherwise be left out, such as elderly women and adopted children.[4] Birth dates were not always entirely consistent between the three surveys, but usually varied by less than 3 years.

Box 5.1 What is a household?

For this study, the term 'household' is used interchangeably with the Bambara term *gwa*, which means a 'kitchen or hearth'. The people of DBG say that *gwa* is equivalent to the more common Bambara term for a household, the *du*. In both cases, the oldest man of the family is the head of the household, and is called *gwatigi* or *dutigi*. The people of the *gwa* or *du* are not necessarily contained within a single compound wall because of growth in numbers and the spread of subgroups into new spaces on the edge of the village. While most millet is cultivated as a collective household activity (known as *foroba*), there are also a series of activities carried out and certain assets held at a level below the *gwa*. In the case of farming, as described in Chapter 4, these fields are described as *jonforo*. Other activities and assets are described as '*i yéré ka…*'[5] to distinguish an individual's assets and activities from those undertaken as

---

[4] Randall, S. and Coast, E. (2016).   [5] Belonging to you, yourself.

foroba. In larger *gwa*, the immediate nuclear family is the core group for certain domains, such as collecting the funds needed for a girl's wedding goods. And the scale of the domestic group can shift from season to season; the rainy season when farming must be done is characterized by a predominance of collective activity and common meals, while in the dry season, everyone is freer to pursue their own interests, and people often cook and eat in smaller groups.[6] Thus, there is a constantly shifting compromise between individual and collective activities.

Equally, some decisions are taken at levels above the *gwa*. For example, there are thirteen *gwa* who currently make-up the Dembélé lineage which co-founded the village 300 years ago. They do not marry amongst themselves, and have a collective approach to marriage relations with other lineages. Thus, it was a collective decision for the whole Dembélé lineage when asked by the Diarra clan of Markabougou in April 2016 whether they would be willing to put a history of dispute and conflict behind them and agree that they could marry in future, as described in Chapter 2.

While I have used the term 'household' or *gwa* throughout this book to describe the large and small domestic groups which constitute home for the villagers of DBG, my demographer friends are not convinced this is the correct term. While *gwa* is the term that people use to describe their own domestic group, it contrasts with definitions used for Government data collected in censuses and surveys which take 'ménage' as the relevant unit, a subgroup within the larger *gwa*. The formal definition of 'ménage' as used by the census is 'the unit made up by an individual or group of individuals, related or not, living under the same roof and recognising the responsibility of the person in charge of the house'.[7]

There is an extensive literature on definitions of the 'household' in the anthropological and demographic literature.[8] This outlines the risks of assuming this term can be used to describe and compare 'households' between very different cultural, historical, and economic contexts, and it critiques the over-simple conflation of residential and economic production units. In DBG, the *gwa* is not an autonomous unit; each is closely tied to many others in this

(continued)

---

[6] As described also for *gandu* relations in northern Nigeria's Hausaland, where Smith notes 'segments of households operate semi-autonomously at some levels but cohere at others'. (1955) p. 100.

[7] In DBG, the person responsible for an individual house is called the *sotigi*, which usually refers to the husband of the woman who lives in this house (*so*). Census enumerators in Mali are instructed to count married sons, their wives, and children as separate *ménages*. See *Direction Nationale de la Statistique et de l'Information (DNSI)* (2008), p. 5. The consequence is a very much larger number of 'ménages' than households or *gwa*.

[8] Guyer, J. (1981); Randall, S. et al (2011).

Box 5.1 Continued

and neighbouring villages. Households are also clearly shaped by cultural traditions. As Netting puts it, 'the household's form and functions are certainly responsive to social norms and cultural rules, embedded in regionally specific, historically persistent systems of marriage, descent, and the rights and duties of kinship.'[9] But smallholder households are also flexible and responsive to shifts in the socioeconomic environment. The long-term relationships between household members can be renegotiated over time as circumstances change. Revised configurations emerge around new forms of livelihood, opportunity, and constraint. Above all, membership of a household or domestic unit helps individuals cope in a context of uncertainty, given varying demographic, economic, environmental, and political conditions.[10]

Demographic growth in DBG

Figure 5.1 shows how the village population has grown. Over the 35-year period, total numbers have increased from 534 in 1980, to 769 in 1997, and to 1589 in 2016. This growth is very largely the result of the increase in the village population, but there have also been a few arrivals from elsewhere who have swelled the numbers of people and households. Overall, they total less than fifty people, and comprise eight new 'households', including the five teachers in the primary school who are accommodated and fed by some of the larger households. Though their numbers are small, they represent a different kind of village resident since they do not farm. At the same time, there has been an outflow of more than one hundred people who have left to settle in Bamako and elsewhere (see Chapter 7 for migration away from the village). Those who have migrated from DBG continue to be registered in the household of their birth, and this is where they pay their taxes. Thus, the actual number of DBG residents in 2016 was 1467.

The increase in the village population over the whole period of 1980–2016 is equivalent to an average 3 per cent annual rate of growth, which is typical of other societies where infant and child survival has been improved by modern medicine, but fertility rates have yet to decline. Most girls marry at 17–18 years of age, which, combined with polygamy and widow inheritance, means that no adult woman spends much time without a husband, and there is no access to modern contraception. These factors mean that women are usually either pregnant or have a small child to care for. From an early age, every girl is adept at bending over to set

[9] Netting, R.McC. (1993).   [10] Moser, C. (2009); Brockington, D. and Howland, O. (2018).

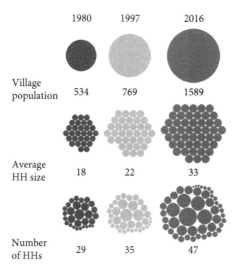

Figure 5.1. Demographic and Household (HH) growth DBG, 1980–2016

an infant on her back, splaying its legs on each side, and knotting a cloth around her waist to hold the child firmly against her, so she can carry on working, whether in the field, drawing water, or pounding millet.

The rate of population growth has however accelerated significantly. While from 1980 to 1997, the annual growth rate was 2.3 per cent; it then rose to 3.7 per cent from 1997 to 2016. This latter growth rate is very high, and it compares to 2.7 per cent for the West African region as a whole, and to 2.2 per cent in Ghana, 2.9 per cent in Burkina Faso, 3.0 per cent in Chad, and 3.9 per cent in Niger. In the case of DBG, this growth results from a significant improvement in access to medicine and health care in the last two decades. Within the overall high level of growth, a look at the childbirth histories of married women in the village today shows a mixed picture, with very few producing the 'ideal combination' of children which people say is needed for Bambara farming households to thrive. This consists of three to four boys to maintain the farm and three to four girls to marry into neighbouring families, in exchange for young women coming into the family as wives. Birth histories show a small number of couples who are childless, several with only one or two surviving children, and a few with seven to eight living offspring.[11] This very diverse experience is one important reason why large complex households are valued since they offer individual couples protection against demographic uncertainty.

---

[11] The uncertainty around successful child rearing is made visible in the names given to children. For example, those born after a long barren period are called Babugu, Cetamalu, Sungo, Mafu, Mulobali, and Nyamanto, and those called Wari, Ceko, and Fako have been born after their father has died.

Households in DBG

The Bambara of DBG form part of the broader Mandé culture, which is patrilineal, polygynous, and gerontocratic, which means that households are formed of men related by blood, who bring women into the household through marriage, and authority within the household is exercised by older men and, to some extent, older women. French anthropologist Jean Bazin, from his work on the history and social organization of the Ségou kingdom, describes the prevalence in the nineteenth and early twentieth century of large groups composed of slaves, established for farming purposes, known as *gwa*.[12] All members of the *gwa* were obliged to work on the collective field known as the *foroba* (or big field) for much of their time, and could then devote themselves to their own plots or *jonforow* (slave fields) in the little time spare, usually first thing in the morning, at dusk, and on the one day off, usually Mondays. DBG shares a pattern of domestic organization similar to that portrayed by other village studies amongst Bambara farmers, which describe households as engaged in producing both crops and descendants.[13] However, the number of people in the *gwa* of DBG is exceptionally large when compared with these other research sites.[14] These large farming groups seem to have been more common in the early part of the twentieth century but have fragmented in most parts of the Sahel, with nuclear family groups increasingly prevalent.[15]

The head of household is a *gwatigi*, who will traditionally sit and work in the *blon* hallway, which separates the village street from the inner compound. The *gwatigi* is the oldest man of the family (unless he is mad or incapacitated in some way). For example, in one household, the eldest man is deaf and dumb, so his younger brother was made *gwatigi*. In another case, the *gwatigi* mainly lives in Ségou, so his younger brother carries out the formal functions of a household head, referring important decisions to his elder brother when needed. They ring each other up at least once every day. The village council is made up of all *gwatigi*, regardless of the number of people in their household. A problem arises with the principle of the oldest man becoming *gwatigi* in the case of illegitimacy, since it is considered wrong that legitimate men be under the authority of a man born out of wedlock. Consequently, to avoid this situation, illegitimate men are required to leave the *gwa* and set themselves up on their own when they marry.

The *gwa* contains the male descendants of a common ancestor, along with their mothers, wives, sisters, and children, and often a few adopted children. The men's common ancestor may be five or more generations in the past, with the details barely known, although someone can usually master the entire genealogy.

---

[12] Bazin, J. (1970).   [13] Lewis, John v.D. (1978); Becker, L.C. (1996).
[14] Discussed in more detail later in this chapter.
[15] Raynaut, C. (1997); Hill, P. (1972); Smith, M.G. (1955).

The men of each generation call each other 'older' or 'younger' brother (*koroke, dogoke*), depending on their date of birth, even though in our terminology they would be second, third, or even fourth cousins. They call the generation above them their fathers (*fa*) and mothers (*ba*), and two generations above are their grandfathers and grandmothers (*moke* and *momuso*). Equally, the generation below are all referred to as *denw* (children), whether male (*denke*) or female (*denmuso*). There is the presumption of equality within each generation, and of hierarchy and respect to those in the generation above. This formal respect for older generations breaks down when it comes to great-grandparents, who are called *tulomasama*, meaning people who have their ears pulled, referring to the way that small infants will snuggle up to an elderly person and pull on their hair and ears. And great-great-grandparents are called *fufafu* since this is considered the sum of their conversation.

People are proud of their family name, and this forms part of the regular greetings they exchange, morning, midday, and evening, and the joking relations they maintain with other lineages, as described in Chapter 1. Women keep their father's name on marriage and maintain strong links to the household and village they come from. A woman's children will have close connections to their maternal uncle, known as *benke*, who is seen as someone who will do their best to provide assistance in times of trouble. A woman's status within the marital household depends on the year of her wedding. The most senior woman of the household is the one who has been there for longest, and is not necessarily the wife of the oldest man.

What do households do?

The *gwa* carries out multiple functions. It is a domestic enterprise—a unit of production which organizes farming of different fields and crops, and it provides food in the form of shared meals for much of the year, which have come from millet stored in the common granary and have been prepared by the women on a rota basis. The *gwa* provides shelter often, but not always, in a contiguous space, and it holds certain assets in common, usually the equipment needed for farming its common fields, such as ploughs, carts, a well, oxen for ploughing, and other livestock. The *gwa* is also the locus of human reproduction, through the organization of marriages, begetting and rearing of children, and the care of the sick and elderly. There are no single-person households in DBG—such a thing would be inconceivable, and practically impossible. Individuals who find themselves on their own will attach themselves to another household for help, mutual support, and protection. There are just too many tasks which need to be done for a single person to be able to cope. In the event of sickness, in a complex household, a man or woman will turn most immediately to their spouse and close kin for help, and only if this route is exhausted, would help be sought from the *gwatigi*.

The *gwatigi is* responsible for managing this domestic enterprise, making decisions about investing in collective assets, sales of cattle and grain, and payment of taxes. He is also responsible for arranging the marriages of men within the household, an investment which will cost 200–300,000 francs in direct payments to the girl's family, and an equivalent sum for the marriage feast and reception of guests. Men expect their first marriage to be organized in their midtwenties, if they are lucky, although, some may have to wait until their thirties. The girl in question will often have been identified from an early age, and cash and other forms of payment made over the years to firm up the agreement. Sometimes a coloured thread is put around her ankle to show she is already spoken for. If a young man sees no sign of his marriage being planned, then his commitment to work for the *gwa* will slacken, and he may either take the process in charge for himself, or spend more and more time away. An increasing number of wives of DBG men now come from Bamako, having been acquired when a young man has been away on migration. The role of *gwatigi* is demanding, especially in the larger households (as described in Box 5.2, page 125). It takes time, patience, and a degree of flexibility to accommodate the diverse characters and interests of the large family group.

Figure 5.2 shows the composition of households in DBG in term of their complexity, 'simple households' being defined as those with a single married man, his wife or wives, and their children, plus his mother, unmarried brothers, and any adopted children.[16] This figure shows that for 2016, twelve out of forty-seven households were 'simple', defined in this way, compared with ten in the two previous surveys, though they are not all the same households. In 2016, thirty-five were complex households, containing the vast majority of the village population, this having grown from 85.6 per cent of people in 1981 to 96 per cent in 2016. This shows that people continue to value and maintain these large domestic groups as

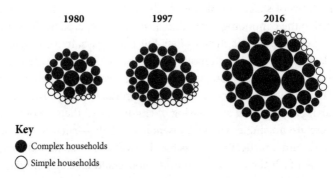

Key

⬤ Complex households

◯ Simple households

Figure 5.2. Simple and complex households in DBG

---

[16] Sometimes referred to as a 'laterally extended household' when including unmarried siblings, or as 'vertically extended' when it includes parents of the couple.

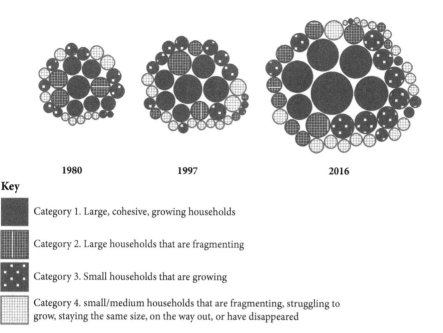

1980   1997   2016

Key

Category 1. Large, cohesive, growing households

Category 2. Large households that are fragmenting

Category 3. Small households that are growing

Category 4. small/medium households that are fragmenting, struggling to grow, staying the same size, on the way out, or have disappeared

Figure 5.3. Household growth and change in DBG, 1980, 1997, and 2016

the principal unit for production and reproduction.[17] Of the ten households in the simple category in 1980, two were still in this category in 2016, and struggling to make ends meet. One of the ten had disappeared; one had broken up into four smaller groups; four have become 'complex' and are managing to feed themselves, and one of the ten has done exceptionally well and is now one of the better-off families in the village. Of the twelve households in the simple category in 2016, eight have been established in the last 5 years; two represent households that set up in the early 1990s; and two are small households that have been in existence for more than 30 years. The data show no tendency for smaller domestic groups to predominate, despite the increase in individualism and private-farm activity. As I found in 1980, large complex households still provide a degree of insurance which offers greater space for individuals to pursue private moneymaking activities than a simple household would allow.

Figure 5.3 shows the increasing number and size of many households in DBG (see also in the colour plates section). Particularly evident is the substantial growth of certain already large households, and the proliferation of small domestic groups. In order to understand and compare the range of different households found in DBG, I have selected a number of typical cases from simple, middle-sized, and large complex households. The figures below present household

---

[17] Lewis, J. v.D. (1978); Becker, L.C. (1990, 1996).

composition by age, sex, and marital status; men above, and women below the line, and shaded in if married.

Small, simple households

Figure 5.4 shows three households which are simple domestic groups in which an adult man has one or two wives and several children and in one case, an elderly mother (also shown in the colour plates section). In the first case, this small household led by HT is the result of a larger household fragmenting on the death of its charismatic leader. It is the most simple of households, with a married couple accompanied by their two adolescent sons, a girl about to be married, and two adopted children. The household was formed in the early 1990s, so there are no data for 1981. In 1998, this household had six people in it, and it had barely grown to seven by 2016. Over this period, three 'brothers' of HT left as a group to establish a new household. They were more closely related to each other than to HT, and found his management as *gwatigi* irksome. They also calculated that as three brothers, they had enough manpower to operate effectively as an independent farming unit, but their departure has been difficult for HT.

The second case involves a poor family which has struggled for many years to make ends meet. The elder brother has been absent for more than ten years, and the younger brother has now disappeared, as well, leaving the remaining members very vulnerable and unviable as a farming unit. The old mother is accompanied

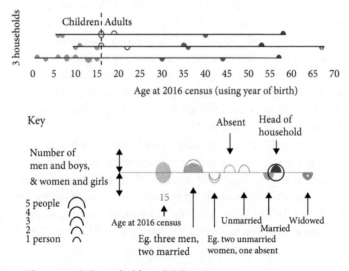

Figure 5.4. Three simple households in DBG, 2016

by her daughter-in-law (who has not been remarried since she is not considered a widow because no one knows if her husband is alive or dead), and several young children, the eldest of which is a 16-year-old son. Their numbers have barely changed from seven in 1981 and 1997, to six in 2016.

The third case involves an illegitimate man who was brought up in the family of the village chief, his mother being from there, but his father coming from neighbouring Misribougou. His mother was then an unmarried girl and, though his father recognized him and gave him his *jamu* Samaké, it was thought better that he be brought up by his mother's kin, rather than by a stepmother in his father's house where no one would be looking out for him. This case exemplifies the broader pattern which relates to illegitimate men, as described earlier. In this case, BS, the household head, has had help in setting up as an independent household, in terms of two young women being found for him to marry, and acquiring a plough team. In other cases, the lot of illegitimate men is much harder, as seen by the case of DD's father (described in Chapter 7), and OS (described below). This *gwa*, having been established in 1990, on the marriage of the household head, has grown in numbers from four in 1997, to twelve in 2016.

Midsized households

Figure 5.5 presents six midsized complex households (also shown in the colour plates section). The first two used to be part of the same household, but they split ten years ago, following disagreement between the two eldest men, now both in their sixties. They have the same father but different mothers, a difference in parentage which often leads to splits as it is said that the jealousy between co-wives is passed onto the children. Children of the same father but different mothers are described as *faden*, while those of the same father and mother are *baden*. *Fadenya* is thus the competitive relationship which exists between sons of different mothers, whereas *badenya* conveys the harmonious, warm, and loving relationship attributed to sons born of the same mother. In the case shown here, both *gwatigi* have married sons who have taken on the job of running the farm and producing their own children, so the continuation of each of the two households looks assured. The man heading the second household illustrated in Figure 5.5 is next in line to be the village chief, and he has been preparing for this role by acting as deputy to the existing chief. Before the household split, the total numbers for 1980 and 1997 were fourteen and twenty-six people, respectively, and by 2016, the households contained thirty-seven and fifteen persons, respectively, their total numbers having doubled.

The third household is an interesting case because it breaks the normal rules. The household contains not only the head of family, CJ, but also his married sister, her husband, and their children. This is very unusual because a girl always

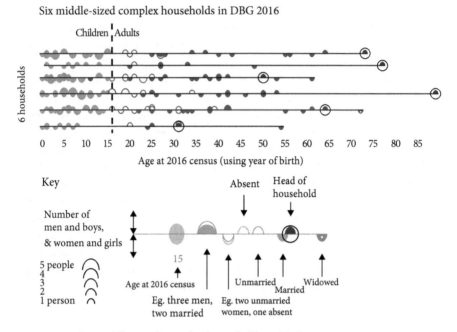

Figure 5.5. Six middle-sized complex households in DBG, 2016

goes to the household of her husband on marriage, not the other way around. It is quite possible that her husband AD will in due course become the head of this household, by dint of seniority. AD is the illegitimate son of the aunt of the household head CJ, by a man in the village chief's family. AD was recognized by his father, and brought up in his father's household, but he was then obliged to leave on his marriage and would have struggled to make a living by the efforts of himself and his wife alone. By joining his wife's family, this gave them a better chance in life, and it brought added strength to the girl's natal family. AD, his wife, and their children now represent 30 per cent of the household and offer an illustration of a Bambara saying that 'if you take a stranger into your family, he will grow so fast he will risk smothering the others'.[18] It will be interesting to see whether and when having two different lineages at the heart of the same household creates a problem. This household also contains two older women, widows of the former household head who died twenty years ago. They have been taken as wives by men from the Toungara family since there are no men of the older generation available to inherit them within this household. Historically this was a slave family of the Toungara. In both cases, the women are well past childbearing age, and they continue to live with their sons, and are visited by their spouses.

---

[18] Similar to the metaphor of 'cuckoo in the nest'.

The household has grown in numbers from 1981, 1997, and 2016, from fourteen, to twenty-one, and to forty-five persons, respectively.

The fourth household is led by the oldest man in the village, who was himself the illegitimate son of a Samaké from Misribougou.[19] His household has grown over the last 35 years from ten to twenty-one, and to forty-three in 2016. His wife of 50 years, with whom he had five sons and four daughters, had died shortly before our interview in 2016, and he was in a very sombre mood. Having been drafted in the late 1940s as a soldier and serving in Indo-China, he brought home both a pension and an open-minded attitude towards new technologies, on his return in 1952. He was the first person to have a bicycle, and he invested money from his pension in buying a plough and acquiring oxen to work the land. He dug two wells early in the investment cycle, and as a result, had a very productive holding of village fields from water–manure exchanges with visiting herd owners. Despite having started with poor prospects, he has become much better off compared with most others in the village. The secret of doing well, he says, is to keep your head down and behave like a snake in the grass. It is a mistake to be too visible and flaunt your wealth or good fortune. This will generate envy, and bring you into difficulty. His main concern when interviewed in late 2016 was that his sons and grandsons have grown up in prosperity and do not know what hard work means. Consequently, he worries that as soon as he is dead, the household will fall into ruin. He pointed to the fall in the household's millet harvest, and reduction in granary size over recent years, as a sure indicator of the trouble to come. Ten years ago, he had washed his hands of his sons because he considered they were managing the farm so badly, and he retreated to his house, eating separately and maintaining no contact. After 5 years, he was persuaded to re-establish relations, but in 2016, he remained sceptical of the family's future.

The fifth case is led by two brothers, the eldest of whom makes considerable sums from fortune-telling and advising people on how to manage their family and wealth. He spends most of his time in Ségou, where he has acquired a piece of land, and built a house. He also travels to Bamako to meet clients. His younger brother acts as household head, but they are in very regular telephone contact, and he always asks his older brother for advice on financial or complex questions. These two brothers were brought up by their older 'brother' (in fact a cousin) since their father died when they were very young. They describe a time of con-siderable hardship, and poverty, following the death of their father, and remem-ber with gratitude the care their older brother provided them. Both brothers have worked very hard on the farm, and they went away on migration most dry seasons, earning large sums to reinvest in the family. Many of their children have gone to school, and several are now in professional training (medicine, communications). In the analysis of millet production carried out in 1980–1981, this household stood

---

[19] He died in June 2017.

out as particularly productive, with a young hard-working field-team, getting their weeding finished early, and a thoughtful household head respected by his younger 'brothers'. The household size has grown from fifteen, to thirty-one, to forty-four over the period 1981, 1997, and 2016.

The final household presented in Figure 5.5 looked highly vulnerable in 1980, containing just a married couple and the husband's elderly mother. They struggled to grow much food and had few livestock. By 1998, they had grown from three to twelve people, as a result of children being born, but the household was still poor, with no well and only two oxen. By 2016, the household had grown to fifteen people, and it is about to acquire a new married woman. She presents an interesting and unusual case. From early on, she had been in love with AT, younger brother of the household head, and had a first child with him, before being married to her arranged husband in a neighbouring settlement. This marriage did not go well, and after 5 years, she came back home and took up with AT again. She was then married off to a man in another neighbouring village, but, again, maintained her relationship with AT and had another couple of children by him. Finally, her father and uncle decided that they had better let her follow her heart and her marriage to AT took place in early 2017. All of her children were noted in the household survey as belonging to AT, and following their marriage, they will be recognized as legitimate. Despite an unpromising start, through luck and hard work, this household looks as though it will survive and prosper.

Large, complex households

Figure 5.6 illustrates four large complex households (also shown in the colour plates section). The first household is that of the village chief, the largest family in the settlement, which contained 185 people in 2016. In 1980, they were fifty-six, and by 1998, their number had grown to eighty-five, so they have seen remarkable continued growth. Currently there are twenty-three married women in the household, with most men having two wives. A household of this size has a series of subgroups within it, each one being made up of the more closely related men, such as full or half-brothers. In this case, the common male ancestor from which all men in the household are descended is probably five or six generations back, a man who would have been born in the early nineteenth century or even at the time that Mungo Park passed by in 1796. Other households would probably have fragmented before reaching this exceptionally large size but, because as the chiefly lineage, they are meant to represent the old Bambara traditions, they continue to live as a single group. Indeed, it is rumoured that when and if the household breaks up, a curse of terrible power will be cast on those responsible for fragmenting the gwa. They continue to be led by the oldest man of the Dembélé family, who is

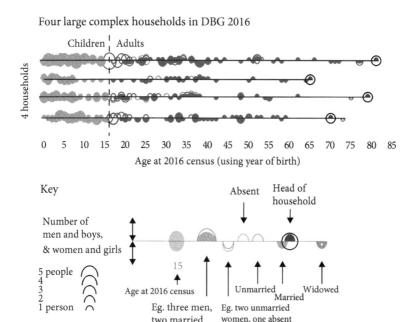

Figure 5.6. Four large complex households in DBG, 2016

currently the chief of the village, they farm a single bush field (*kongoforo*), and maintain a set of collective farm assets which are used for their joint farming activity. At the same time, in order to provide sufficient independence and auton-omy for people within the household, each of the subgroups of brothers farms a 'private field' from which to fund some of their expenses. In this case, the village fields around the settlement have been divided up amongst the subgroups, and they are referred to as *jonforow*, or 'slave fields'—fields cultivated for the benefit of individuals or subgroups, rather than for the whole collective enterprise. People within each subgroup know, in the event of a split, which assets they will be able to take with them, though subdivision of the wells would be more difficult. The current *gwatigi* and village chief is in his late 70s, and when he dies, the next younger man of the same generation will take the role of head of household. While it might be the obvious moment for the household to break-up, people fear the powerful curse and seek to accommodate the desire for autonomy within the larger domestic group. On the *gwatigi's* death, his role as village chief will be transferred to the next oldest man in the wider Dembélé family, who leads another household, as shown in Figure 5.5.

The second household illustrated in Figure 5.6 demonstrates the results of successful investment in marriages, and domestic assets. In 1980, the household had an exceptionally high dependency ratio, with a very large number of small children relative to adults. When I asked MT, the then household head, how they managed to feed so many children, he just chuckled, chided the children for eating so much, and said they would be an excellent workforce for the farm in future. Luckily, for him, the bet has paid off. They have grown in number from twenty-three to thirty-three to sixty-six over the periods 1981, 1997, and 2016, respectively. And there is a cluster of men in their 30s and 40s who are fulfilling MT's dream of mobilizing a big farming team out in the field.

The third household is led by the last surviving brother of his generation. One of the better-off households, they came to DBG in the late nineteenth century, seeking shelter when their home village of Markabougou was taken by N'To Diarra, so they are not members of a founding lineage. However, they have done well, acquired a significant cattle herd, and produced several hunters of great repute. They have grown from 36 to 39 to 104, over the years from 1980, 1997, and 2016, respectively, the recent rapid expansion being due to the marriage of many young men born in the 1980s and 90s. A small nuclear family has split off recently because of a dispute to be described on page 134, but this has barely dented their overall numbers and strength.

The fourth and final household in the table is a case of good management over several generations, which has brought about a transformation of their situation. Their population numbers have grown from 37 in 1980, to 56 in 1997, to 119 in 2016. Bina, the elderly head of household in 1980 described to me how, in his youth, they had been amongst the poorest in the village. They had been taken by the French administration in the 1940s to settle the *Office du Niger* irrigation scheme and were told they must do at least 7 years before being allowed the option of going back home. The colonial reports confirm this was indeed the policy, it being thought that after 7 years, these dryland farmers would recognize the huge advantages of irrigated farming and never want to return to their sandy bush settlements. But Bina's family decided, after they had done their time, that they wanted to come back to DBG, and fortunately, were allowed to do so by the irrigation authorities. On their return to DBG, the large number of young men in the *gwa* invested their energy in making ropes for sale, and put whatever cash they could gather into oxen and plough teams. During the wetter, more favourable decades of the 1950s and 60s, they earned good money cultivating groundnuts, from which they built up a substantial herd of cattle. This has given them a strong base from which to expand further, funding marriages for the many sons of the family, and allowing several to set up shops which generate profit for the whole household. In 1981, Bina confided to me that their success had generated envy in others, and they needed to be careful not to display their good fortune since this could invite some form of retribution.[20]

---

[20] A similar worry to that expressed by OS, when discussing his household's wealth, p. 169.

Common interests, conflicting demands in Bambara households

A *gwa* is characterized by the common activities and assets shared by its members, and their collective identity. In principle, the men of the household are meant to devote most of their time to collective tasks, leaving some time free for individual pursuits. For farming, this takes the form of working 6 days a week on the common millet field, drawing on the household's labour, animals, and equipment, as shown in Chapter 3, Figure 3.19. Despite the widespread use of oxen-drawn plough teams, the agricultural system demands much hard work in the few months of the wet season, when households depend on mobilizing labour for rapid sowing and weeding of fields, which makes the difference between a good and a mediocre harvest (see Figure 5.7, and in the colour plates section). The farming enterprise relies on having a hard-working team of young men, under the orders of the *chatigi* (or work chief). Members of the farming team travel out to the fields from first light, on foot, riding the donkey cart or pedalling their bikes, hoe balanced on the shoulder. The work oxen are led and cared for by teenage boys, who take them off to graze and bring them home at night. As described in Chapter 3, the fallowing of land after 4–5 years means that over the years, the bush field moves farther and farther away from the settlement. Some households set up camp in makeshift huts on the edge of the bush field for several weeks when the rapid growth of weeds demands long days crouched over the soil with

Figure 5.7. Young men from the family of the village chief come back from migration to help sow the bush field, June 2014

the hoe. In this fashion, the energies of the young men are focused on getting the weeding done. Each morning, women and girls follow the men out to the field once they have prepared the midday meal, which they carry out on their heads, if they cannot find room to travel on a donkey cart. And they will bend their backs to the task of weeding with the hoe along with their menfolk. Young men who have gone to Bamako for the dry season will come back for a few weeks of plough-ing, sowing, and weeding the big household field, seeing this as an essential part of continuing to be a member of their *gwa* and a means to show commitment to fill-ing the collective granary. Staying away for the farming season signals the weak-ening of ties between young men and their family since both sides know the value of their labour in the field.

On Monday, by tradition, no work should be done on the household's millet field, and people can either rest or pursue their own interests, such as going to market or cultivating a field of sesame, maize, or groundnuts. Monday is the trad-itional market day in Ségou, so the ban on millet farming on this day relates to freeing people to travel to the big weekly market. People in DBG used to frequent Ségou market, despite it being a good 12-hour walk to the south, but now they prefer going east to Dougabougou, which is closer, and there are usually trucks willing to transport people and their goods to and from DBG for a small fee. Groundnuts used to be the crop cultivated on Mondays, but, given the dry years since 1970s, there are only a few small plots of groundnuts grown by individuals for the pleasure of having a snack rather than as a commercial activity. Sesame has replaced groundnuts as the crop which individuals want to grow in order to make money.

The bush field (*kongoforo*) is the symbol of this collective enterprise by the *gwa*, and the millet harvest from this field is stored in one or several granaries controlled by the *gwatigi*, from which certain meals are cooked and expenses paid. As described in Chapter 3, bush fields can be enormous, in the largest cases stretching over more than 100 ha, equivalent to a field of 1 km square. The harvest from the village-field millet (*souna*) is stored in a different granary, as the millet is a different variety and does not store as long as the bush field (*sanyo*). Thus, in each *gwa*, you usually find a big bush-field granary, a smaller village-field granary, and a series of little granaries owned by individual women and men.

As shown in Figure 3.19, outlining the annual cycle of activity, once the main weeding season is over in September, many young men will disappear off on migration, with a few returning to help harvest, thresh, and store the crop. However, some young men must stay behind in DBG to water the animals, repair the compound, and prepare the land for the next farming season.

After many years of farming, men hope to retire from fieldwork and invest their time in other tasks, such as hunting, running a shop, making ropes and granaries, and fattening sheep for sale. Except in the smallest *gwa*, where every-one sets off for the field each day, there is usually someone left at home to look after small children, care for animals that have not been sent out to graze, and carry out other family business. A man now in his midsixties, G.D. describes how he started farming, aged 12, and he did this for 35 years. When his brother's sons were old enough to be serious members of the farming workforce, he was able to retire at around 50 years of age, and has since been very active as a fortune-teller, earning large sums which he invests in educating the younger members of the family, as well as in a series of assets.

When young men go on migration, they are meant to give most of the cash they earn to the household head since the young man's time and effort should belong to the collective household, whether at home or away. It is considered only fair that migrant earnings come to the *gwatigi* to pay taxes, marriage costs, and buy new farm equipment since those who have stayed in the village over the dry season to water cattle have not had the chance to fill their pockets with cash. However, as described in more detail in Chapter 7, household heads today complain that they see less and less of the cash which is earned, with most young men holding onto their money and buying fancy clothes and a motor-bike, rather than handing it over for the family's needs.

Challenges of being household head

Of the twenty-nine household heads present in 1980, there were five still playing this role in 2016.[21] They remark on how the job has changed, with new demands and greater responsibilities for people managing these large domestic groups, as described in Box 5.2.

Box 5.2 Changes in the role of household head from 1980 to 2017

'Managing four households in the past would be easier than managing one household today. People used to have respect for the *gwatigi*, but not now. Then, all household affairs would be for you to decide. Now, there's a lot which is no longer in your power. Some people don't tell you what's going on, they don't ask your advice. If you see that my household is well-managed, its because I have a good temper. But some people don't want to be managed—it makes you sad and upset. The time when you were here before, there were not many households with more than 30 people. But now, take

(continued)

---

[21] Four of whom have died since 2016.

Box 5.2 Continued

---

the family of the village chief. They alone have grown to more than 180 members. If someone says they can manage such a number, in truth, it's very hard.'

'Humanity and people have also changed. Not only has the number of people multiplied, but their manners have changed. There are many kinds of people, those who are knowledgeable, those who know nothing, those who respect others, those who respect no-one. People's needs have also moved on. Before, one granary could feed the whole household, but now with the large increase in numbers, three granaries of the same size would not be enough. Today, also, there is not just one way of doing things. There is one way for the household and a different way for the individual!'

'Taxes still come from the *foroba* (joint estate). Once they're paid, most other things come from individual money. If we agree to farm a field of sesame, and we sell the harvest, we'll put the money aside. When the time to pay taxes comes around, then the money can be used for that, and anything left over will be put aside for other things that may arise. For example, if someone is ill in another town, then some of the money might buy petrol to go and visit them, and give them some money. Some of it will be used to pay the salary of the herder looking after the sheep and goats. There is such a big difference between how we do things now, and the olden days when you were here before.'

Interview with JD, in his mid-60s, head of one of the largest households, which he has combined with running a shop. July 2017.

The position of women and girls

DBG belongs to a patrilineal society, in which women are brought into the household by marriage. Girls have no choice as to whom they marry, and, while it is not expected that they will love their husband, it is hoped they will get on with him and the rest of his family. As in all societies, relations between man and wife run the full gamut from disdain to strong passions. One man is said to have put medicine into a village well to try to make his wife love him, but it did not work, and now no one draws drinking water from this well. A second example, from the sixth household in Figure 5.5, provides an example of a 'head-strong'[22] woman who, after two loveless marriages, finally gets to marry the man she loves. A third case involves a man who is mocked for being so in love with his wife; he is

---

[22] '*A kungolo ka gelen.*' / 'Her head is very hard.'

described as firmly under her thumb. In a fourth example, an elderly man is distraught at the death of his wife of 50 years. A fifth example concerns a newly widowed woman unable to accept her dead husband's younger brother, who is due to inherit her and who insists on following her affections by choosing a man of the next generation for her husband. In a sixth and final case, a woman complains that her husband's affections have been completely captured by his new wife, but she acknowledges that this means she is freer to travel to visit friends in neighbouring villages.

Many women expect to be married several times in the course of their life, usually through widow inheritance; that is to say, on the death of their husband, they will pass to his younger 'brother', the next man by age in the household. Women are promised to a particular man in marriage but will have been negotiated and acquired by the man's family, and payment of bride-wealth will have come from common household funds. There is often a significant gap in age between husband and wife, which explains the frequency of widowhood. Where the recently deceased has more than one wife, the widows will be shared between the two men next in age. Widows are never passed upwards to older brothers, nor are they meant to be inherited downwards, by men of the subsequent generation. However, given the frequent large gap in age between husband and wife, this does occasionally happen. In a few cases, the widow may leave the household altogether, such as when there is no younger brother to take her, or if she has been very unhappy and has poor relations with other women in the family, and if she has no children. In such cases, she may return to her father's house, or marry a man of her own choice.[23]

Each married woman has her own two-room dwelling within the compound. Women say they prefer to marry into a larger, more successful household since they can share the tasks with others and have some free time for their own moneymaking activities. Their tasks start before first light when they get up, make the fire, fetch water from the well, heat washing-water for the husband and any guests, cook breakfast, wake and wash young children, and sweep the yard (see Figure 5.8 in the colour plates section). After breakfast, they pound millet, cook food for the farming team, and take food and water out to the field. After hours of work in the field, they return to the village in the late afternoon, collecting firewood on the way home, and then start the evening round of fetching water, pounding millet, cooking food, washing up, and preparing for bed. During the dry season, the burden of domestic tasks is less intense, because they do not have to leave for a day's work in the field. However, fetching water, cooking, washing clothes, and caring for young and old still need to be done, and it is not until a woman gains a co-wife, or a daughter-in-law, that her work slackens somewhat

---

[23] Divorce is uncommon, in contrast to Hausa society in northern Nigeria and Niger. (Smith, M. (1981); Cooper, B.M. (1997); *New York Times* (2019)).

Figure 5.8. Drawing water from the well early in the morning, a regular daily task for women, 2014

and she can travel more easily to visit relatives. Women's domestic duties are largely unchanged since 1980, except some will get help from their children in transporting water from the well, using the family donkey cart.

Women are members of an age group, based on the year of their marriage, which provides mutual support. There are also a range of other associations set up by women to promote self-help, savings, and joint activity. These include the two women's associations, one for each of the two wards of the village, each with a president and several other office holders.

Girls have their marriages planned by the *gwatigi* in consultation with the girl's own father and mother. Every household has a set of marriage relations with a number of other households, both within the village and with neighbouring settlements, with whom young women have been exchanged over the generations. These networks are called 'marriage paths' or *furusiraw* because they are the dusty tracks down which young women are taken to their new home. They will take these paths on regular visits back to their father's house, and these are the routes which a woman's children will take when looking for help or advice. As noted earlier, a child's maternal uncle (*benke*) is seen as kind and indulgent towards his sister's offspring, and as a good source of support in times of need.

Women say they prefer to be their husband's first wife, though, once married, a woman may look forward to a second wife coming to help with domestic tasks and give time to be able to travel, without incurring too many complaints from her husband. There is often 10–15 years difference in age between first and second wives, so it can be difficult for a first wife to see a younger wife arrive, and jealousy between wives is recognized to be a problem. Husbands are enjoined to behave fairly to each of their wives, in terms of dividing their time equally between them. Hence, a man normally spends two nights in turn with each of his wives, and a woman is usually responsible for cooking dinner on those nights when her husband is with her. However, many co-wives get on well, and many a husband complains of them ganging up against him.

A woman will look forward to the day when her eldest son gets married because this means her daughter-in-law will replace her in the farm-work team and she can retire. Freed from daily work in the field, she can then focus time and effort on farming her own field, and pursue a set of activities which enable her to earn money. She will also spend a lot of time preparing her own daughters for marriage, by helping to purchase the goods which each girl will need to take with her to show she comes from a respectable family with means.

Women's position has evolved over the 35 years since I first visited DBG, in part because of families being better equipped, in part because of women being significantly better off, and because of changes in attitude, as described by HC in Box 5.3. However, many things have stayed the same, such as responsibilities for cooking and fetching water, and the considerable time and money spent collecting the goods which a girl needs to take on her marriage, as will be seen in Chapter 7.

Box 5.3 Two women's views of change in DBG since 1980

'Today, farming is easier than in the old days. Then we did everything by hand. But now we have ploughs and carts, so people can plant a field which is a lot bigger. When I married into DBG, women didn't have the chance of farming their own fields, but today, women have a sesame field and a millet field for themselves. Every woman who is in a large household can expect to get a few days' help with ploughing, and some women pay for 3 to 4 days of ploughing in addition.'

'When I married into DBG, it was all *foroba baara*.[24] Old women used to have a little plot of tomatoes, and they'd give the produce to the *gwatigi* to liven up the sauce. But now people work for themselves. But that also means our children don't agree to work together. You'll find old women have a sesame field, each child has a field apart, each married woman has a field apart—everyone is pursuing their own individual wealth here in DBG. You'll have seen we're not

(continued)

---

[24] Working for the collective estate.

Box 5.3 Continued

spinning cotton anymore. If we want *fini mugu*[25] we buy it from villages towards the west—women in Jessourna still spin cotton, and so do women in Taiman.'

'Many of our young people go on migration to the big city. They learn many things there and bring back their ideas to the village. It's thanks to them that this village has seen big changes. For example, we now have a market, which takes the village forward. You'll see the market tomorrow.'

Interview with HC, now in her 50s, married into a large household which has seen better days. She was President of the Women's Association until 2015.

'If I compare now with the time of my childhood, back then farming was much harder than today. We'd farm by hand but now, ploughs have multiplied. And the number of carts has also grown. Before, we would have to carry things on the head, out to the far-off field. We'd spend the whole day farming, and then come home in the dark, we'd pound the millet and cook the food to give men at night. Today, if you've prepared the food, it's put in the cart, you sit next to it and out you go to the field. Back then, the wells would dry up, we'd sit by the wells for hours, waiting for them to fill.'

'Long ago we used to spin cotton, and get it woven into cotton cloth. But now machine-made cloth has become common, cotton is no longer worked here, you buy it instead. You can't find weavers either. If you say you're going to do a bit of cotton cloth for yourself, it's not worth it as you don't make any money.'

'Sesame brings in more money than millet, or maize, it generates more cash than anything else. Our young girls who go on migration to Bamako, if they've cultivated a small sesame field, they can make 100,000, or 200,000FCFA. Those who go off to Bamako on migration don't make anything like the same money. Last year I was ill, so I didn't manage to do anything but my son cultivated a small field for me, and when it was harvested it filled a small sack which I sold for 50,000F. Sesame brings in the cash quickly.'

'We've stopped cultivating fonio because of the work involved. Fonio and *sunan*[26] cultivation both happen at the same time, If you ask men to come and cut the fonio, they say they're busy with the *sunan* harvest. Women can't harvest the fonio themselves, and if you can't find people to cut it, it all goes to waste. Fonio cultivation has really declined here in DBG. In the old days, we collected *ncin*[27] from the bush. But you don't get much from it, so we shifted to cultivating fonio instead. You can't cultivate *ncin*. It's not domesticated. As for harvesting *nzamara*,[28] the work is tough and it leaves prickles in your fingers.'

Interview with MD, in her 70s, born and married in DBG.

---

[25] Homespun cotton cloth.   [26] Village-field millet.
[27] *Panecum laetum*, a wild grass.   [28] 'Cram-cram', *Cenchrus biflorus*.

Women, marriage paths, and social networks

Of the 315 married women in DBG in October 2016, 128 came from other house-holds in DBG, representing 40 per cent of all married women. There are then a further 151 women from thirteen settlements, from which 4 or more women have married into DBG, making up 48 per cent of all married women. Of these, the three most important are Jessourna (twenty-four), Misribougou (twenty-two) and Taiman (sixteen). Jessourna 15 km away to the northwest, was settled by members of the Traoré family from DBG, so they consider themselves the same lineage. Until now, the Traoré of DBG had considered themselves too close in kinship to consider marrying anyone from the Traoré family in Jessourna. But, recently, they have reassessed the situation and agreed that the passage of time means they have grown sufficiently distant for such marriages to be possible, though none as yet has been arranged. In the case of Misribougou, 10 km away to the southeast, this was settled originally by the Samaké, with whom there are multiple marriage relations with many DBG families. The village of Taiman, 25 km to the northwest, is especially closely linked to the Tangara family, with whom they have long-standing marriage relations. Bamako has now become a place where men look for wives, because of their being there on migration, with ten women from Bamako now married into DBG families and resident in the village. Many of these women will have come from a rural background themselves. The remaining 12 per cent of women (thirty-six in total) come from a scatter of settlements near and far, with whom there are many fewer connections.

The origin of married women in DBG also demonstrates the continuing importance of social networks and status. There are, for example, settlements close to DBG, but without any marriage ties to the village. Noumoubougou, for example, is closer than Misribougou but is a blacksmith settlement, and, hence, their families do not marry into noncasted families. Equally, certain other villages are known to have been settled by slaves or former soldiers from the Ségou kingdom in the nineteenth century, and thus, are not part of DBG's social network, such as Djibougou 15 km to the southeast and Nienkintola 10 km due south. And it was only in April 2016 that the long-standing dispute was formally healed between the Dembélé of DBG and the Diarra of neighbouring Markabougou, a conflict which dated from 1895.[29] As yet, however, no one has arranged a marriage between these families, despite this now being possible.

Household growth and fragmentation

In many societies, there is a regular cycle of household establishment, growth, and gradual decline, as first a new couple marry and set themselves up as a new

---

[29] Described in Chapter 2.

unit, then have children, and ultimately see their children marry and leave home to set themselves up elsewhere.[30] In practice, however, there is great diversity in household forms and their evolution over time. In the 1970s, in the village of Dorayi, northern Nigeria, Hill recounted that nearly all men continued to live in their father's home after marriage, leading to large residential compounds, containing 106 people in the biggest case, but in most cases, they had separate farming activities.[31] Fraternal *gandu*, where brothers work together in a common field, was also dying out. Whitehead's work in northern Ghana in the late 1980s describes a similar situation in which the wealth of different households lay traditionally in the number of people under the authority of the household head. She describes the fragmentation of large complex households and the multiplication of small, nuclear family units, which are less able to marshal the people and assets required to farm effectively, and hence, are more vulnerable to risks. In her field site in 1989, the largest household was seventy-three people strong, but the average size was only twelve people, and the economically most vulnerable averaged fewer than seven people.[32] Raynaut's survey of changes across the Sahel confirms these trends of household fragmentation to be widespread.[33]

Recent household surveys across several rural sites in the Ségou region show that average household size varies between 12.6 and 15 people, which compares with an average of 33 people in DBG in 2016.[34] One of these surveys in the Ségou region found that 30 per cent of people lived in households of more than thirty people, which compares with 75 per cent of people in DBG. Thus, this pattern of large domestic organization is remarkable even within the Ségou region. In the case of DBG, are the days of these large complex domestic groups numbered? Over time, will a more typical pattern of small to medium-sized households emerge? It is difficult to imagine further growth in the largest households, which could attain a size of several hundred people in another 35 years. But the great flexibility they exhibit in internal organization means they can often succeed in balancing individual and collective interests and needs, while maintaining the overall institution intact.

In DBG, households have no systematic pattern of growth and division, as male children usually remain within the household once married, and there is no specific moment at which the larger group breaks up. The death of the household head can be a spur to smaller groups separating themselves off, but many households survive such deaths and go on to further growth. There are also numerous cases where household break-ups are caused by factors other than the *gwatigi*'s death. There is a Bambara saying that there are three 'strangers' who can

---

[30] Chayanov, A.V. (1966); Goody, J. (1958).   [31] Hill, P. (1972).
[32] Whitehead, A. (2006) p. 285.   [33] Raynaut, C. (1997) p. 337.
[34] Sourisseau, J. et al (2016).

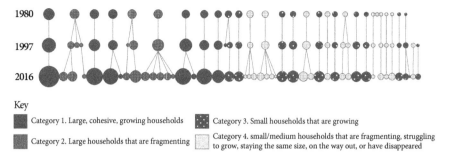

Figure 5.9. Household fragmentation DBG, 1980–1997–2016

destroy a household, or family (*du*): a wife by turning her husband against his brothers, a child by being loved more than other brothers' children or if one brother has no child until late, and wealth, by encouraging some within the household to take their assets for themselves alone.

In 1980, I reviewed examples of household break-up in the recent past, of which there had been five over the previous 30 years. Two of these involved a household fragmenting on the death of the household head; two were due to conflicts between brothers, leading to their separation; and one involved the establishment of an illegitimate man as a separate unit on his marriage. Conflicts of authority, questions of widow inheritance, and personality differences are the main causes of dispute and fragmentation. People recognize, however, the acute difficulties facing small households, the powerful disapproval and shaming of those involved in causing a household to break-up, and the possibilities of avoiding break-up by renegotiating the terms binding the different elements within the household.

Figure 5.9 illustrates what has happened to the size and structure of forty-seven *gwa* in DBG over the period from 1980 to 2016 (also shown in the colour plates section). As can be seen, there has been substantial growth in household size, with some growing far more than others have. Also evident is the number of cases where households have broken up. In the period 1980–1997, there were four such break-ups, whereas in the subsequent period, there were seven cases. Given the vulnerability of small, nuclear households, the decision to set up by yourself is always risky. Some men, such as those of illegitimate birth, face no option. Others are ejected following a major dispute, such as BD, as described below.

Household break-ups, 1980–1997

In this period, there were four cases of household fragmentation, all of which were provoked by the death of the household head. Long-standing differences between men in each of the subgroups prompted them to part company and set up on their own. In one case, two of the separating subgroups then merged to form a single household for some years, while in another case, the second subgroup has disappeared as the household has moved away from the village.

Household break-ups, 1997–2016

There were seven cases of households fragmenting in the period 1997–2016, but in only three of these was the break-up due to the death of the household head. Taking the other four cases, the first involves a split between two half-brothers, as described earlier, in relation to Figure 5.5. In the second case, S split off from B because he wanted his own autonomy. In the third case involving SD and BD, a fundamental and acrimonious dispute erupted. The latter had two wives. The first wife of BD, who had five sons and one daughter, was very possessive and not at all pleased to see the arrival of a second, much younger wife, and she became increasingly jealous and unpleasant to her co-wife. The rest of the family counselled BD to be firm with her, and insist on good behaviour. By this stage, the second wife had a son by BD. One night, when all the children were sleeping in the house of the first wife, the son of the second wife was found dead, which greatly shocked the family and the village. While there was no concrete proof of the first wife's guilt, her previous behaviour made everyone very suspicious of her, and they demanded that BD punish her in some way. He refused to do so, and the family head demanded that he leave the household because they could no longer tolerate having them around. BD is now farming by himself, and he lives separately with his first wife and six children, his second wife having returned to her family home. In the fourth case of NT and JT, the latter decided to separate off from his elderly uncle with whom he did not get on. Having several close brothers who left with him, his household is now a reasonably viable group of thirty-two people. His uncle's family, by contrast, is small and precarious, as a result of his nephews leaving.

Of the three households that split on the death of the household head (ST, ND, MT), the case of ST's household exemplifies the dysfunction that can develop between different 'sons' of the household. None of the brothers could get on with each other, and their poverty meant they were unlikely to do well in farming. There were few assets which might act as glue to hold the members together, and the man in charge of one subgroup has now left the village to an unknown destination. It is likely that the other subgroups will follow suit.

Disadvantages of being a small group

There are several disadvantages of being a small household, which are largely the converse of the benefits from large household size. First, there are a multitude of tasks to be done to grow enough food; maintain the farm's equipment; water the herd of livestock; ensure the cooking, water collection, and care of household members; and have confidence in the longer-term survival and prosperity of the group. There are clear economies of scale in moving from a nuclear family to one involving several adult men, their wives, and families, which means that one or several can go on migration to earn cash, while an adult man stays behind to water livestock, repair the compound, and prepare the field for the forthcoming farming season. Hence, diversification of incomes and activities is much more possible in large households, which is explored in more detail in Chapters 6 and 7. Equally, given the uncertainty around success in producing and rearing children, having several married couples in the household producing children, which represent descendants for the household as a whole, offers some insurance against the failure of any single couple to produce enough descendants.

Conclusions

There has been rapid demographic growth, especially in the last 20 years, because of improvements in infant and child survival. However, demographic performance remains uneven between households and couples. The village of DBG demonstrates the persistence of very large domestic groups, which are larger than comparable households elsewhere in West Africa. These remarkable domestic institutions work as a farming group, a residential unit, an economic enterprise permitting livelihood diversification, and a generator of children and descendants.

Institutions are key to managing risks in an uncertain setting. There are multiple benefits from remaining within large households, which include economies of scale and the maintenance of assets, providing a critical mass of labour for farming and many other essential tasks to be done. Larger groups find it easier to gather the capital to invest in key assets; they face less risk from failure to reproduce; and there is greater space for individual income earning and increased autonomy. Chapter 6 explores in more detail the relationship between household size and accumulation of assets. Such assets, especially cattle, can be converted into future household growth, by paying the costs of marriage.

Household break-up is not just the result of the death of the household head. This itself does not necessarily catalyse fragmentation, and many households stay as a single group, despite the deaths of a succession of household heads. The break-up of a *gwa* happens for a variety of reasons—such as conflict over assets, or women, illegitimacy, or unacceptable behaviour. Household break-up and the bitter words uttered by opposing factions make it hard for people to get back together after such a split, while the strong identity of each family and lineage makes it uncommon for small insecure households from different clans to join together, even though it might make practical sense.

6

Investment and prosperity

Gesedala ani nafolo sorolen, u bee kakan. Waati dola i sen be sanfe, waati dola i sen be jigin duguma.[1]

Introduction

If you drive past the village of Dlonguébougou (DBG) and many of its neighbours, you might dismiss these low-lying, mud-brick settlements as stuck in a poverty trap, following traditional patterns of farming, and unable to respond to new markets and business opportunities. This chapter shows you need to look more carefully and observe in the few visible signs of modernity, such as the cluster of solar panels and TV aerials, an indication both of how much income and assets have grown over recent decades and of people's openness to take up new technology and innovation. As described by Himanchu et al for their village study in India, 'contrary to the picture of a stagnant, unchanging rural backwater, the people of Palanpur have been constantly changing, adapting and absorbing new ideas and technologies to create better lives for themselves and their families'.[2]

This chapter illustrates the big increase in assets in DBG over the last 35 years, as well as changes in the scale and pattern of investment made by households and individuals, and their current distribution between households. This evidence shows how farming households have seized new investment and market opportunities, channelled high levels of cash into productive farm assets, and diversified into a broad range of activities to strengthen their household's portfolio of income sources.[3] Many African governments have courted domestic and international 'investors' to acquire land and 'modernize' the farming sector since it is assumed that ordinary farmers are incapable of such a task and getting rid of the hoe as a symbol of backwardness has been the focus for policy. President of the African Development Bank, Adesina, said in 2017: 'Hoes and cutlasses, bulls or oxen, have

---

[1] Riches and poverty are like the feet of a traditional weaver—at one time, your foot is rising, and the other one is on the ground, but then they swap round, and the other rises, while the first falls.

[2] Himanchu et al (2018) p. 108.

[3] Evident in Toulmin, C. et al (2000); Faye, A. et al. (2001); and recent work by Brockington and Noe in Tanzania (forthcoming).

Land, Investment and Migration. Camilla Toulmin, Oxford University Press (2020). © Camilla Toulmin.
DOI: 10.1093/oso/9780198852766.001.0001

no place any longer in African agriculture: they belong in museums, not on the farms. We must rapidly mechanize agriculture in Africa, with low-cost, affordable tractors and equipment, to raise labour productivity and value added per worker to global levels.'[4] In the case of DBG, farmers combine the old and the new, retaining the hoe for certain tasks and using it alongside oxen-drawn ploughs, donkey carts, and mobile phones. This ability of households to invest in new assets and activities depends on their control over household labour, access to migration earnings, and the success of the farm economy.

Measuring economic growth and wellbeing—national data

The economic statistics needed at both national and local levels to describe economic development in Africa are frequently patchy and of poor quality because of a combination of factors.[5] These include limited collection of production, income, and expenditure data; reliance on assumptions and extrapolations from previous data series; and infrequent updating of economic baselines. Consequently, much of the analysis undertaken of macroeconomic trends, differences between countries in terms of their economic performance, and examination of how economic growth has been distributed across the nation is based as much on fiction as fact. Young (2012) notes that 'existing GDP and poverty statistics substantially under-estimate true economic performance in Africa'.[6]

Particular weaknesses include the very limited regular collection of data from major parts of the economy, such as the rural agricultural sector, which continues to supply incomes and employment to the majority of the population.[7] The contribution of the large and diverse informal sector to incomes and jobs, while recognized in aggregate is largely unquantified, and there are significant illicit funding flows which escape scrutiny. Agricultural output is often estimated on the basis of a formula linking harvests to an estimate of total area cultivated, adjusted by a rainfall variable to account for wetter and drier years. Cash crops may be better counted, particularly where they are subject to central marketing boards, but their accuracy depends on whether farmers deliver their crop to the marketing board or seek parallel markets paying better prices. There is very limited tax-based information because of widespread evasion and the large number of enterprises unregistered for tax purposes. In terms of other statistics, human population numbers in most African countries probably are reasonably captured at aggregate level, but, with high levels of seasonal movement between

---

[4] 'Betting on Africa to Feed the World'—The Norman Borlaug Lecture delivered by Dr Akinwumi A. Adesina, President of the African Development Bank and World Food Prize Laureate 2017, at Iowa State University, Des Moines, Iowa, USA, 17 October 2017.
[5] Jerven, M. (2013, 2015).   [6] Young, A. (2012).   [7] Jerven, M. (2013).

rural and urban areas, the timing of the population census makes a big difference to where people are counted.[8]

Basic economic data for Mali are no exception to this general pattern for Africa. In 2016, the total population was estimated to be 18 million, growing at 3.6 per cent per annum—one of the highest rates in the world. Mali's GDP in 2016 was estimated to be $14 billion, growing at around 5 per cent per year, giving a per capita income of $743 in nominal terms, and $1,963 at purchasing power parity. Cotton, textiles, food processing, transport, telecommunications, livestock, and gold mining constitute the main sectors showing in GDP statistics. Most modern economic activity and government expenditures are concentrated in the capital Bamako, which accounts for more than 80 per cent of estimated GDP. Strong monetary and financial discipline is maintained through Mali's membership of the Union Economique et Monétaire pour l'Afrique de l'Ouest (UEMOA), and the associated currency, the CFA franc. Critics of the franc zone argue that the currency is overvalued and makes it impossible to establish manufacturing and other enterprises which can be competitive globally, as noted in Chapter 2.[9] Mali is placed in the bottom twenty-five countries worldwide for poverty and human development, at 164 out of 187 by the IMF, and at 175 out of 188 according to the UNDP's Human Development Index.

Nationally, it is estimated that 45 per cent of the population fall below the poverty line, which is set at 178,000 francs, representing 54 per cent of those in rural areas, but only 5 per cent of the population in Bamako.[10] The regions of Sikasso, Ségou, Koulikoro, and Mopti all show rates of more than 51 per cent of the rural and urban population falling below the poverty line.[11] The Ségou Region had been considered one of the better-endowed parts of Mali, thanks to Ségou city's long-standing political and economic importance, and the presence of the *Office du Niger* irrigation scheme. The region has an estimated 3 million people, and, in 1998, it was estimated to have an income per head of 176,000 francs, one-third that of Bamako. No current estimates exist for income per head in Ségou Region, but the disparity with Bamako is likely to have persisted. The *Office du Niger* irrigation scheme, Comatex fabric mill, and Sukala sugar factory are the main sources of modern employment in the Ségou Region. However, recently there are concerns that Ségou is not on the principal transport routes from coastal West Africa, through Sikasso, to Bamako and Mauritania, and Ségou risks becoming a backwater. Equally, the growing insurgency in the centre of the country is having

---

[8] The particular case of Nigeria and its population census is well-documented, given the highly charged political stakes associated with political representation, federal funding allocations, and numbers of people.

[9] Nubukpo, K. (2015).

[10] INSM (2018). The surprisingly low figure of 5 per cent for Bamako may be due to most of the poorer informal settlements lying outside the formal boundary of the city.

[11] INSM (2018).

major adverse effects on the region's economy. Within the Ségou Region, the communes of N'Koumandougou, where DBG is found, and Bellen just to the north, are amongst the poorest for this region.

Measuring economic wellbeing and growth in DBG

The only official statistics available for DBG refer to the village population, and that of the commune of which it forms part. The population census is not fully accurate since it under-reports the human population by 10–15 per cent, and tends to leave out older women, adopted children, and infants.[12] Despite the absence of quantitative economic data, the people of DBG acknowledge that they have become better off materially since 1980, with access to many more diverse goods. They also point to the much higher expectations held of the wedding 'trousseau', which girls aspire to take with them when they marry, as evidence of increased wealth.[13] Interviews with young and old alike also make clear that control and distribution of incomes and wealth have changed greatly, with household heads losing their grasp on younger folk, who now make their own choices. I have tried to document changes to both incomes and asset holdings to get a sense of how economic wellbeing has changed since 1980–1982.

I have collected data on asset ownership in 2016 to compare with 1980–1982 and 1997, as a change in asset ownership acts as a partial, though imperfect, proxy for changes in incomes. As Brockington and Howland acknowledge, 'attention to assets matters a good deal if we are to study poverty dynamics'.[14] In judging the relevance of changes in asset holdings since 1980, it is important to ask how income and assets are linked. When people experience a rise in income, they tend to invest this in assets rather than increased consumption, whereas a fall in income is often taken in reduced consumption rather than sale of assets, and trying to 'make do' until conditions improve. In times of stress, poorer households will try to hold onto limited livestock holdings rather than sell them since sale of work oxen, for example, would put them in a much more difficult position in the farming season to come.

When starting the 2 years of fieldwork in 1980, the original intent was to conduct twice-weekly interviews with the household head, to fill in together a large questionnaire covering every activity on and off the farm, and all sales and purchases. Because of the very large size and diverse structure of DBG households and the household head's consequent inability to speak for his

---

[12] This shortfall of 10–15 per cent becomes evident when a comparison is made between the official government survey results and the household survey undertaken by Karen Brock and Sidiki Diarra in 1997.

[13] *Konyo minanw,* or wedding equipment.   [14] Brockington, D. and Howland, O. (2018) p. 15.

many members, it became evident early on that we would need to abandon these questionnaires in favour of a lighter-touch approach. This was made possible by living in the village, earning people's trust, and observing many transactions as they took place.

Over the 2 years of fieldwork, I collected income and expenditure data over a 12-month period at a household level, for twenty-six of the twenty-nine households. The major elements of these household budgets, as shown in Figure 6.1, consisted of crop sales, livestock sales, migration earnings, and trading profits, while expenditure included livestock and farm equipment purchases, marriage costs, tax payments, and food. The average cash expenditure per household was approximately 150,000 francs (equivalent to 7,500 francs per person). This figure excludes the subsistence value of grain and livestock consumed by the household, and it does not cover the very considerable private incomes generated by some people in DBG. Typical incomes at individual level were estimated, recognizing the big differences between men and women, and between those working in the family field whose time was severely constrained, and retired folk, who could spend much greater time on private activities.

From the 1980 data, it can be seen that millet provided nearly half, livestock more than a quarter of the resources used in cash and barter transactions, and migration made up 22 per cent. By contrast, trading income on average was almost negligible at 3 per cent. But there were very high coefficients of variation so that households differed greatly depending on their circumstances. Migration earnings were particularly important for smaller households, while trading profits represented 27 per cent of revenue for the small number of households with such a business. Expenditure patterns also varied greatly from one household to the next. While average wedding costs per household were 25,000 francs, for those actually celebrating a wedding, this could rise to more than 200,000 francs for this event. Equally, if a household had to purchase a new ox that year, this would require 100,000 francs. Even in 1980, it was clear that as household size grows, the range of expenses for which the household is responsible tends to diminish. The largest households could generate a significant millet surplus, which meant their members were granted a degree of autonomy over time and income, which would not be possible in smaller grain-deficit households. The more distant kin ties between men in larger households also meant that there was less pooling of assets and incomes between different groups of 'brothers'.

In terms of individual income earning in 1980, for men of working age it was rare to be able to earn more than 15,000 francs cash, given the many demands on their time. Women of working age were able to generate a larger amount from private fields, winnowing, and grain appropriation at harvest time. If they were lucky, they could amass millet and cash worth around 30,000 francs, but most of it disappeared into their granary, which ended up feeding her husband and children through much of the dry season. The remainder was spent on buying cotton, cloth, shoes, soap, and hairdressing. Retired men and women could earn

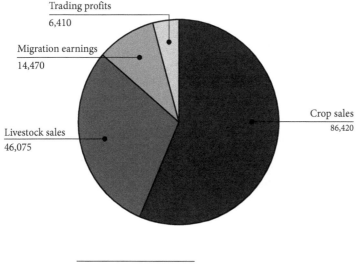

Mean value per gwa (CFA franc)

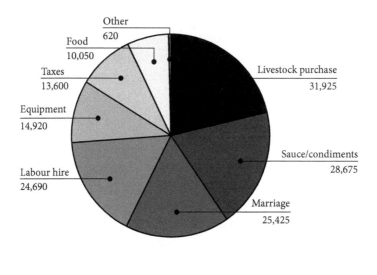

Mean value per gwa (CFA franc)

Figure 6.1. Household income derived from different sources and expenditure (average per HH), 1980

significantly larger amounts, from private fields of millet and groundnuts, fattening sheep and goats, rope making, trading, and cloth-dyeing activities (see Figure 6.2). A good season could bring in 50,000 francs. I noted that the magnitude of private-income sources for retired women helps explain the competition amongst older men to marry recently retired women, where there is no obvious candidate

Figure 6.2. Making rope from a shredded plastic sack, DBG, 2017

to inherit her, as they can hope to benefit from her companionship, hard work, and generosity.

Alongside the income and expenditure estimates at household and individual level, we collected data on the size of the millet crop by household, the value of total asset holdings, and changes in their numbers. A simple calculation of average income per person, which combines household and personal incomes, with the cash value of millet consumed during the year for 1980–1981, gives a total of 50,000 francs per person for the 12-month period covered, of which 27,500 francs (55 per cent) was represented by the cash value of millet consumption; 15,000 francs (30 per cent) came from private income earned; and 15 per cent represented household cash spent per person on tax and other payments. However, it must be remembered that this presents an 'average income' per person, in a context where there is huge diversity between households and individuals in their income-earning capacity. The figures imply a very low level of average income in 1980, equivalent to less than US$100 per year, and this demonstrates the importance of subsistence-food consumption as a share of the total.

For 2016, it has not been possible to construct a 'typical' level of income for individuals in DBG, as was done for 1980–1981, because of constraints on my undertaking detailed field-research. However, rough estimates are possible for incomes earned by different kinds of people, based on interviews about people's different activities, migration earnings, and purchases of food and gifts, and other expenses. Elderly men and women like MD can hope to get 50,000–100,000 francs from a field of sesame, from which to fund small gifts and purchases of sugar, sweets, and other snacks. A more ambitious sesame farmer told me in 2014 that he had sold 640,000 francs of sesame, having spent 150,000 francs on costs, netting close to 500,000 francs. A man with a sewing machine can earn more than 100,000 francs over the year if business is brisk in the dry season, while the owner of a shop is able to bring in a much larger sum. Women of working age earn cash through a sesame plot, providing hair-plaiting services, running a small trading activity, and growing vegetables—all of which might bring them 100,000–150,000 francs, depending on how much time they can invest (see Figure 6.3, colour plates section). Young women on migration might hope to come back after many months away with 100,000 francs in cash or goods. Young men who do well on migration can make enough to buy a motorbike and fashionable clothing, totalling 300–400,000 francs, but many will be less successful. Preparing charcoal for sale has become important for some men, especially in the period before harvest, when there is little to do in the fields. In October 2016, there were more than 300 bags of charcoal waiting for collection by traders from Ségou, each selling for 1,250 francs, equivalent to 375,000 francs.

Other ways of making a bit of extra cash include having a bag full of medicines for sale, and selling cooked food at the weekly market. Thus, as a rough guide, individual incomes today span from 50,000 to 400,000 francs, depending on age

Figure 6.3. Women and girls earn money from hair-dressing, 2014

and activity. Taking the midpoint gives an average income of 225,000 francs, but there will be many in the poorer households with less than this. A large contrast between the period 1980–1981 and today concerns the importance of millet in the overall household budget. The analysis of millet harvests in Chapter 3 showed average yields per person are now only a third of those gained earlier, at 183 kg for 2016–2018, compared with 502 kg in 1980–1982. This is equivalent to one-tenth of the average income, in contrast to 55 per cent in 1980–1981. Today there is no millet surplus which can be sold to pay taxes or buy farm equipment. Indeed, the quantity harvested is not sufficient to feed all members of the household, so individuals have to provide for their own food needs for a significant part of the year. Information on private incomes must also be seen in the context of rapid shifts in social values and loyalties. Individuals are both proud of their earning capacity but also reticent to make this public, for two reasons. First, they recognize that such hubris is unwise since vaunting your moneymaking abilities could invite envy and court disaster. Second, there is evident tension between collective and individual activities and duties. Hence, people are embarrassed to admit they are doing well in terms of private earnings, especially when the overall household budget is in disarray.

In 1980, the village of DBG sent a 353,600 francs to the commune headquarters at Doura in tax payments, and by 2016, this had risen nearly fourfold to 1,386,350 francs. Tax is levied on adults (currently 1,700 francs per head[15]), livestock, farm equipment, guns, and motorbikes. Even before the colonial conquest, villages within the Bambara and Peul Empires had to pay tribute to the precolonial state, in the form of grain, cowries, labour, and honey. Following the colonial conquest, the people of DBG were required to pay a head tax, first in millet or cowries, and then in cash. Other taxes were added over time, such as for cattle, horses, rifles, carts, bicycles, sheep, and goats. In 1980, taxes were paid with little hope of seeing anything in return, except peaceful relations with the *chef d'Arondissement*. As noted in Chapter 1, the first day I arrived in the commune in April 1980, the *chef* had detained the chiefs of several neighbouring villages and left them sitting in the baking sun, to punish them for late payment of tax and delivery of their grain quota. Today, every household is keen to pay their taxes since laggards are identified and shamed amongst the family heads. When the harvest has failed, earnings from migration must be used for this purpose. With the establishment of local government in 1999, the villagers still grumble about paying taxes, but they recognize that they are starting to receive more benefits in return, such as the primary school and market. However, the commune budget remains small, at 16 million francs, equivalent to approximately 1,000 CFA francs/head; hence, there is not much room for investing in infrastructure or expanding services.

---

[15] Equivalent to $2.90 per person.

Investment in Assets, DBG 1980–2016

Currently, these assets include:

- Livestock holdings—cattle, sheep, and goats and donkeys and horses
- Plough teams
- Well digging
- Shops
- Solar panels
- Other assets, sewing machines, bicycles, and motorbikes

Table 6.1 presents the change in the number of different assets in DBG between 1980 and 2016. Valued at current prices for 2016, the cumulative total shows that over the last 35 years, there has been a fivefold increase in capital formation at village level, from 51,112,600 to 328,336,000 francs.[16] There has been an increase in the number of all assets, except for horses, which have fallen from ten to four over this period.

Figure 6.4 presents the value of productive capital assets in DBG for 1980 and 2016, which highlights several important features of the village's capital base and

Table 6.1. Changes in Total Assets, DBG 1980–2016[17]

	1980	2016	Change in Numbers	Approx Unit Value Today FCFA	Cumulative Value FCFA
Cattle	602	685	83	150,000	102,750,000
Work oxen	120	189	69	250,000	47,250,000
Small stock	698	951	253	25,000	23,775,000
Donkeys	45	352	307	70,000	24,640,000
Horses	10	4	−6	350,000	1,400,000
Ploughs	48	121	77	25,000	3,025,000
Carts	20	168	148	85,000	14,280,000
Wells	27	51	24	175,000	8,925,000
Shops	6	13	*	5,000,000	65,000,000
Solar panels	0	172	172	30,000	5,056,000
Sewing machines	3	26	23	85,000	2,210,000
Motorbikes	5	81	76	375,000	30,375,000

Values have been estimated at the average village price, as follows: cattle = 3–4-year-old female; oxen = fully grown ox for ploughing; small stock = average goats and sheep; wells = cost of digging; and*shops = approximate capital invested in stock, in 1980 tabletop with c ten items, and 2016 shops housed in a building with more than one hundred items.

Abbreviation: FCFA, *franc de la communauté financière africaine.*

---

[16] Equivalent to $620,000.
[17] The value of each asset has been estimated at today's current price.

Asset values 1980 prices

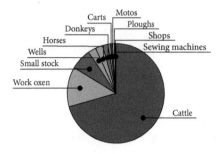

Cumulative value FCFA in 2016

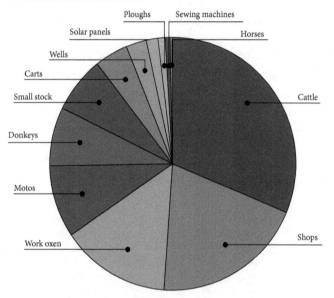

Figure 6.4. Relative importance of assets by value, DBG, 1980 and 2016

how it has evolved over 35 years. First, in 1980, livestock made up an overwhelming share of the assets held by the villagers, representing 85 per cent of the total sum. Cattle were by far the largest component, followed by work oxen, and sheep and goats. The latter, while low in individual value, achieve importance because of their large number. In 1980, horses were significantly more important than donkeys were, because their individual value was much greater. Remaining assets of significance were made up of carts, wells, motorbikes, bicycles, and sewing machines. By 2016, there had been a great diversification of assets acquired, as well as a substantial increase in their overall value, the total sum having multiplied by a factor of five over the 35 years, in comparison with a threefold increase in the village population. In terms of their relative proportions, by 2016, livestock had fallen to 61 per cent of the total asset sum, of which cattle remained of greatest importance, followed by work oxen and small stock. Donkeys have multiplied greatly in number and their overall value is now far greater than that of horses. The remaining 39 per cent of asset values are made up of shops and motorbikes, representing 20 per cent and 9 per cent, respectively, while wells, carts, sewing machines, and solar panels make up the remaining 10 per cent.

This shows that over the 35 years covered by this study, annual capital investment in the village averaged 7.6 million francs. This is a very significant sum of money, devoted each year to improve the productivity and income-earning possibilities of households in the village. None of this money has come from government, banking, or donor sources, but it is the product of hard work both within the village and from people bringing back cash from migration. Taking current prices, the average value of assets held per person has more than doubled from 95,716 francs in 1980 to 206,630 francs in 2016.[18]

However, the distribution of assets is by no means equally spread across all village households, with some much better off than others. The actual distribution of assets amongst all village households in 2016 is shown in Figure 6.17 (shown in the colour plates section). The smallest households tend to focus on acquiring a plough and a cart, as the essential assets before looking for oxen and small stock. The largest households have a diverse portfolio, containing all available assets, which gives them much greater economic resilience.

Table 6.2 presents data for a selection of households, to explore differences in ownership patterns according to size. This is the same sample of households described in Chapter 5 to explore the varied patterns of household size and organization. The table also shows that total asset holdings are greater in large than in small households, and it makes evident the continued strong association found between household size and capacity to acquire and maintain livestock and other assets found in 1980–1982.[19]

Many successful households today are built on the legacy from a previous good period, during which assets were built-up in the form of a cattle herd. Such cattle have then been converted into growth in household numbers, by financing the costs of marriage, which leads to an increased labour force in future, if all goes well. The case of ST, the second largest household described in the previous chapter (Figure 5.6), shows how labour and hard work can be converted over time into a broader, more secure portfolio of people and assets. The family had been very poor when they arrived in DBG in the mid-nineteenth century. The

[18] Equivalent to $387/person in 2016.
[19] Toulmin, C. (1992); an association also evident from Whitehead's work in Northern Ghana (2006).

Table 6.2. Distribution of Assets by Household Size: 2016

	3 Small HHs	6 Medium HHs	4 Large HHs	Village Average, Nos/HH
Cattle	4	14.3	48.5	14.3
Small stock	4	23.0	51.5	19.6
Donkeys	3	6.3	23.0	7.4
Ploughs	1.3	3.0	6.3	2.5
Carts	1.3	3.8	8.5	3.5
Wells	0.7	1.3	2.3	1.2
Shops	0	0.5	1.3	0.3
Solar	0.7	4.3	13.8	3.6
Sewing machines	0	0.8	3	0.6
Motorbikes	0.3	2.3	6	1.7

Abbreviation: HH, household.

current household head, now in his 60s, remembers when he was a small child in the 1950s, that the compound was filled with baobab bark being prepared for rope making, and men of his father's generation were hard at work, competing with each other to make money. The wealth generated from this joint activity was invested in oxen and a couple of ploughs, which allowed them to expand into groundnut cultivation, the harvests from which were then invested in cattle. The cattle have provided bride wealth for a series of marriages, which have been blessed with children.

The characteristics of each of the investments in this broad portfolio are described below, along with its risks and returns and how these have evolved since 1980–1982.

Livestock holdings: cattle, small stock, donkeys, and horses

Cattle are the traditional form of holding wealth for farmers and herders alike. As described in Chapter 2, the North Bank of the River Niger was the grazing zone for the kings of Ségou, and large cattle herds—often the product of raiding— were kept there in the guard of Peul herders belonging to the king.[20] Until the early 1960s, all of the villagers' cattle were managed in a single herd, which suggests a total herd size of no more than 120 animals. Today, they are grouped into seven different herding units, averaging just under one hundred animals each. If you only own two or three cattle, you will add them to the herd of a neighbour

---

[20] Bambara farmers in this area have traditionally given their cattle, sheep, and goats to be herded by the Peul, so farmers can concentrate all their energy on their fields.

Table 6.3. Distribution of Cattle Holdings All Households in DBG in 1980 and 2016

	1980	2016
Total no. cattle (excluding work oxen)	602	685
Cattle/pp average	1.09	0.43
HHs with 20+ head of cattle	10 HHs (34%)	14 HHs (30%)
Average cattle/pp	1.87	0.69
No. of HHs with 10 or fewer cattle	18 (62%)	32 (68%)
Average cattle/pp	0.31	0.21

Abbreviations: HH, household; pp, per person.

and take joint responsibility for them. Table 6.3 shows that in 1980, there were 602 cattle owned by Bambara households in DBG, managed in six herding groups. Such ownership was highly skewed, with large households having a disproportionately large share of animals per person. Thus, for example two-thirds of the village cattle herd was owned by five households, with an average herd size of seventy-eight head, equal to 2.5 cattle per person. Whereas the nineteen households (65 per cent of village households) with 10 or fewer cattle owned 11 per cent of the village herd and had an average of 0.4 cattle per household member. Hence, in 1980, there was a strong tendency for household and herd size to be positively correlated.

By 2016, total cattle numbers (excluding work oxen) had risen from 602 to 685, but given the tripling of human numbers, this implies a fall of more than 50 per cent in animals per person. The reasons given by the villagers for such a fall include cattle disease, shortage of fodder, sales of cattle to pay for marriage costs, sales of cattle to buy grain after poor harvests, theft, and poor reproductive performance attributable to over-milking, which has led many households to now herd the animals themselves. As was seen in Figure 6.4, there has also been a shift from cattle into other forms of capital investment. The distribution of these cattle holdings remains highly skewed. The four largest households own an average of forty-eight head; ten households have between twenty and forty head of cattle, while thirty-two out of forty-seven households (68 per cent) have ten or fewer stock. One of the owners with the largest herd in 1980 has subsequently split into five subgroups, leading to the fragmentation of its herd amongst the different parties. Fortunately, for them, the original herd was sufficiently big for each subgroup to gain both oxen and breeding females in the distribution of assets. A second large-herd owner has suffered falling grain yields and harvests, and has sold several animals to purchase grain. A third has had to pay for more than ten marriages over the last ten years, each of which has taken a heavy toll on the family herd. There has thus been a large fall in the number of cattle per person owned by farmers in DBG, from 1.09 to 0.43 per person, so they are now less important as a store of value.

Cost, maintenance, and returns from cattle

Cattle are usually purchased from visiting herders present around the village in the dry season, and it is common to find both the speckled grey cattle of Peul origin alongside a few dark-red Maure cattle (see Figure 6.5 below and in the colour plates section). Some purchases are also made between villagers. Females are usually kept in the herd, so far as possible, in the hopes they will calve again, only being sold-off finally for meat when their chances of breeding are considered nil. Today, a 3–4-year-old female sells for around 150,000 francs but will only fetch 70,000 francs when elderly and sold for meat.

In 1980, there were six herding groups; each one cared for by a hired Peul herder. There was a lot of grumbling from Bambara cattle owners about the behaviour of their hired herders, especially the over-milking of cows. Several cattle owners said that you must look for a herder with some of his own cattle, and avoid hiring a herder with a large family because he would be under pressure to find milk for them. Some herd owners, recognizing the pressure on milk supplies from hired herders needing to feed their family, tried to help by ploughing the herder's field. But they recognized it was difficult to supervise milking behaviour closely. One herd owner said that all of the calves born to his cows in the 1981 rainy season were dead by the following year, and he attributed these losses to the hired herder taking too much milk from his cows.

By 1997, there were seven herds, all cared for by hired herders. Relations had become increasingly difficult with Peul herders, but with Bambara cattle owners

Figure 6.5. Village herds contain the red Maure and grey-flecked Peul cattle breeds, 2011

wanting to focus their labour on cultivation in the rainy season, they continued to use hired herders for their cattle.

By 2016, the system for cattle herding had changed greatly. Only two households in DBG retained hired herders to look after their animals: the village chief and one of the shopkeepers. In the latter case, this is a place where many visitors stop-off for company, tea, sugar, and cigarettes, including many Peul and Maures, so he has maintained good relations with both groups. Everyone else had chosen, some years ago, to take back their animals and find a young man from within the family to look after them. The villagers' animals are now grouped into seven collective herds, with the tasks of watering and herding of animals during the farming season being shared amongst those households with cattle in the herd. They say this shift in herd management is principally to ensure that the calves survive the rigours of the long, hot dry season, having had too many succumb in the past to weakness from not having had enough milk from their mothers (see Figure 6.6 below and in the colour plates section). They also accuse the hired herders of claiming animals have been lost in the bush, when in fact they have stolen them.

Cattle provide a range of returns, from their milk and dung, their offspring, and the financial capital they represent, which means they can be sold when need be, to realize a cash sum. The analysis of returns to investment in cattle in 1980–1982 showed that while overall returns were low, and negative in years when calf deaths were high, cattle were very important as a store of value for meeting future needs,

Figure 6.6. As evening falls, calves are let off the rope and allowed to drink milk from their mothers, 2011

such as marriage costs and emergency expenditures, given few other options for holding wealth. Dung from the household's herd was also an important input for raising millet yields. I noted then that the return on capital invested in cattle might be higher if they were cared for by a member of the herd owner's own family, rather than by contract herders since there would be less risk of over-milking, but there would be a significant opportunity cost to withdrawing a young man from work in the field to care for the herd.[21]

Milk used to be the principal part of the herding contract, and Peul women would come into the village each morning with a calabash of milk to sell, so they could buy grain and other foodstuffs. In 2016, given that most cattle herds are managed by the Bambara themselves, there is less tension around levels of milking, so calf survival is said to be higher. In the rainy season, those with cows in milk will only take a small amount for household needs and leave the major part for the young animals.

Investment in breeding stock comes after the household's work-oxen requirements have been fulfilled. No one has a cattle holding which does not include work oxen. The largest cattle-herd owners operate several plough teams since they are amongst the largest households in the village and have abundant supplies of farm labour.

Sheep and goats. There were 951 small stock in DBG in 2016, compared with 698 in 1980. Sheep and goats are owned by individuals; older men tend to invest in sheep, spending time fetching fodder from the bush, and fattening them up for sale or slaughter at festivals and weddings. Goats are mainly women's property, giving a little bit of milk for breakfast *moni* porridge and afternoon *dégé*. In the rainy season, the sheep and goats are under the care of a hired herder and are taken out in the morning, to be herded away from the fields. Watered in the compound, their dung is a valuable source of soil fertility for women's farm plots. In the dry season, sheep and goats are allowed to wander freely, to forage around the village, and make their own way home in the evening.

Donkeys and carts. Donkeys have become widespread, with all households making acquisition of a donkey cart a high priority. Women say the adoption of donkey carts has made a big difference for them, as they no longer have to carry heavy burdens of food and water out to the field, and bring firewood back. Their numbers have grown from 45 donkeys in 1980 (1.8 per household), and 111 in 1997 (3.2 per household), to 352 in 2016 (averaging 7.4 per household). They have become so indispensable that girls save up for a donkey cart to add to their wedding trousseau. Because they are reasonably light, a woman can handle a donkey and cart, so they offer a means for her to fetch and carry firewood from the bush, as well as visit neighbouring settlements. Donkeys are put in the care of a boy in

---

[21] Toulmin, C. (1992) p. 195.

the household, to feed and water them. Households without a child often adopt young boys and girls from a related household to help with tasks such as these. If the donkey is lucky, they will get some of the cowpea and groundnut 'hay' stored after harvest, alongside fresh grass and weeds brought home from the field. When not needed for work, they are usually hobbled on the edge of the field during the rainy season, and tethered in a shady part of the family compound in the hot dry season.

A donkey costs 70,000 francs and a cart 85,000 francs. Returns come in the form of transport services, a small amount of dung for the field, and their offspring. As can be seen from Table 6.1, donkey carts have become more common than ploughs (168 vs. 121), and the number of donkeys has grown nearly eightfold over 35 years. The largest households have an average of twenty-three donkeys, and 8.5 carts (nearly three donkeys per cart). While the carts are light enough to be pulled by a single animal, when heavily laden, a pair of donkeys is needed. Donkey carts are especially important for those with a trading business or shop since they are the means by which to transport goods bought at the big weekly market in Dougabougou. The large household led by ST, for example, which has four shops, forty donkeys, and sixteen carts (see Figure 6.7, below and in the colour plates section).

Donkey carts are especially important to incoming farmers seeking land in DBG and neighbouring areas. In June, setting out from villages such as Tekena, N'Golobabougou, and Temou, each household usually brings two to three donkey carts with people, food, seed, and farm equipment for the forthcoming season. The carts also allow farmers to come in search of water from DBG when there is not enough drinking water in bush ponds.

Horses. Horses used to be the transport of choice for older men, and they retain some of their prestige from precolonial times. In the olden days, a powerful and

Figure 6.7. Donkey carts are invaluable for transporting water to the field, 2011

beautiful horse was highly coveted, as is clear from the numerous stories which involve horses and disputes, such as between DBG and the warlord N'To Diarra, from neighbouring Markabougou. Horses were valuable as a military asset, giving armed men the capacity to raid and carry away people as slaves, particularly children. As late as 1900, a first-class horse was said to be valued at five to twenty slaves, or up to one hundred cattle.[22] The colonial records highlight the huge significance of horses as a means of transport and military asset. The North Bank region in the early nineteenth century was able to muster 600 armed cavalrymen, alongside 1,000 foot soldiers. Mungo Park, as he travelled through the area in the 1790s and met many travellers on horseback, found himself scorned because his horse was weak and so was obliged to drive it in front of him. Horses are still very expensive: a luxury commodity costing 350,000 francs in 2016. They can also be acquired through *serenkoro*, an arrangement whereby you agree to look after a mare and, in return, gain every second foal.[23]

In 1980 there were ten horses kept in the village, largely by old men who needed them to travel to weddings and funerals and to conduct business in neighbouring settlements. They were reluctant to set out for a day's journey on foot, would not submit to cycling, and did not have a motorbike. By 2016, only four horses were kept in DBG, one of which has been acquired recently by one of the wealthiest men in DBG, who spends much of his time away in town, and can afford the pleasure of a horse. He says:

> I bought a horse. If you go there you'll see it tied up behind the kitchen in our compound, it's got a reddish coat, its two years old. Once it's gelded, I will ride on it, to go to the field, I will enjoy myself on the horse, and go off to other villages. Once I am on its back, I will race about. If you want to look after animals, get a horse to look after. If it gets lost, it's easier to find than a motorbike. If I want to travel somewhere, I can get on the horse.[24]

While they continue to confer prestige, there are other forms of transport available. Today, old men needing a lift are more likely to ride pillion on the motorbike of one of their sons, or take the donkey cart. Horses are costly to maintain, and the limited fodder supplies are usually given to working animals, such as the family's donkeys.

Plough teams

Heavy mouldboard ploughs were first introduced into the Ségou Region in the 1930s, with the establishment of the irrigated *Office du Niger* and the spread of

---

[22] In comparison with today, when one horse equals two to three cattle in value.

[23] *Serenkoro* also applies to donkeys, and it is a means by which households with spare labour can acquire an animal.

[24] Interview, March 2017.

groundnut cultivation. They were sold on credit, with the debt to be repaid over a number of years. Farmers in DBG were fearful of taking out loans with government agencies, and so it was not until the 1950s that the first ploughs were bought by them. OS claims to have bought the first plough to DBG, having the advantage of a military pension, following his time away fighting in Indo-China. Combined with his illegitimacy, which put him at arms' length from the big old families, he was under less pressure to conform, which allowed him to take the risk of trying this new invention.

The early heavy ploughs were made for breaking-up deep clay soil, in the irrigation scheme. In villages like DBG, they were subsequently replaced by much lighter two-bladed ridging ploughs, made by local blacksmiths, which were all that was needed for the light sandy soils found around the village. A single-bladed weeding plough was added to the household's list of essential farm equipment in the 1970s. They are used to break-up the soil between the lines of millet, which speeds up the subsequent weeding done by a team of hoers.

In 1980–1982, much of the bush-field millet was sown on unploughed land, in holes rapidly dug on the old field surface, in order to seed land as rapidly as possible. Plough teams were only used for preparing the new land to be added to the bush field in that year (usually 20–30 per cent of the surface area). But today, farmers aim to plough all bush-field land, to keep weed growth at bay. In 1980 and today, all village-field land is ploughed because there will be substantial weed growth by the time the workforce starts to sow these fields.

Table 6.4 shows the pattern of plough-team ownership for 1980, 1997, and 2016. In 1980–1982, most households had both a plough and a pair of work oxen (twenty-six out of twenty-nine households), and only one had neither plough team nor oxen. Typically, a household without sufficient oxen hired or borrowed an animal from someone else, such as by exchanging access to their well for the loan of an ox for the forthcoming farming season. Others were able to borrow an animal from a household with a new untrained ox, or in exchange for providing watering labour over the dry season. Plough teams can also be hired, as is often done by women and old men who want help with their private fields of sesame and millet, on days when the plough team is not needed for the household millet

Table 6.4. Oxen Plough-Team Holdings, DBG 1980, 1997, and 2016

No. of work oxen owned	% Bambara village HHs 1980	% Bambara village HHs 1997	% Bambara village HHs 2016
0	10	20	13
1–4	66	49	53
5–8	14	17	19
9–12	10	11	9
12+	0	3	6
	100	100	100

field. There was no general market in plough-team hire in 1980–1982. Given the uncertain rainfall, the best time available for ploughing is tight, and everyone wants his own equipment if possible.

Those with work oxen typically sell-off older, mature animals, which can fetch 200,000 francs, and replace them with a younger beast for 50,000–80,000 francs, thereby freeing-up some capital for other purposes, such as tax payments and wedding costs. Aside the cost of purchasing work oxen, their maintenance is significant since they need to be watered throughout the dry season and given extra feed in the run-up to the start of farming. They are thin and weak at the end of the dry season, so people store groundnut hay and cowpea leaves to build the oxen up before ploughing begins.

By 1997, there had been a significant shift in ownership of work oxen, with an increase in the number of households without a full complement and needing to hire. This was due to the impact of cattle disease on oxen numbers, and an increase in the number of small asset-poor households. As a result, only 49 per cent of households in 1997 were able to rely on their own animals alone for ploughing,

---

Box 6.1 Household GG: the slow process of acquiring a plough team

Household GG consists of a widow and her young family. They had split off from a larger household when the widow's husband was still alive, following a dispute between him and his younger brother. At this time, the oldest child was 14 years old, and the youngest had only just been born. Soon after the split, the husband died, and his younger brother offered to take them back into the larger household, but the widow refused. The split had been acrimonious and left them without equipment, animals, or wells. In the first year after the split, they cultivated the bush field by hand. A wealthier neighbour saw their plight and lent a plough and pair of oxen. The surplus from the first year's harvest was used to buy a plough and donkey cart. In the second year, the widow rented an ox from a Maure household for cash, and paired it with an ox borrowed from her sister in a neighbouring village. In the third year, an ox was rented from the same Maure, and a second animal acquired from another village household in exchange for having provided watering labour the previous dry season. By the fourth year, the millet harvest was enough to buy an ox, and in the fifth year, a second animal was purchased using the earnings from migration. Thus, this household has been able to acquire a full oxen plough team over 5 years, in which there have been reasonable millet harvests.

Source: Brock, K. and Coulibaly, N. (1999).

the remainder needing to hire and borrow animals for this task. This has led to the development of a local market in oxen plough- team services, with transactions in the market replacing help from relatives. Where possible, households tried to build-up their own oxen holding, as described in Box 6.1.

By 2016, six households had no work oxen at all and had to borrow animals or hire a complete team to get their fields ploughed. These are amongst the smallest households in DBG, several being the result of a recent fragmentation of a larger domestic group. BT has always chosen to hire work oxen rather than purchase and maintain a pair, and he pays 50,000 francs per year per animal, which he considers makes sense for a small household with limited labour. One of the six is household GG, presented in Box 6.1, which has lost the hard-won oxen because of disease and several poor harvests. Some of those without their own oxen can negotiate access to an animal from family or neighbours, get a 6-month loan from the Maures in exchange for access to their well in the dry season, or get help from incoming farmers.

At the other end of the spectrum, Table 6.4 shows that in 2016, three households (6 per cent) owned more than twelve work oxen. This means they can field six plough teams at a time, of particular value to speedy land preparation in the family's large bush field, and they can then be used for preparing sesame plots. No one has yet invested in a mechanical means to prepare the land, nor hired a tractor from Ségou, although such equipment is available for hire closer to the city.

Returns to plough teams

Analysis of returns to oxen plough teams in 1980 showed that the investment gave a positive return to all households. Larger households gained better returns because the labour costs of watering and maintaining the oxen were spread over a larger unit. In 1980–1982, the highest returns came from households which combined investment in plough teams with expansion of well-manured village fields. Bush-field millet, at that moment, generated lower returns from plough-team use because yields per hectare were significantly lower. In almost all cases, the investment paid back over a single year, the exception being the smallest households, which took 2–3 years. Households without their own plough team had lower than average yields of both village- and bush-field millet. Great speed is needed to weed the fields during the short rainy season, to give the millet a chance of getting enough water and nutrients. Without a plough team to prepare the land before sowing, or to quicken the pace of weeding work, it is difficult to keep the millet in good condition. In 1997, returns from oxen plough teams had shifted from village- to bush-field millet, given the fall in manure available and associated decline in *sunan* millet yields. Hence, most energy was invested in expanding the bush fields. This shift in relative yields has continued so that in 2016, the returns from investment in oxen plough teams come principally from rapid cultivation and weeding of extensive bush fields and being hired out to individuals for use in preparing land for sesame.

Well digging

Wells have always played an important role in this dry region, as seen by the host of legends associated with the discovery or drying-up of wells, such as the fall of the Ghana Empire as described in Chapter 2. Equally, as described in Chapter 1, the founding of DBG by the current inhabitants involved the surprise discovery of an old well in a thicket by the billy goat belonging to the Traoré family. Today there are five public wells in the village used for drinking water and washing clothes. In addition, there are fifty-one private wells, dug by individual village households, to establish watering contracts with visiting herd owners.

Until 1960, only the Dembélé family of the village chief had the right to dig wells in the village's customary territory. In a region where water is scarce, the person who owns a well exerts power over people and livestock, through controlling access to water. After Independence in 1960, individual households in DBG started digging their own wells, led by Bafin Toungara, who was head of one of the other two founding families, and leader of the rival Marka community. This was a successful test of chiefly authority, and their assertion of control over village affairs. Only one of the founding families could contest the Dembélé clan in this way.

Growth and distribution of wells

Figure 6.8 shows the growth in the number of wells in DBG since 1960. Over the 1960s and 70s, there were sixteen wells dug, predominantly by the most powerful households of the village, in terms of their settlement history and size. In the early 1980s, there was a widespread boom in well digging, with twenty-seven being dug in the 4 years between 1980 and 1983. The last of these years saw fifteen wells dug, of which two were first wells; ten were by households which had already dug a well; and three households were investing in a third well. By the end of 1983, only five households did not have a well of their own—all of them amongst the smallest, poorest, and least viable of domestic groups in DBG. Given the big increase in number of wells dug in 1980s, it might have been expected to bring about a fall in the water table, but the villagers say there is no clear evidence for this. Annual renewal of the water table comes from rainfall, and perhaps the wells are not close enough together in most cases to affect each other's draught. However, there has been some discussion as to whether the big new irrigated sugarcane plantation 30 km away might have added water to groundwater levels, since villagers remark that none of the wells has dried up recently.

Table 6.5 shows the breakdown of well ownership by household. By 1997, there were forty-six private-household wells operating. One household had four wells,

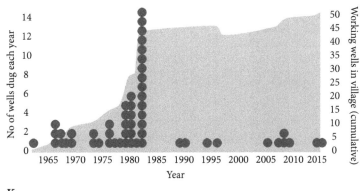

Key

Cumulative number
of working wells
in the village

Number of wells dug
each year

Figure 6.8. Wells dug in DBG, 1960–2016

Table 6.5. Distribution of Wells by Household, Village
Bambara 1981, 1998, and 2016

Number of wells/HH	1981	1998	2016
0	7	7	16
0.5	0	2	0
1	17	12	18
2	5	10	7
3	0	3	5
4	0	1	1
Total HHs	29	35	47
Total wells	27	46	51

Abbreviation: HH, household.

while three others had three each. The number of households without a well
remained at seven, and one well was shared between two households.

By 2016, there were fifty-one private wells. Between 1997 and 2016, only seven
wells were dug, and two had collapsed completely, as a result of the wooden
beams making-up the top structure having slipped. Several others have fallen into
disrepair and need to be dug out to deepen the draught of water they can hold. As
can be seen from Table 6.6, there are now sixteen households without a well, and
these are amongst the smallest and poorest households, with little or no labour
to invest in getting a well dug, nor assets to sell to hire someone else to do it.
However, the rationale for well digging has also changed, as described below.

Table 6.6. Comparison of Sixteen Households with no Well Compared with the Village Average in DBG in 2016

	16 HHs No Well	Average All HHs
Household size, no. people	11.7	31.2
Cattle holding/HH	2.8	14.6
Combined asset value FCFA/HH	1,129,100	6,985,000

Abbreviation: HH, household, FCFA, *franc de la communauté financière africaine.*

Costs and returns from wells

Digging a well in DBG is the task of 2–3 months, depending on how much labour is available to the household, or whether they must rely on hired labour (see Figure 6.9, below and in colour plates section). The total cost of getting a well dug is given as 175,000 francs in Table 6.1, which also represents the average amount of labour that has been invested in the well. Villagers talk about there being 'water-pathways' underground, which you need to tap into for a successful well.[25] Although every well has found water within the fields close to the settlement, prospective well diggers usually resort to the advice of a trusted *marabout* to identify the best site. Given the saucer-like depression within which DBG sits, the depth of the well depends mainly on the location and the thickness of the sandy layer to be dug out before reaching the harder rock where water is found (see Figure 6.10). This layer of sand can be from 3 to 6 metres in depth, and it requires a criss-cross construction of timber be built to ensure a stable wellhead. It is clearly visible when you bend to

Figure 6.9. The first day of digging a new well, 1981

[25] *Ji siraw.*

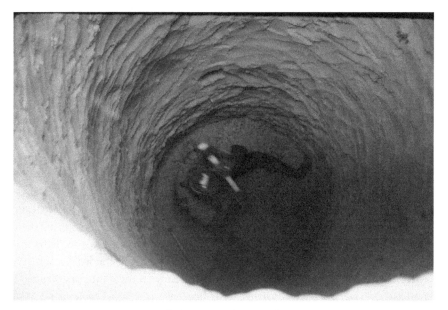

Figure 6.10. One week into well digging, and the shaft is about 4 m deep, DBG, 1981

look into the well, and the topmost wooden trunks bear deep grooves in the wood from the ropes of people pulling up their buckets over the years.

Analysis of returns to well digging in 1980–1982 showed that the main benefit at that moment was to gain access to the dung of animals watering there. An extra well around the village would marginally improve access to domestic water supply, but the well was dug principally to acquire dung. A household having dug a new well would expect to both spread manure over the existing field plot and cut a new plot which could benefit from building up its fertility over time. The highest returns were found for larger households which had expanded their village-field area and invested more plough-team days to ensure timely weeding of the village-field millet crop. Lowest returns came to households which had no plough team of their own and had to hire in the equipment for a few days. The boom in well digging in the 1970s and 80s generated substantial benefits to early investors, who gained much higher yields of millet because their soil was made more fertile. I estimated that most of those digging wells in the late 1970s and early 1980s got their money back in less than 3 years.[26] But given the large number of households who started to follow suit, and the harsh drought of 1984, the boom in well digging was then followed by a fall in returns, and slowdown in new wells dug.

---

[26] Toulmin, C. (1992) p. 154.

This was because the large increase in animals drawn to water at DBG could not be supported on pastures around the settlement. Visiting herders would no longer agree to limit their movements so that the animals were brought back to manure the village fields each evening since this meant their animals missed the better, more distant pastures.

By 1997, returns from well digging had declined significantly, and people's enthusiasm for investing in a new well had fallen as a consequence. By 1997–1998, there had been a shift in the type of watering contracts, with only 41 per cent involving the exchange of water for manure, while the remaining wells were either offering water against payment of cash (26 per cent) or offering water in exchange for an ox (33 per cent). Typical payment for a season's watering was 50,000 francs. In 2016, returns to a well are much lower than in 1980–1982, because of heavy pressure on grazing resources and the reluctance of visiting herders to bring their herd back each night to bed them down on the village field. Most wells have a visiting herd watering there for part of the rainy season, but the herder agrees a fee for the week or a month, rather than committing to the entire dry season.[27] Households have not been repairing wells that have run into problems because the returns are not seen as worthwhile. As with other investment cycles, it is the smallest and poorest households who were not able to seize the opportunity early on, or who only managed to jump on the ladder once the best returns had been gained by others.

Shops

Many individuals run a small trading business from their house, selling kola nut, snuff, and various other commodities brought back from a visit to market. There are also a number of households which have constructed a dedicated shop (*butiki*), of which there are now thirteen in the village. These businesses have grown in scale from the small tabletop trade of 1980, when there were six regular traders, with ten to twelve items for sale, to several hundred items found in *butiki* today, as shown in Box 6.2.

Most shopkeepers invest in solar panels to be able to offer their customers light, radio, TV, and cold drinks, which are especially popular during the Ramadan fasting month. They take both cash and millet in payment for goods, and sell the accumulated sacks of grain to visiting traders. TD has become a particularly successful trader and shopkeeper. The youngest of three energetic brothers, he lives on the edge of the village, and his shop is always full of Peul,

---

[27] Typical watering fees are 50,000 francs for the entire season, or 10,000–15,000 francs per month.

Box 6.2 What can I buy in Babu's boutique?

Items in Babou Dembelé's shop, 1980
  Tea (green), sugar, soap, cigarettes (Liberté only), salt, petrol, sweets, kola, and dates.

Items in Babou Dembelé's shop, 2016
  Tea (green), sugar, soap, cigarettes (many brands), salt, petrol, sweets, kola, dates, nail varnish, chocolate biscuits, scissors, rattles for babies, honey (local), biscuits (chocolate), rope (nylon), rope (baobab), string, razor blades, lamps, milk, soap powder, spare parts (bike), spare parts (moped), tyres, clothes, well pails, plastic pots, cooking pots, knives, tomato concentrate, bike pumps, thread, cotton fabric (local), cotton fabric (manufactured), batteries (several sizes), tea (brown), coffee, aspirin, flip flops, kerosene, matches, cold drinks, telephone cards, fertilizer, chains, mosquito coils, mosquito nets, padlocks, underclothes (pants, bras), maggi cubes, rice, and much more.

Maure, and incoming Bambara farmers who all spend time and money at his shop. One of the first two households to buy a solar panel in 2004, he now has four. Everyone acknowledges that he has done really well. In some ways, his family history may have helped by setting him apart from his neighbours, and by exerting fewer social pressures.[28] His cattle herd has grown from a pair of work oxen in 1980, to more than fifty animals today. His household numbers have grown from six in 1980, to fifteen in 1997, and to forty today. Of the thirteen shops in DBG today, six were already operating as a small trading business in 1980. The thirteen are spread across nine households. Of these, seven have a single shop; one has two; and the family of ST has four shops, each one run by a man in his 40s or 50s who has retired from the family field. This family also has a large number of donkey carts that form part of this trading business. As could be seen from Figure 6.17 (in the colour plates), shops are disproportionately owned by larger households, within which it permits an adult man to focus on trade rather than work in the field.

DBG's weekly market, established in 2012, is held on Wednesdays, and it offers a further opportunity for people to shop. There are more than fifty stalls selling foodstuffs (e.g. dried fish, cooked snacks, and meat), shoes, second-hand clothing, medicines, and telephones, along with a range of services—cycle repair, barbering, hair plaiting, blacksmithing, and fortune telling.

---

[28] His family is one of the former slave households who chose to stay behind in DBG following abolition in 1905.

Solar panels

Figure 6.11 illustrates the rise in solar panel investment in DBG, over the period 2000 to 2016. The first solar panels were purchased by GD in 2000 for 175,000 francs each, a purchase that was followed by TD in 2004, who bought one for 150,000 francs. In both cases, they wanted to generate electricity for charging phones, and to earn money charging up batteries for others. They also wanted to provide light for the household and shop, as well as music and TV for customers. GD has always been quick to pick-up on new opportunities and technologies, as he spends much of his time in town. From 2010, there has been substantial acceleration in the purchase of solar panels, such that today, there are more than 170 panels in the village. Most of these have been bought by individuals—young and old—for light, music, and charging batteries. The maternity clinic has a set of three large panels to power a refrigerator (see Figure 6.12). There is as yet no system to connect these individual purchases into a village-wide energy network, nor is solar energy used to power 'productive' activities, such as a mill, or other machinery, though one travelling barber carries out his work with a razor electrified with solar power.

Figure 6.13 shows the large fall in average price for solar panels over this period, and clustering of purchases of lower price panels in the last 5 years. Solar panels are purchased in markets such as Dougabougou. They come from both China and Germany, the latter being more expensive but generally considered to be more reliable. Their prices depend both on origin, but also on their size and voltage. Small panels are available from 10,000 francs while the largest and most powerful panels are currently between 80–140,000 francs.

In 2006, a German-funded project (PACT Ségou) constructed a small building in DBG and equipped it with four solar panels, which could charge people's batteries for home use. It operated for 5 years, but made a regular deficit, because villagers could get their batteries recharged more cheaply elsewhere in the village. Having shut its doors in 2011, it reopened in 2017, having been equipped with a

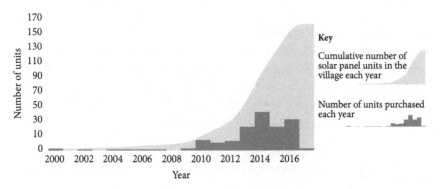

Figure 6.11. Purchase of solar panels, growth in numbers DBG, 2000–2016

Figure 6.12. Installing solar panels on the roof of the maternity clinic, DBG, 2009

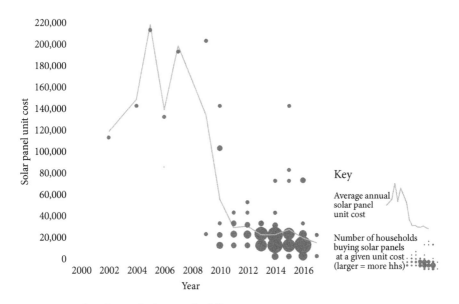

Figure 6.13. Purchase of solar panels, fall in prices DBG, 2000–2016

brand-new deep-freeze, which is now being used by the man in charge to make ice and frozen juice for sale.

As could be seen in Figure 6.17 (colour plates section), even the smallest of households has one or two panels, since their low cost means that they are afford-able for people in all households regardless of size and wealth.

Other assets, sewing machines, bikes, motorbikes...

Figure 6.17 (colour plates section) illustrates the portfolio of assets held by each household in the village. Purchase of sewing machines, bikes, and motorbikes repre-sents an individual acquisition, rather than a collective household asset, and it is usu-ally the product of migration earnings. Sewing machines arrived in the 1970s, and they are seen as a valuable tool for men to earn income from a craft while remaining in the village, and so are often the asset of choice once men have stopped going away on regular migration. They reap a reasonable income, given the growing demand from women and girls for pretty blouses, and young men's desire for matching shirts and trousers (see Figure 6.14 below and in the colour plates section). Bicycles were first acquired in the early 1950s. They are mainly pedalled by young men and boys since it is hard work making progress on the soft sands and rutted tracks around the village (see Figure 6.15, below and in the colour plates section). Motorbikes are now widespread, and they are much more powerful than the five light motorcycles owned by villagers in 1980. Most of the eighty-one motorbikes in DBG are of Chinese manufacture, and they cost between 250,000 and 500,000 francs, depend-ing on size and age. They are valued greatly as a means for young men to show-off in front of their girlfriends, visit neighbouring villages, and run to the market at Ségou. The village council has had to ban motorbikes from being ridden through the settlement because the speed and panache of the riders were a menace to pedestri-ans. Because of their speed and manoeuvrability, they have also been used by jihadist groups to carryout 'drive-by' assassinations. Consequently, the Governor of Ségou banned all use of motorbikes in certain communes, including N'Koumandouguou, for several months in 2017, and anyone caught riding a motorbike in certain com-munes, including that of DBG, was subject to a fine, as well as seizure of the bike. Mobile telephones are a personal investment for whoever can afford one, and are predominantly owned by younger men and women, and a few older men with the need for regular contact with family and clients (see Figure 6.16).

Farm investment strategies—the overall picture

The composition of a household's asset portfolio shifts over time as a result of several factors—past performance in farming, returns from livestock and other

Figure 6.14. In the dry season, older men can earn some extra income in the village with their sewing machines, 2014

assets, cash earned from migration, decisions to convert one form of asset into another, and the tensions and divisions within the domestic group. Over time, a household will hope to increase both physical and domestic assets, converting a harvest surplus into productive farm assets and marriage payments, which then generate a larger future workforce and continued diversification. Large household size plays a key role in the process of accumulation. Larger domestic units are better able to generate the capital required for investment, and can overcome problems with the indivisibility of certain investments. It is easier for larger domestic groups to diversify production activities, and to take risks early in the investment cycle, when returns are higher than later on, such as was seen for well digging. A large and diverse workforce is itself an asset of value, and part of a household's income will be devoted to maintaining and expanding the size of the domestic group, through ensuring early marriage for young men and second wives for those already married. However, departure of young men on migration represents a threat to this strategy, as will be seen in Chapter 7.

It is difficult for a small, poor household to farm effectively since their small workforce is stretched by the multiple demands of managing oxen, donkeys, and

Figure 6.15. Boys prefer to go to the field on bicycles, DBG, 2014.

Figure 6.16. Mobile phones are a popular purchase at DBG's weekly market, DBG, 2014

small stock, and leading the plough and getting the weeding done promptly. A combination of good luck and a better-than-average harvest can generate sufficient surplus for investment in farm equipment, and the subsequent gradual build-up of people and farm assets. But it takes a long time, and the odds are stacked against success. The consequences of one of their number falling ill are more serious, as are the risks of not producing sufficient offspring for the future. Equally, young men who have gone off on migration may feel less ready to return to a household with limited farm equipment and few means to assure their marriage costs are paid.[29] Villagers say prosperity and wealth go in cycles, and they point to the feet of a traditional weaver as illustration—at one moment, the left foot is up, and the right foot is down, but then they shift positions. A poor man may take two generations to see his household prosper, while the better off can expect to see their wealth diminish and dissipate. Having built-up his household from nothing to be well-endowed with cattle and wells, OS was convinced that on his death, his sons would quarrel and fragment the family's good fortune, because having it too easy as a child leads to laziness. Others say it is impossible to do well if you come from a poor family because you have none of the equipment needed to get started. As was seen in Chapter 5, of the ten households which were small and poor in 1980, four have succeeded in significantly improving their lot; two are in broadly the same position; one has disappeared; and three are fragmenting and likely to disappear in the next few years. This suggests it is still possible to rise, like the foot of a traditional weaver, through good luck and hard work, but of those who try, half do well, and half do badly.[30]

Risks and returns from investment

Returns on investment depend on a range of factors which are themselves subject to risks: First, is climate. Returns to agricultural and livestock investments rely on weather patterns improving or at least remaining broadly the same. Rainfall is highly variable in terms of its distribution within the cropping season, and from one year to the next. Equally, it increasingly falls in a very patchy fashion, especially at the start and the end of the rainy season, so that neighbouring fields can receive significantly different amounts. Such variability is built into cropping practices, with bush fields spread over a large area, and cultivation of two different varieties of millet. Sesame, maize, and Bambara groundnuts provide further diversification of cropping patterns. Farmers say they have abandoned longer cycle-crop varieties, and they seek ever-more-rapid seeds to grow. The cropping system would need to adjust even further, if rainfall were to halve or the wet season to shorten further.

---

[29] Described in greater detail in Chapter 7 on Migration patterns.
[30] The Bambara insist that *gerejege* matters, that is to say 'good fortune', which comes from God.

Second, is land availability. Past investment strategies depended on there being abundant land around the settlement for bush-field millet and pasture to maintain manure levels on village fields. Referring to the situation in 1980–1982, I wrote:

> large tracts of land to the north of the village have never been farmed before because of the lack of ponds from which the workforce could get drinking water during the cultivation season. However, with the widespread ownership of donkey carts, these areas are potentially cultivable as drums of water can be transported out to the field. Population growth within this and neighbouring villages and the continuous movement into this area of farmers from zones further south will gradually check the current land use system, by reducing the length of time for which land can be fallowed before its re-use. However, unless there are a large number of immigrant households, this point must still be several decades away.[31]

The large number of incoming farmers from further south, especially since N-Sukala was established in 2009, means that the land shortages which might have taken several more decades to eventuate have now arrived. It was clear by 1983 that the inflow of animals seeking water and grazing around DBG was placing serious pressures on forage availability and damaging the nutrition and condition of village herds. The returns a villager hopes to make from well digging have fallen as a consequence and now take the form of cash or access to an ox to be used for ploughing in the rainy season, rather than dung. Returns to investment in cattle as an asset have also fallen, as grazing is scarcer; cattle wealth per person and per household has declined, as livestock have been sold; and people diversify into other assets.

Third is the extent to which local Bambara communities can maintain control over access to land and water within their village territory. Although control over these resources was, in theory, vested in the state following Independence in 1960, in practice, villages continued to exercise much of their traditional power in this respect. The Bambara of DBG maintained a powerful *komo* cult, which supported their customary control over land. They have been bitterly hostile to both Peul and Maure settling permanently and digging a well within what they see as their territory. The high returns to well digging in the past depended on maintaining their monopoly over well digging, from which the Bambara were able to set advantageous terms. If land and water were to be freely available to all, there would be rising pressure as more and more farmers flood into the area, and well owners would lose their monopoly. The new agricultural land tenure law (*Loi Foncier Agricole*) and associated decrees specifying how the legal provisions will

---

[31] Toulmin, C. (1992) p. 201.

be applied in practice have yet to be put into effect. The new law specifies that people who have been using land under customary occupation can get their rights of use recognized through a formal attestation and certification process, to be carried out at commune level. If incoming farmers were able to assert rights to the land they have been given by the villagers, this would fundamentally change the power balance between them and the village of DBG.[32]

Fourth, several of the assets in a household's portfolio are less reliant on agriculture, land, and climate. For example, shopkeepers in DBG have done well out of the inflow of migrant farmers, since they are regular customers. In the evenings, many people flock round the TV and lights of the village shops for company and entertainment. Some households are investing in the education of their children, and more than twenty men from DBG have set themselves up in town, as they see the urban economy to offer many more openings than in DBG.

Fifth, the stability and management of the domestic group remain very important foundations for investment, as do good cooperative relations between family members and spouses.[33] The household remains the principal unit for farm production, investment in assets, reproduction of household members, mobilization of labour, and insurance against risk. Some households are better able to take advantage of new opportunities because they can mobilize labour and capital, and take risks in the early stage of any investment cycle. Hence, the maintenance and renewal of the domestic group remain important determinants of growth in assets, and a focus for investment, through the traditional system of marriage. Were systems of marriage to change, and women no longer willing to accept the choices made by their fathers, this would affect significantly patterns of household organization, labour mobilization, and investment.

Conclusions

Most people in DBG say they have become better off since 1980. They have increased income and wealth, and the business of farming has become easier, thanks to widespread adoption of ploughs and donkey carts. DBG is known for its *fadenya* or competitive rivalry, which pushes individuals and families to outdo each other in getting the biggest harvest, having a large cattle herd, and acquiring new assets. This *fadenya* or competitive rivalry between people has contributed to a sequence of investment booms, described in this chapter, which have brought

[32] The village chief was alive to the risks of incoming farmers seeking firm rights to land, and he insisted that our research should not map and measure the field boundaries for incomers in the same fashion as for villagers.

[33] As clearly demonstrated by de Weerdt, (2010) and Brockington and Howland (2018) for Tanzania; Mushongah, J., and Scoones, I. (2012) for Zimbabwe; Whitehead (2006) for Northern Ghana.

increased income and wealth. The strength of *fadenya* and competitive rivalry has also led to a big shift in values and behaviour in favour of individual incomes and wealth, at the expense of the collective household estate.

Each investment cycle follows a similar pattern to that of solar panels, illustrated in earlier in Figure 6.11. One person brings back a new idea; two or three people copy it; while others watch and wait. When it is shown to be a good thing, everyone else follows suit as soon as possible. However, many of the best returns accrue to those who took the risk early in the investment cycle, with later-comers getting lower returns. There are also a few households which have not done well over the last 35 years, and who have been unable to invest in these new opportunities. They tend to be amongst the smallest and poorest domestic groups. Looking forward, it is not clear what the next cycle of investment will be. Taking the far-sighted GD as the model, he considers the best things are to invest in education of children and build a house in town. While he is a regular visitor to his home village, as he remarks in Chapter 7, he no longer sees a future for himself in the village.

7

Leaving the village on migration

Anka den minnu jɛnsɛnnen don dinɲɛ fan bɛɛ fɛ. Ka koro, den dɔw tun bɛ wolo yan, fo ka taa u se furu ye, u tɛ taa dinɲɛ fan si fɛ. Bi, o t'a la.[1]

Introduction

For millennia, the Sahel has been a region of movement. The open landscape has been easy to cross on foot, horseback, camel, or cart. Today, trucks criss-cross the region, carrying goods to market, and people away on migration. The wide Niger River has been a major transport route, its long black canoes travelling long distances with passengers pressed tight against sacks of grain, salt, and fish beneath the canvas shade. The marked contrast between the Sahel's wet and dry seasons shapes patterns of movement, forcing herders to take their animals south at the end of the rains. Its variability from year to year mean that after a bad harvest, farmers must move to find work in more favoured regions, while a good harvest in one village will pull in large numbers of people from neighbouring settlements. Periods of prolonged drought or conflict push people to move longer distances and settle further south in areas with higher rainfall, where land is more abundant, or to other ways to earn an income, while education and off-farm opportunities draw some rural dwellers to move to town.

The resilience of Sahelian people has depended on them being able to adapt by diversifying activity and moving to exploit new sources of income. In West Africa, many people have moved from rural to urban centres, both as temporary migrants and long-term settlers. The urban population for the West African region has grown by a factor of fourteen since 1960, from 14.5 per cent of the population to 47 per cent in 2017. For Mali, in 1960, only 11 per cent of the population was resident in urban centres, but recent growth has been very rapid. Today, Bamako is one of the fastest growing cities in the world, at 5.7 per cent per year, and the urban population is reckoned to be 40 per cent of the total population. Apart from the capital Bamako, other cities of significance are

---

[1] 'Our young folk have scattered across the world, in all directions. In the old days, there were many young men who were raised and reached the age of marriage without setting off to see the world—today it's not like that at all.' Village chief Danson Dembélé 2014.

Land, Investment and Migration. Camilla Toulmin, Oxford University Press (2020). © Camilla Toulmin.
DOI: 10.1093/oso/9780198852766.001.0001

Sikasso, Ségou, Kayes, and Mopti, but each of these has only 200,000 to 300,000 people, compared with more than 3 million in the wider Bamako region.

Across the Sahel, migration is a vitally important part of village life and household economics, with both men and women relying on cash earned in town to supplement other earnings. Dlonguébougou (DBG) is no exception to this. In years of poor harvest, leaving home for many months not only contributes cash for essential expenditures, such as tax payments, but also relieves pressure on the household granary. In 1980, most men planned to be absent for some weeks or months, but there were no unmarried girls from DBG migrating to town to earn cash. By contrast, today, all girls expect to spend a year or more away from home, raising part of the money needed to fund their marriage costs. People have mixed feelings about migration; some greatly enjoy the excitement of being away, exploring new places, and trying their luck with risky pursuits, such as gold digging, but others say how difficult it is to live in a big city like Bamako, where everything costs a lot of money, and people's manners are so different from those in the village back home. Improved living standards have been achieved by calling on resources outside the village, and movement to town has brought back not only cash but also new ideas and ways of living. As is also the case today, such new ideas were not always popular. In the colonial reports from 1910, village elders were reported as complaining that young men were coming back from migration to cities with worrying new ideas, such as abandoning the traditional religion and building a mosque.[2]

Migration in history

A combination of extensive trading relations, the search for better land and grazing, conflict between kingdoms and groups, and pursuit of religious instruction has led to a mosaic of peoples and cultures across the West African region. The establishment of the colonial administration, in the late 1890s, brought peace and allowed people to travel with far greater safety. Peace also meant the opening up of areas which formerly had been out of bounds, because they were considered too insecure.[3] The large colonial irrigation scheme, the *Office du Niger* in central Mali, brought tens of thousands of people from elsewhere to settle and farm the land, many being moved more than 500 km from the Mossi plateau of what is now Burkina Faso. In the 1930s, many young men from Mali also walked westwards to work as *navetane*[4] labour on the peanut fields of Senegal. Forced labour on projects such as the *Office du Niger*, and construction of the

---

[2] Rapport Politique, cercle de Ségou 1910.   [3] Raynaut, C. (1997).
[4] *Navetanes* describes seasonal migrants used for groundnut cultivation in Senegal and the Gambia, drawn from the Wolof word for 'rainy season'.

administrative buildings in Ségou took men away from home for several months during the dry season, and, by 1938, a recruitment drive was underway for young men to join the army as *tirailleurs sénégalais*. The French colonial administration was rightly worried that the combined demands made on the population were driving people away, and putting food production in jeopardy. As described in Chapter 2, by 1944, an estimated 200,000 Africans under the French colonial administration had moved to settle in the Gold Coast (now Ghana), drawn by economic opportunities, such as mining and cocoa production, and driven by French colonial demands for labour services and taxation.

Since Independence, Côte d'Ivoire has been the principal magnet for people from Sahelian countries, given its large economy and currency in common with the rest of the franc zone. The Economic Community of West African States (ECOWAS), established in 1975, agreed a protocol on free movement of labour amongst member states in 1979, which has made it easier for people to move between the fifteen ECOWAS member states without visas, using only their national identity card. In the 1970s and 80s, Nigeria's booming oil economy also drew in people from poorer neighbouring countries, though occasional bouts of xenophobia linked to economic downturn and political turmoil have plagued both Nigeria and Côte d'Ivoire, forcing migrants to flee.

A further factor spurring people to migrate were the harsh, widespread droughts of 1972–1974 and 1983–1984, which pushed millions of Sahelians further south, in search of better-watered lands and grazing. By the late 1990s, there were an estimated 5 million Sahelians living in Côte d'Ivoire, many of them settled in former forest regions, the land having been cleared for coffee and cocoa plantations. In many cases, they left part of the family back home in Burkina Faso and Mali, thereby maintaining a foothold in their natal villages.[5] For decades, Sahelians have also been going north to the Maghreb, where many Tuareg provided recruits for the then Libyan President Gadhafi's army. Malians are amongst those trying to cross the Mediterranean to reach Europe, while others travel elsewhere in Africa. There is also now a significant community of Sahelian traders in Guangzhou, China, and the Malian government has established a consulate there.

Cross-Saharan trade routes have seen a profitable revival, thanks to a range of illicit activities, such as smuggling of cigarettes, kidnap and ransom of foreigners, and the transit of cocaine from Latin America to Europe, through Guinea Bissau and Mali. In the hands of Tuareg and Arab traders and armed groups, control of these routes is very lucrative, money from which fuels the civil wars and insecurity wracking the Sahel. Violence, kidnap, and extortion provide significant benefits to those running these businesses, and mean good wages can be paid to young recruits, who get status, cash, and guns.

---

[5] Brock. K. and Coulibaly, N. (1999).

The government of Mali has a Ministry responsible for its diaspora community, given the large numbers living elsewhere. It is estimated that there are 4.5 million Malians living out of the country (equivalent to 25 per cent of the current resident population), of which 3.5 million are elsewhere in Africa (of whom 2 million are in Côte d'Ivoire). The number of Malians in France is reckoned to be at least 300,000, but numbers are difficult to confirm, and many people have dual nationality. Remittances are a large and valuable source of foreign exchange earnings for the country as a whole, and they provide much-needed cash for individual house-holds. Certain villages are the proud recipients of a new mosque or deep well, thanks to one of their 'sons' having made money overseas. The World Bank esti-mated that migrants sent home remittances worth $530 million per year in 2013, equivalent to 5 per cent of Mali's GDP, but this is probably an underestimate, given that much money is sent informally and, hence, is less easy to track.

Migration in DBG

Dafé Dembélé, who was chief of the village in 1980, first travelled to Senegal in the 1920s. He went to work in the peanut fields, taking 6 weeks to get there on foot.[6] Even in his 80s, he could still recite the names of the villages through which he had travelled to get there and back. He followed in the footsteps of his father's generation, including his uncle, who had made a similar journey 10 years before, having run away to Dakar with the girl he loved. Today, young men still have itchy feet and really enjoy setting off to explore the world. Travelling in twos or threes, they usually know someone along their route who can take them in and guide them on their next steps. The decision for any individual to migrate is nor-mally discussed with the household head since a few people must stay at home to help water livestock and prepare the fields. But old men say it is hard to hold young people back from setting off, and they recognize, with frustration, the limits to their authority.

Patterns of migration in 1980

In 1980–1982, migration was an important element in household revenue and a rite of passage both for young men and, increasingly, for young women. In 1980, unmarried men set off to town as soon as the millet was harvested and threshed, but very few young men stayed away for more than 6 months, and they brought earnings back to the household head to help pay taxes, buy a new plough, or put

---

[6] The Bambara term for going on migration is *taama*, people say, '*a taara taama la*', 'he has gone off on migration'.

towards the costs of marriage. Typical amounts brought back by migrants were between 10,000–25,000 francs.

Unmarried girls earned a bit of cash from 2 or 3 months' migration spent harvesting and winnowing millet in neighbouring villages, being paid in grain which could then be sold. Known as *namaden*,[7] if successful, a woman could bring home several hundred kilos of millet, to be sold or exchanged for wedding goods. The system of *namaden* provides a means for women to earn significant amounts of millet, of especial importance in years of poor harvest. Women and girls lodge in the house of a relative, and go out to work for others during the time they spend away from home. In return for every 2 days of work, they are paid a large basket of millet spears which, when threshed, gives 3 or 4 kg of millet grain. They also earn millet from winnowing work, and if staying with their uncle, they will be given further gifts of millet when they set off back home. In 1982, the first girls set off to work in Bamako, finding a maid's job usually in the household of a distant relative, working for 3–4 months, and bringing back cash to help buy their wedding goods.[8]

In 1980, many household heads were worried about young men going away on migration, as they feared such youths might be absent for several years, during which time the household would be deprived of their labour on the farm. The receipt of remittances was not seen as an adequate substitute for the loss of weeding labour, and prolonged absence was a signal that this 'son' might disappear completely. Occasionally young men stayed away from the village for the whole of the rainy season, and, though a brother might be sent down to fetch them, sometimes it was hard to find them or persuade them to return home. Only rarely did a young man decide to move away permanently, finding a woman to marry in town, and settling there. In 1980, there were six men who had been absent for more than 2 years, three of whom did subsequently return and rejoin their household. However, the most productive years of a man's life, so far as farming the millet field is concerned, are considered to be those of his late teens and 20s, while he is still unmarried and full of energy. Passing several rainy seasons away from the farm at this stage deprives his household of an important source of farm labour, the effects of which are particularly harsh on smaller households.

In 1980, the pattern of absenteeism across households was not associated with patterns of wealth, and there was no evidence for poorer households losing more people in this way than the better off. Both the general poverty of the Malian national economy and the relatively high productivity of agriculture in DBG encouraged young men to head back home after a few years away. Poorer villages in the neighbourhood, such as Dofinena, had higher rates of out-migration to Ségou and Bamako, with a number of men establishing themselves permanently in town. When close relatives become urban dwellers, this promotes further

---

[7] Literally 'young people who have come'.   [8] '*Konyo minanw*', 'wedding utensils'.

migration from these villages to town, as the risks of migration are reduced, and prospects for finding employment and shelter increased.

Patterns of migration in 1997

By 1997, as can be seen in Table 7.1, there had been significant changes to the pattern of migration, compared with 1980, concerning the principal occupations pursued by migrants, their destination, and the size of revenue they brought back.[9] Looking at the distribution of migrants by age and gender, Brock found

Table 7.1. Comparing patterns of migration from 1980, 1997, and 2016

Year	Frequency/Timing	Location/Work	Money Earnings
1980	Every young man after threshing December to June; some married women and unmarried girls from start of harvest	Men go to Ségou for weaving Married women and girls go to neighbouring villages to work as *namaden* for millet harvest and winnowing	Most are given to *gwatigi*, 10,000–25,000 francs Women keep millet to feed the family, and girls use earnings to buy wedding goods
1997	Every young man after weeding; some married women and unmarried girls from harvest time	Men go to Côte d'Ivoire for latrine and well digging, gold and diamond mining Girls go to Bamako to work as maids Married women go to neighbouring villages to work as *namaden*	Most are given to *gwatigi*, 25,000–50,000 francs Women keep millet to feed family, and girls keep cash to buy wedding goods
2016	Every young man and many girls from Sept/Oct till June; married women as *namaden* at harvest time and a few to town in the dry season	Men go to Bamako street for trading, cloth beating, labouring, gold mining, and to Kayes + Europe Girls go to Bamako to work as maids, and to Niono for rice Young men and girls go to N-Sukala for sugar cane Married women go to neighbouring settlements to work as *namaden*, and to Bamako to earn cash	Migrants keep most of their money Small gifts, 10,000–25,000 francs to *gwatigi* Women use millet to feed family, and seek cash for daughter's wedding Girls keep cash to buy wedding goods

Note: Cloth beating involves using wooden hammers to beat the expensive brocade cloth used for festive clothing, giving it a much-appreciated sheen.

[9] Brock, K. and Coulibaly, N. (1999) p. 124.

that almost all men had been on migration, whatever their age, but for women, the pattern was different. Women aged 50 years or more had never been off to the city to work but had only done the harvest in neighbouring villages. Younger women, by contrast, had almost all spent some months away in Ségou or Bamako. Travel as a *namaden* remained very significant, and in 1997, a year of reasonable harvests, sixty-four women left DBG to work on the harvest elsewhere, while sixty-nine women arrived in DBG for the same purpose. The principal purpose of migration for women and girls remained acquiring the cash needed to purchase the wedding goods they are expected to take on marriage. In 1980, this cost between 7,500–10,000 francs, but by 1997, this had multiplied seven times because of a larger number of more expensive items being considered essential and because of rising prices. By 2016, it had risen ever further to 400,000–500,000 francs, and it has become a significant burden for a girl and her family, as described later in this chapter.

In comparison with 1980, when there were six men absent for more than 2 years, by 1997, Brock found eleven such absentees, mostly from very poor households, or large complex households where relations had broken down. There had also been a clear shift in migration patterns between 1980 and 1997. Weaving cloth in Ségou was the main source of dry season income in the 1970s and 80s, but very few people were still doing this in 1997. Machine-made cloth and cheap second-hand clothing had displaced hand-woven textiles, except for a few special outfits, such as the hunter's tunic, worn on ceremonial occasions. Instead, people were travelling further, either to Bamako for a variety of labouring jobs, or to Côte d'Ivoire, where the well-digging skills of men from DBG could earn them a good wage.

Brock describes migration as serving 'an important social function in maintaining the prevailing system of labour management. It allows a young man some independence in a system which places a high level of control over the activities of individuals.'[10] The example of OS illustrates this point. As the head of a better-off household, with a couple of wells, large cattle holdings, a shop, and a mill, OS has generally forbidden his children from going off on migration, saying that the household can meet all their needs. Several years ago, one of his sons persistently pressed him to be allowed to go to Côte d'Ivoire along with his age-mates, and finally he relented. He worked for 3 months and then returned. His father did not ask for any of his cash earnings, but noted that 'he found it was the same thing over there, and afterwards he was happy to come back and settle here'. In the 1950s, OS had himself spent 3 years away in the French colonial army fighting in Indo-China, and after a traumatic period there, he was convinced there was nowhere better than DBG.

[10] Brock, K. and Coulibaly, N. (1999) p. 123.

Patterns of migration in 2016

In October 2016, all unmarried men were seeking to depart, often planning to stay away for the next 9 months, returning when the millet fields were being ploughed for sowing. A number of young men had already left, but returned for a few days to take part in the *sogo* mask festivals to celebrate the forthcoming harvest (see Figure 7.1). Widespread access to mobile phones now means that they can be called back for marriages and festivals. Unmarried girls combine spending a few months in Bamako, with getting several weeks' work on the N-Sukala sugar cane plantation and being employed to plant rice seedlings around Niono, some 80 km away to the northeast. A series of interviews with young unmarried women from DBG living in Bamako illustrates their common purpose in preparing for marriage. Married women also set off to earn cash, especially if they have a daughter's wedding to prepare, such as DT interviewed in Bamako (see Box 7.1).

Wages in Bamako are low, with girls expecting to earn no more than 10,000–15,000 francs for a month's work as a housemaid today. In 1997, Brock noted that in years of high millet prices, girls and young women earned more by staying around DBG working as *namaden*. Today, many young women say you can make much better earnings by farming a sesame plot, from which to harvest more than 100,000 francs if you are lucky, rather than spending 5–6 months in Bamako,

Figure 7.1. Two wild beasts join the *sogo* festival dance, October 2010

Box 7.1   DT, a married woman, stays in Bamako for a few months[11]

DT is staying with her cousin, who is now living on the edge of Bamako. She came for 3 months to earn money to pay some of the costs of her daughter's forthcoming wedding. But it is not the first time she has come to Bamako, having spent more than a year here twenty-five years' ago, before she was married. Then, she worked as a housemaid—cleaning, shopping, cooking, and washing clothes—in order to earn enough to buy many of her wedding goods. This time, hoping to turn a profit from petty trading, she has bought a large cardboard box of mosquito coils, and is going house to house in the neighbourhood, selling individual packets. She reckons she should make 5,000 francs if she sells all the packets over the next week.

As she says:

When I was here before, you didn't earn a lot each month—you got 5,000 Francs, but you could save most of it. Now wages are higher but the price of everything has increased hugely, so you need a lot more money. Today, the things you can buy for 100,000 Francs, you'd say you'd got nothing! While in the past, if you spent 15,000 Francs you'd fill up the place. The things you need for a wedding have also increased a lot. This year my daughter is getting married, so she's been here in Bamako since the previous hot season. Once the rains approach, she'll go back home to prepare for the wedding. It's mainly the responsibility of the girl herself to collect the money needed for her wedding, but her mother and father will also help out, and your relations will add a few things. She's been in the care of my husband's younger brother who found her work here in Bamako. Nowadays, most of our people go and work in town, but once the rains begin, they go back home and plant their sesame field. That's where people get the money they need today.'

---

where it would be fortunate to come back with more than 50,000–70,000 francs. However, like young men, all girls want to have a bit of time away in the big city, even if it is not terribly lucrative. As HC says, many of the good things which have come to the village are a result of people who have gone to town, bringing back ideas and new ways of doing things that make a positive difference to people's lives.[12] Also, some girls admit that it is impossible to save money if living at home in the village, as anything earned will be called upon by other members of the family.

---

[11] Interview, Bamako, March 2017.   [12] See Box 5.1 in Chapter 5.

For some household heads, the love of setting off on migration has gone much too far. Danson Dembélé says when he was young, you needed permission from the household head to leave the village, and all the income you gained was given to him on your return. But now 'everyone makes up their own mind, they scatter across the land, to all corners of the world'. And to add insult to injury, echoing the 1910 colonial reports mentioned earlier, he says young men pay him no respect, and rarely bring him a gift on their return from town.

Ten young women from DBG in Bamako

Testimony from a group of ten young women from DBG who spent the dry season of 2018 in Bamako confirms the general picture described by DT in Box 7.1.[13] All of the girls worked as domestic servants, doing a combination of cleaning the house, preparing food, and washing clothes. In many cases, the job was found through a relative, or the person they were lodging with. In one case, the girl described knocking on doors within the neighbourhood to seek housework, before she found a job. Most girls stay either with a relative or in their place of work. Five of them arrived together and lived with a man from DBG now resident in Bamako. For some it was the first time, for others it was the fifth or sixth visit to Bamako to earn money.

All the girls said the reason they came to Bamako was because:

> there is nothing to be earned in DBG, there is no work, and no means of earning money. This last year has been particularly bad, because the millet harvest was not good. The rains stopped early, and we have a lot of trouble with birds, due to the Chinese irrigation scheme. Peul herders also let their animals into our fields and ruin the crop. It is difficult earning money at home too, because you cannot build it up—if you've earned a lot of millet, then you need to contribute what you have to feed the rest of the family. There is work in the dry season at N-Sukala with the Chinese, but it is not an attractive job. It is very hard work, you have to get up before dawn to travel there, and often they don't pay you for the work you've done.

Girls need to collect enough money to buy all the wedding goods they need to take on marriage. The numbers and costs of things considered essential for a young married woman have grown enormously since 1980. Now ideally you need to bring with you a table, a bed, six chairs, a TV, an armchair, a wardrobe, a chest, lots of clothes, and a donkey cart. The cost of this adds up to more than 500,000 francs, and it must be gathered together over a period of years by the girl and her

---

[13] Interviews with ten young unmarried women in April 2018.

mother.[14] Neither the fiancé nor his family is expected to make any contribution to these goods, though they will have paid a formal marriage sum to the girl's family, of 200,000–300,000 francs. The girls recognize the challenge of collecting this large sum of money, given that most of them only earn 10,000 to 15,000 francs a month for their housework. Several years of work in Bamako can contribute, but sales of sesame from their private field are also part of the answer. The money girls earn is usually given to a relative, who looks after it until it is time to return to the village. Before she leaves Bamako, the girl goes shopping and spends most of the money, purchasing whatever she can afford, before taking it back home, though she might hold onto a small amount of cash to give to her relatives.

When asked why there has been this huge escalation in the cost of marriage, one girl said it has come from the pattern of life they have seen in town, where there is a lot more money around. However, she noted that town-dwelling men are expected to make a major contribution to these costs in town, unlike men in DBG. Some of the better-off families in DBG have also set this new trend, because they have the means to provide well for their daughters. But it is hard on poorer families because they have to try and keep up, and ensure their daughters receive respect from their new in-laws. One girl acknowledged that the trend for ever-more expensive weddings also comes from the girls themselves since they compete hard to show how well they are doing. They say that if they do not put on a good show at their wedding, their co-wives and in-laws will criticize them and their family.

Of the ten girls interviewed, most were about to be married and knew who their husband would be. One young woman was already married and had joined her husband, temporarily in Bamako, while another had had a baby out of marriage. In one case, the girl's marriage arrangements had broken down, and she did not know whom she would marry and was keen to get this settled as soon as possible. Regardless of her uncertain marital destination, she was collecting the money and belongings that she would need to be ready for her wedding, whenever it happens.

The girls have mixed views about life in a big city. The main attraction is to earn money in Bamako, but they say they find the way of life and behaviour of people in the city unattractive. 'Some people wander about without anything to do, while others are dressed in rags.' All of them say they would rather be back home. 'I am happier back in the countryside, that's where my fathers, and mothers are, that's where my older and younger siblings are.'[15] And many of them say that if there was an irrigated market garden in DBG to grow vegetables in the dry season, that would mean they could stay at home and earn money instead of coming to Bamako.

---

[14] About £700.
[15] *Brussikono de kadi ne ye, ne faw be yan, ne baw be yan, ni korow ani dogow be yan.*

Migration as part of the life cycle for men

Regardless of the village chief's complaints, migration is central to the life cycle for men. Makono Dembélé's experience of migration is a typical example. Now in his early 60s, he started with farmwork in neighbouring settlements when he was 15, and then set off to Côte d'Ivoire in 1977, aged 22. Retiring from migration in 1998, aged 45, he had been away almost every year, usually for 6–8 months, and mainly to Côte d'Ivoire, where he could earn good money digging latrines and wells, and sometimes mining for gems. The total earnings he can recall for each of the fifteen years spent away on migration come to 1,809,750 francs, giving an average of 120,650 francs each year of travelling.

Makono Dembélé

I first went to Côte d'Ivoire, in 1977, to dig wells and toilets, for the Agni and Busu people in the forest-lands. At that time, there wasn't big money in well-digging, you'd earn 300 Francs per metre, so if you dug 20 metres you'd earn 6,000F. The following year, I went with three age-mates from DBG, for another 6 months to dig wells there again. The year after that was 1980, that was the year you first came here to DBG. I left on September 22nd, the festival was going on in Ségou,[16] so once that was over, we found a truck to take us to Burkina Faso, which was called Haute-Volta then. There we caught a train to Côte d'Ivoire, to go well-digging again, but that year we didn't earn much money, so we came back home. I gave 25,000 francs to the *gwatigi*, and bought a radio for 30,000F. That was the radio that Sidiki bought for 30,000F, so I could buy myself a carte d'identité.[17]

The following year, we took a taxi to Koutiala, and then onto Burkina Faso, and found a train which took us to Feregese.[18] Once we got to Feregese, our money ran out, so we started walking. Although the money had run out, we had some couscous in an old sack. When we felt hungry, we'd look for a bowl and ask for some milk to add to the couscous so we could drink it. After walking for some time, we came to a town where there was a sugar-cane field. There was a big boss who called to us 'come to the cane field'. So we four went to clear the field of all the old cane stalks, and earned 3,500F. Then they asked 'can you dig latrines?' We said 'yes!' and each metre earned us 6,000F. After we'd done that, we went on to Bouaké, where we found my cousin Kefa living there, and he gave me a lot of his well-digging work. So we earned enough money in Bouaké to take a train further on to Abowili. Once April came, we returned home and the

---

[16] The anniversary celebrations for Mali's Independence Day.
[17] Sidiki Diarra my research assistant.   [18] Ferkéssédougou, Côte d'Ivoire.

following year I didn't go away. The year after that I went to work as a weaver in Ségou for several months.

The following year, we did 6 months' work in a place near Korhogo. We were digging for diamonds, and when we came to sell them, we made 200,000F which we split with our patron. We both bought bicycles in Bobo Dioulasso, and decided to cycle back home, which took three days. We left Bobo on Sunday evening, and spent all Monday cycling, and on Tuesday we reached Ségou. We were strong young men then, we could pedal like mad!

After that year, we went back to do more diamond digging in Côte d'Ivoire, but by then our luck had run out. I came with C that time, at another time with B, and then with B's younger brother—always well-digging. Then the year that Sidiki was back in DBG with Karen (Brock) which was 1997 and 98, I went with my older brother's son, to show him the way. We made 370,000F that year, in 3 months, so we bought some things for ourselves and gave the old man 60,000 Francs. Since 1998, I haven't been back to Côte d'Ivoire.

I never dig wells by myself. You need two or three people with you. You might agree to work with Ivorians on some other work, but for well-digging, I would only do it with another person from Mali. Ivorians don't know how to dig wells, and they don't like getting into a deep hole. Now, many of our young men go to Bamako, and Kayes, to earn money by *finigosi* (beating cloth), but gold-digging is also done by many.

Now, no money is given to the *gwatigi*. These young men won't get up to help out their old man. It's for their own purposes that they go on migration. One or two may give him something, like 25,000F, or 50,000F, some don't give him anything at all. They say—I've bought a solar panel, or a battery, or a TV which everyone can watch. In the old days, you knew there was no oxen or plough in the family, so you did your best to find the money to buy them. Whatever you see in our family compound today—plough, cart, donkey, cattle, motorbike, radio, solar panels—they all came from migration money, from myself, my brother, and our sons. Today, anyone can farm a field of sesame, and fulfil their wants. Last year, the money we got from selling our *foroba* sesame harvest came to 150,000F.[19] Our young folk who had sown the sesame field, said let's contribute the harvest to the family. So we were able to pay our tax bill with this sesame money—it came to 42,200Francs. When it comes to sowing sesame, you look for people to hire to make the field bigger. It's sesame that's been giving us our cash today.

In 1986 I had attended a literacy course, and I was then asked to be in charge of collecting up the taxes for DBG, as well as keeping the administrative records— all the people who have been born and died. So that is my main task today.

---

[19] This is one of the very few households that have a collective household field of sesame.

Gold mining: BD talks about his migration experience

BD is a young man in his late 20s, and a son of the large chiefly household.[20] He has recently married, but continues to enjoy a few months away each year. Interviewed in his courtyard, with a gleaming new motorbike on one side and a large music player on the other, his migration has earned him good money. He is dressed in baggy jeans and tee shirt, and sports dark glasses and a big smile.

Right now, you can see we're farming. When that's finished we'll have a month of sitting around waiting for the millet to ripen, and once that's over we'll start the harvest. If that's done, young people are free to go off and search for their own needs. We go off and spend 3 months searching around, and whatever money we succeed in getting, we'll bring it back. When we get back home, we'll show some of what we've managed to get to the household head. But he won't see any of the things we've bought for ourselves.

The three months I spent away, I ended up gold-mining. The first time I went was in 2008. Before that, I had only gone to places nearby, to dig wells in neighbouring settlements. After that, I left Mali behind and went to Senegal, where I spent three months, then went on to Guinée where I spent another month, before coming back to Mali. Two of us went, and we stayed more than five months. This year, I went with one of my older brothers, for 3 months. First we went to Senegal but found nothing. Then we came to Kenieba and found a little.[21] By the time we got there, we were both really anxious, and with the little we gained we said to ourselves 'let's go back home'.[22] The rainy season had started, my family had already gone to the fields for at least two days. We had found something for our own immediate needs, but there was not much left to buy anything for the family.

There are lots of different ways to dig for gold. Some dig a hole, a man's height, and if they have good luck they can find something. Some dig a hole 7 times a man's height, and yet others will go for 27 times a man's height, and find something. It's all to do with luck. That's gold-digging for you. Then sometimes the hole will cave-in and fall on top of people. Not one person will escape, they'll all be dead. But not two days will pass before people will start digging in that hole again. After all, Allah can kill you even if you're not digging for gold!

There are always people sitting there, buying gold for money, but they won't accept it unless you've washed it in Omo. One gram today is worth 15,000F. Before we got 22,500F per gram, but the gold buyers say that war somewhere has brought the price down. The quality varies—the best gold is number 26. I don't know how these numbers work, but the gold-buyers know the difference. Then

---

[20] Interviewed in June 2014, in DBG.
[21] In the far west of Mali, on the sites where gold has been mined since the era of ancient Ghana.
[22] *Anka taa so!*

there are several machines people use to dig for gold, which make a noise when they get close to a place with gold in it. It even sets off a cry if you've got a piece of metal on you. Some people go and fetch several lorry-loads of mud from the river bed, break it into pieces and then wash it through with water. The gold separates out, and you share it between the people who have done the work. Everyone has their own way of working there.

Getting your food is not easy. When we've gone there, we buy food and prepare it ourselves, which is better than buying expensive food from the cooking women. You would never guess you could find a sleeping place in the goldmines. You're out in the bush, not in a big town. You can try and build yourself a hut, sleep out in the open, or rent a room for 4,000–5,000F each month. There are so many different kinds of people there, from other countries, they're not all from Mali. Right now, once the farm work has finished, I want to go back there again but to a different area. The first place I went has become very crowded.

Between DBG and city life

GD is the second of three brothers from a family that has been doing well over the last 35 years, growing from fifteen in 1980 to forty-seven in 2016. Two of the brothers have been successful migrants and have brought significant sums back home for investment in a range of assets. In 1980–1982, in the analysis of millet production, they were also amongst the most successful farming families, with a hard-working team of women and men, arriving early in the field and getting the weeding completed early in the season. And for the period 2016–2018, their harvest was much better than most. After his elder brother's death 10 years ago, GD became the household head, but he lives most of the time away from the village in Ségou. Sitting in his half-built house on the edge of the city, GD says:[23]

> I myself started farming when I was 12 years old and, from then till the moment I withdrew from the field, I completed 38 years of farming. Today I am 66 years old, and I have always had plenty of business, thanks be to Allah. Of all the people in DBG, if you were to add up all their wealth, everyone would agree I have done the best, out of everyone in the village.
>
> Look outside the doorway and you'll see my *jaatigi* SD lying on the mat.[24] I spent 23 years in Ségou weaving in his household, coming for several months each dry season. Then I did 7 years weaving in Bamako. After that, I took up the work I do now, which is fortune-telling and giving advice. I agree a contract with my client which says 'I will do such and such'. Last year, I was given a building

---

[23] Interviewed in October 2016.
[24] 'Jaatigi' means 'landlord, or person who provides shelter to migrants and other travellers'.

Figure 7.2. Leaving the village and building a house in Ségou, 2016.

plot by an entrepreneur in payment for services (See Figure 7.2). We've got a contract for four years, for which I have been given this land we're sitting on now. He hasn't paid anything else. But if I was to sell the land, I could get 500,000F, maybe even 600,000 or 700,000F. Last year, I invested more than 1,750,000F to construct this house, and there's more to do this year. This is how I now spend my time.

I alone am the household head (*dutigi*). We've done well under my headship, and everyone in the household is on my side. In the village, I am a big person. Look! Eight households in DBG have asked me to look after their affairs. Whether it's to do with a death, a marriage, or children, nothing can get past me, I have the final word. I have bought everything except a car or a camel. Last year, apart from the two plots of land, I bought a horse. If you go to DBG, you'll see it in our compound.

In the old days, once you were ten years old, you'd be given to an old man who'd teach you what you need to know. Our hunter-teacher would take us out into the bush and we'd follow his footmarks. If he killed an animal, we'd fetch it and bring it back home. At that time, there wasn't a single boy in DBG who didn't know how to manage a rifle.

I started fortune-telling fifteen years ago. My teacher for *bugurida*[25] was B. There was also M, who had been in military service, who taught me how to read and write. When I started earning money, I put learning aside. But many of my children are now studying. I don't need to advertise my business, I don't talk about it on the radio. People know I am here. They come to me for business, and afterwards they will talk to others about what I can provide. As night follows

[25] Making signs in the sand from which you can divine the future.

day, people will come and find me. The money I have acquired means I can build a house in the big town, my children will learn how to speak French, and get a job and build their own house. Out in the bush, I don't have any further business. This is what I think matters most, to prepare my children for the future. But in the village, no one else is thinking like this.

The people in the household (*du*) in DBG keep me in touch. We've divided responsibilities into three. Looking after the animals, cattle, sheep, goats, that's the job of my eldest son. The next son, his job is managing the field. When it comes to talking, and village discussions, my younger brother sorts it all out. He doesn't go to the field anymore. But if it's a money question, I do it.

My main concern now is about health, which is the foundation for everything else. Health matters to everyone—women, girls, children, boys, men. My own son B has gone to Bamako to study medicine. Another son of mine is here studying. If he doesn't become a lawyer, he will learn how to be a journalist. I put them into a lycée in Ségou, and the three of them cost 150,000F, 200,000F, 250,000F each year. Until they get a government job, I will pay for them.

Moving away from DBG

Figure 7.3 shows that by 2016, twenty-three men had left the village definitively, settling in Bamako and elsewhere, more than double the eleven men who had left in 1997, and many more than the six who were absent in 1980. With their wives and children, this made up more than one hundred people no longer living in DBG. In some cases, the men have married women from Bamako, the late planning of their wedding being one of the main reasons a young man decides to stay away for longer.

The people who have left DBG come from a wide range of households (see Box 7.2). Some are from very impoverished homes, where they could see little prospect of acquiring the assets needed to be a successful farmer. Others come from large, successful households where they would have had a reasonably comfortable life. They occupy largely unskilled trades, with farm work, selling bread, and being a cloth beater being the most common activities. Working as a tailor or transporter of goods requires a bit more skill and capital to acquire the machine or vehicle. A couple of men are involved in selling medicines, which is a risky business, in which boxes of cheap drugs are bought in Ghana and Nigeria, and sold illicitly in Bamako. One of the migrants had recently had his entire stock seized by the Bamako police, and was in severe difficulty as a result (see NT interview). Two young men have reached Europe: one is in Spain, and the other in France. The latter was badly beaten on arrival in Marseilles and spent some weeks in hospital in Paris, though is now recovered. The former reached Spain, found work, and is sending money home. He came on a visit in 2018 but has now returned to Spain.

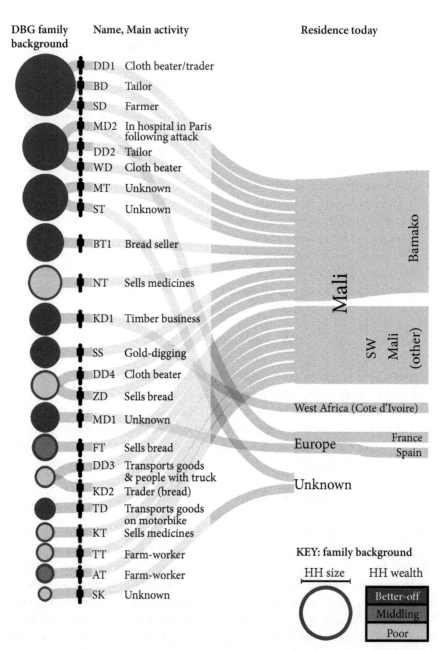

Figure 7.3. Patterns of male migration by household and destination 2017

Portrait of DD

DD and his older brother KD present a typical example of young men leaving an impoverished household to earn their fortunes, recognizing they can expect little from their family back home. The eldest of the three brothers also spent a considerable time away from DBG himself, before deciding to go back to the village and make a go of being a farmer.

Born in 1969, DD is the third son of a very poor man, CD, himself the illegitimate child of a daughter from the chiefly household. As someone born out of wedlock, CD was brought up in his mother's family, but he had to leave and set up on his own when he married. Life was a struggle to grow enough food to feed his family. His three sons had a hard time as children, especially the youngest DD, whose mother died when he was still small. His father managed to find another wife to join the family, but the job was too hard for her, and after a year or so, she returned to her father's village. CD then had to call on his old mother to help them out, so she came back to look after her son and three grandsons, despite being in her 70s. When we arrived in 1980, we found the elderly woman hard at work, pounding millet, washing clothes, and fetching wood, all tasks she would have hoped to have left behind in her 40s. The low status and poverty of the household meant that no one was willing to lend them a girl to help with these chores.

DD is now settled in Bamako, as is his older brother KD, though they live on opposite sides of the city, 40 km apart. DD's house is to the west of Bamako, in a peri-urban area, which is gradually filling up. He built the house on land that he was shown by the village chief, and for which he paid 750,000 francs. The legal status of the land holding is not clear, however, and is at risk until DD acquires a formal title. By contrast, his older brother KD is still renting a couple of rooms, and selling bread in the market, close to the bus station. DD observes that you need to develop a skill if you and your family are to thrive in Bamako, and selling bread offers no path for making progress.

He says:

I drive a van which transports people and goods around town. It's a white Mercedes pick-up truck, which takes 3 people in the front and lots of baggage in the rear. I rent it from the owner, at the cost of 15,000F per day. If the truck goes wrong or I am sick, then the owner is reasonable and does not demand full payment, so I am lucky. The owner of the truck is a young man I met at the main Bamako market, who noticed I was a hard-working man. He trusts me, so he asked me to become his driver, and gave me all the paperwork to do to acquire the van. People call me up to ask if I can shift goods from one place to another. My mobile phone is my work tool, and I must guard it carefully from my son when he reaches out to play with it. Sometimes people ring you up the night before to get you to come at dawn the following day. My business has gone well due to good luck, and the confidence people have in me. Not only do I carry goods, but I also take money from one person to deliver to another.

I didn't move to Bamako definitively when I left the village, things were more unsettled at that stage. It wasn't until 1986 that I first came and worked mainly in the market loading and un-loading trucks. In 2000, I went back home because my old father was ill, and stayed for two years with him. But I was desperate to move away from the village. Life was impossible. I moved definitively to Bamako in 2002, following the death of my father. Since then, I have been back for three visits to DBG but never longer than a fortnight, the last time in 2009. I love DBG, it's my home but there were too many problems for me to stay there. Problems and oppression pushed me away.[26] After my grandmother died in 1984, there was no peace or happiness. As a family, we received absolutely no help at all from my grandmother's family. I went back to DBG in 2009 to find a wife for my older brother KD, but no one gave me any help. Actually, a couple of men even sabotaged the plans we had made for KD to marry X, a young woman from Niaro who has now been married off to a member of the chief's family.

There are many young men from DBG and the North Bank who turn up in Bamako once the weeding is finished, so he gets an update from them and clearly enjoys being in the loop on local news and gossip. He is up to date with news of the N-Sukala sugar cane plantation, and he has heard that the Chinese have been seen driving pickets into the ground to extend the area they farm.

DD has two wives, both of whom he met in Bamako. The first has not been able to have children, despite having had a lot of expensive treatment. He has married a second wife, and they now have a son of 4, and a baby daughter. His second wife comes from the Ségou region, and he sent someone to go and ask formally for her father's permission to marry her. His first wife lives with them and helps with the cooking, and the care of the young family.

When asked what he likes about Bamako, he says: 'If you work hard, you can make money. I'd like the car to be my property, which it will be very soon, as I have nearly finished paying off the loan to the owner. Then I will think about getting a second car and expanding my business.'

DD does not want to go back and settle in DBG because there is too much unhappy history there. He sends money to his eldest brother via Orange-Money from time to time. At the moment, he has his female cousin staying for 3 months, who is earning cash for her daughter's forthcoming wedding (see Box 7.1). DD sees his life starting to get easier once he has paid off the loan on his van. But there remain considerable risks, such as the status of the land on which his house is built, whether he will succeed in raising children, and their readiness to learn the skills needed to thrive in Bamako.

---

[26] *Toro ani degu*, indicating the difficulties faced by the poorest households in the village.

Box 7.2 Interviews with a dozen male migrants from DBG in Bamako, 2019

These long-term migrants, in their 20s and 30s, do not plan to return to the village. Many are married to girls from DBG, though second wives tend to come from Bamako. One had planned to set off to Europe, but his brother had needed the cash more urgently, so he let fall his migration plans that year. He is still keen to go if the opportunity presents itself. They see a large number of seasonal migrants from DBG who pass through Bamako, stopping for a couple of nights with kin, on their way to the gold-mining areas in the southwest.

They are pursuing a range of occupations; house building, selling bread, cloth beating, *maraboutage*,[27] sewing, petty trade, transport of goods, and clothes making—since one takes his sewing machine around the outskirts of Bamako, Koulikoro, and gold-mining sites. He is always on the move. Finding work is not always easy, it can take time. But if you are lucky and you ask for help from relations, you can find something to do.

Most are living free of charge in partially completed villas on the edge of Bamako, in exchange for looking after the property and protecting it from others. One DBG migrant is taking care of land and a half-built house belonging to the young man from DBG who has been in Spain for several years, who is investing his earnings in Bamako property. One migrant has a room for which he pays 5,000 francs per month, where he lives with his wife and four children. All of them are saving up money to purchase a plot of land on which they can build a house on the outskirts of Bamako.

People say their main reason for being in Bamako is to earn money to help out their family back home, but several have stories of bitter quarrels which explain why they left the village. And they all remark on the expectations held by villagers that migrants to town will always provide help. 'However good the harvest in DBG, they have never sent me a grain of millet. Those in town should always help those in the village—never the other way around!' And with the fall in millet harvests, their families need them to be earning cash even more. Some have plans to invest back in the village; with plenty of land available, they talk of planting an orchard of fruit trees, setting up a chicken farm, or establishing a market garden—anything to create employment for the young people of the village.

Increasingly young men do not bother to ask permission to go off on migration. In a bigger household, where there are ten workers, then it is not an issue for

(continued)

<hr/>

[27] Using Islamic learning to divine the future, making amulets to protect people from harm, and providing remedies for sickness.

Box 7.2 Continued

---

three or four people to go off on migration. But in smaller households, it creates a big problem because there will not be enough people to do everything that needs to be done. Cattle are now left in the hands of 8 year olds, so it is not surprising they do not do well.

There are five young men in further education: one has trained to be a teacher; another is studying pharmacy; and another has studied agriculture. But they say it's difficult without parents to support them. One lodges with his uncle and does some private teaching to earn a bit of money. Another has done 9 years of training and is now working in a factory making fruit juices, earning 70,000–75,000 francs per month. They concur 'we have no one from DBG in an administrative job who could help us with all sorts of things such as finding jobs.'

Source: Interviews conducted by Sidiki Diarra January 2019, Bamako.

Portrait of NT

NT has been living in Bamako since 1994. In an interview in Bamako, he describes some of the difficulties of life in the capital, including his mother's unhappiness and nostalgia for her friends and kin back in the village.[28]

We were recruited from DBG in 1985 to do military service. They had come to recruit us, because of the conflict with Burkina Faso. We were taken to Doura, then on to Ségou. Those who weren't fit enough, they were able to get out. Those who were fit, they'd be given a uniform. Fighting wasn't at all what we wanted to do, but it was an obligation. They said 'Your fatherland risks being in a hole, you need to stand up and fight for it!' There were lots of us from DBG, not just me, and there were four of us who stayed. We did four years in the military, and once our time was up, we said 'we're leaving'—so we left. It isn't easy work, if you're not educated. I had not learnt how to read and write, so I realised that I was never going to advance in the army. You spend a long time, with a rifle in one hand, *kiriti karata*.[29] Only those who had had some education could get ahead.

After the army, I came to Bamako and went on to Guinée, where I was digging for gold. I did quite well. I would dig a hole, and climb into it. A little bit of money is what I got, not a lot. In terms of my finally settling here completely, that was in 1994. I married in 1998 a woman from DBG. Living with us here, we

---

[28] Interviewed in March 2017.
[29] Describing the noise of standing to attention with a rifle.

have my children and grand-children. I have had 3 boys and 2 girls, and my sister's two children also live with me. I am glad there is now a school in DBG. All of my children here are in private school. I have to pay fees every month, for some it's 6,000F, for others it's 3,000F.

Now I am selling medicines in the market. I will get a large box of pills from elsewhere, such as Nigeria, that's where many of them come from. But there are a lot of troubles with this trade. Last year the government seized all my boxes of medicine. They came to my store at the market with two cars and filled them with all my stuff. It's been really exhausting, it's worn me out completely. All my boxes were taken away and sold to other people. I tried my best, and offered them money (250,000F) but they wouldn't agree. They took everything. They even took the money from out of my hand. I was left with neither my pills nor my money. Now we have absolutely nothing! We'll get the strength to carry on, but I am not sure how.

Bamako is better than DBG. In a place where you've got lots of people, that means there are many more chances to earn some money. Also, if life at home had been easier, I would have made my future there. We were born there, we were raised there, but if you have nothing, what can you do? If you have something, then you stay. Look at OS's son G, we're age-mates. He has stayed, because his father is well-off, but if you have nothing, you've got to get up and leave. You need a plough and oxen, at least, to be a farmer. But even if you do have the equipment, if it doesn't rain, then it's all ruined. We people from DBG, many of us stay in touch. Whoever has a child to be named, we all gather and pass the day together.

DBG is sweet to me…it's where I was born and grew up, the place you're born is always sweet to you. But since my older brother K died, I don't go so often. I am responsible for my wife and children, who are with me here. My older brother BT called me to tell me that they didn't have enough food. I have just bought millet for them and if the rainy season comes, I will send it to them. I bought millet at 12,500F a sack, but today you couldn't get it for that. I managed to buy 5 sacks.

My children all say of themselves that they are Bamako people. When the rainy season comes, I had wanted to send my children back home, but my mother says they shouldn't go. 'If they go, they will fall ill', she says. Being here is not so good for my mother, she finds it difficult. If she falls ill, she goes home to DBG to cure herself. If I say 'you're not going', she disagrees, we argue and fight. If she insists then I have to send her off. She'll do a bit of time there, then I will call the family and ask them to help her get back here. If she spends a bit of time at home, she gets what she doesn't have here. Sometimes, she falls ill in the village, and I worry she may have died, but when I get there I find that our family has exaggerated how ill she is. I would be ready to burst into tears, but I find her there still alive. I call her and say she should come home to Bamako, I need her. She says Bamako is not good for her, there is nowhere to go for a walk. If she was at home in DBG she would go and see her friends, they would have a chat, brew tea, and even spin some cotton.

If you have nothing, it's hard living in Bamako. At the beginning, if you get a little money, you can manage to sort things out, but now it's got a lot harder. You need money for everything—rice money, sauce money, rent money, drinking water money, school fee money, that's life in Bamako. Before your family gets big, you need to gather some money together. But the burden is heavy if you haven't got money, and if you haven't got money it will be hard to find more. I came here in 1994, at which time I wasn't married, so I was going off and buying merchandise, which is easy if you don't have a wife and family to look after. But if you've gone ahead and taken a wife and brought her here, and you haven't got a lot of courage, then it's not easy.

Changing patterns of migration 1980–2018

The significance of migration from DBG has changed since 1980, with all young men and women now taking part, for 6 to 9 months of the year. It has become much more central to patterns of work, but now largely serves to provide individuals with the cash they want rather than supplying the larger household with what is needed. The village of DBG now has twenty-three men, and their families established mainly in the cities of Bamako, Ségou, and Kayes, a presence which helps their kin find a place to stay and seek work. Because all twenty-three men were born and raised in DBG, they have strong attachment to the people and place, even though it is tinged with difficulty and bad memories for some. Close connections are maintained through occasional visits back home, hosting of relatives from the village when they come to town, and keeping in touch with others from the same village and wider region. The ubiquitous mobile phone has made such connections much easier. But their children do not know the village well, and think of themselves as Bamako folk.

Apart from sesame cultivation, there are currently few opportunities to generate income in the village, and since most people are poor, there is not much of a market for goods and services in the village itself, or surrounding area. Cities like Bamako offer much greater possibilities given the very large number of people and their higher incomes. Young women also mentioned the need to get away from their family to earn money, since otherwise their earnings would be called on to meet a range of family needs, such as buying medicine and providing food in the hungry season.

A viable livelihood in the village depends on access to cash from migration. In the past, migrant earnings made it possible to invest in farm assets, such as ploughs, carts, and oxen. Today, migrant earnings are mainly used for personal consumption, such as purchase of a motorbike, a solar panel, fancy clothes, or a mobile phone. As with farm production, there has been a significant shift from collective *foroba* provisioning, to individual cash earnings, associated with a loosening of control by household heads over the time and product of younger men's labour. Competition and jealousy between people and households have driven a process of accumulation and conspicuous consumption, especially amongst young people who are keen to look more fashionable than their rivals do.

As NT's story shows, becoming a migrant is a result of several factors and events. It is not necessarily a one-off choice, but you fall into it, in his case because of being drafted into the army. After some years, however, especially after the death of a parent or close kin, people say, 'from this point on, Bamako became my home'. Family circumstances are important, especially if your household does not have a good supply of farm assets, because farming demands a certain level of investment to do well. Delays in a marriage being planned also discourage young men, and make them more likely to stay away. However, it is clearly hard to leave the village behind, and migrants speak with great emotion about the landscape and settlement, the muddy pond next to the village where they learned how to swim, and the fun they had with all their brothers and sisters. Old women like NT's mother are pulled in two directions, finding it very difficult to adjust to life in the capital, despite their grandchildren being there, and wishing they were chatting with their friends and neighbours back in DBG.

However, there are several positive aspects to migration. For individuals, apart from earning cash for themselves, it is an opportunity to go and explore the wider world and acquire a stock of hair-raising stories to be recounted many times over in later life. It also provides freedom from the stifling atmosphere of village life, where everyone can watch your every move. Larger households can 'reward' their young men for the hard work put into weeding the millet by giving them time off to pursue their own interests. And in a year of poor harvests, having several people away for much of the year takes pressure off the family's granary. For a few like GD, leaving the village is essential to building a new life for his children, which involves education, setting up in the city, and getting a salaried job, preferably with government. As he says, 'I have no further business in the bush.'

8

Facing an uncertain future

Bolokoni kelen tese ka foy ta.[1]

Introduction

This final chapter considers the future facing the people of Dlonguébougou
(DBG) and the wider region, based on how life has changed since 1980, the
current forces at play, and likely future scenarios. The previous chapters have
described how people have coped with multiple problems and made the best of
new opportunities over the past 4 decades. These problems include changes in
rainfall patterns, increased scarcity of land and grazing, demographic growth and
household change, and the impacts associated with establishment of a large irrigated sugar cane plantation 40 km away. This longitudinal study has shown that
high levels of risk and uncertainty persist because of a combination of rainfall
variability and drought, disease, misfortune, and adverse impacts from government
policy. In response, people hedge their bets in farming, investment, sources of
income, and social networks to protect themselves as best they can. Membership
of a large household and maintenance of social networks provide some protection
from risk. The very large domestic groups found in DBG (average size thirty-
three people, with five households more than one hundred–people strong) are
much bigger than those found elsewhere in West Africa, and they constitute a
remarkable institutional form within which people balance rights and responsibilities, through a combination of collective and individual activities.

One of the most striking changes for DBG is the move from land abundance to
increasing scarcity over the last 25 years, with the arrival of large numbers of
migrant farmers from farther south and east.[2] There have been many adverse
externalities associated with installation of the new sugar cane plantation, both
within the immediate vicinity of the scheme, owing to damage from bird pests,
eviction of farmers from their customary farmlands, and pollution of water
supplies, and over a much wider area, as a result of the displacement of thousands
of people. Investment in irrigated agriculture is usually judged by the balance

---

[1] 'A single finger can pick up nothing', meaning that people need to work together to achieve
anything of note.
[2] Similar to a process across the Sahel, as farmers seek land in former grazing areas, prompted by
diverse pressures. CILSS (2016).

Land, Investment and Migration. Camilla Toulmin, Oxford University Press (2020). © Camilla Toulmin.
DOI: 10.1093/oso/9780198852766.001.0001

between costs and returns within the scheme itself, but it can be seen that a proper assessment should include costs and benefits over a much wider region.

There have also been big shifts in attitudes and values within the village community, from focussing on collective activity by mobilizing the household labour force to much greater interest in individual gain.[3] In 1980–1982, villagers said that their strong commitment to collective activity at that time was a recent shift, associated with the decline in the importance of private groundnut fields because of the droughts of the 1970s. It is not clear where these shifts in attitude stem from, but it is no doubt linked to worldwide trends in consumerism. The current focus on individualism in DBG expresses itself in a strong consumption boom, with many people enjoying the spread of shops and the acquisition of new goods. People say they have many more wants and needs than before, with fancy clothing, a mobile phone, and a motorbike in big demand. The *chef du village* complains that this individualism has gone too far: 'when we're not together, like now, all our fortunes are damaged. Whatever anyone finds, they put it in their pocket...it's everyone for themselves.'[4] As another elderly villager comments: 'in the past, the household was rich and individuals were poor, but now individuals have money and the household is threadbare.'[5]

The shift towards individualism stems in part from the values picked up through migration, and in part through the age-old tension between individual and collective interests encapsulated in the terms *jonforo* and *foroba*.[6] While the villagers always had connections outside the settlement, these have greatly multiplied as many people spend long periods away, earning money, seeking a new life, and bringing up their family in the capital, Bamako. Although people who have left still maintain links to the village, they say their children will be city dwellers. A few village families are investing in the education of their children, to give them professional qualifications beyond secondary school, but many cannot see the benefit of sending their children, especially their daughters, to school.

Most people in the village agree that they are better off since 1980, thanks to new activities and investments. There was an acceleration of well digging in the 1970s and 80s, which led to a big expansion in water–manure contracts with visiting herders and much better millet yields, while in the 1990s, many people set up shops. Sesame fields became widespread in the 2000s, while solar panels are

---

[3] Hart (1982) states that the erosion of cooperative work groups is the consequence of commercialized farm production and increased cash sales, leading to increased individualization and growth of private property. However, he also notes that in some places, the demands of commercial agriculture have led to the establishment of larger cooperative farming groups, attributable to economies of scale.

[4] Interview, DBG in June 2014.   [5] Interview, MD in February 2019.

[6] Meaning 'private or individual field', versus the 'big field' conveying the sense of joint estate, as described in Chapters 3–5.

today's newest asset. Each investment cycle follows a similar pattern. One person brings back a new idea; two or three neighbours copy it; others watch and wait; and when it is shown to be a good thing, everyone else follows suit as soon as they can. However, the highest returns accrue to those who are able to invest early in the cycle, as with well digging. If you want to be a successful farmer, you need significant investment, in the form of equipment (ploughs, carts, work oxen, donkeys, wells, and cattle), and control over labour. Farming is difficult for the smallest, poorest households because they lack essential assets and can mobilize few workers. Their long-term future looks bleak in the village, unless they have a lucky break.

Many farmers recognize they must change their agricultural methods, given the big fall in soil fertility, and loss of grazing around the settlement. The villagers of DBG no longer hold a monopoly over access to water, grazing, and dung, and most farmers use small amounts of chemical fertilizer, mixed with seed at sowing time. Some form of agricultural intensification will be essential to improve crop yields. However, rainfall trends are unpromising. Although the village has received a higher volume of annual rainfall in 2016–2018 than in 1980–1982, it is more unreliable, especially at the beginning and end of the wet season. There are also many uncertainties linked to government policy and action for villages like DBG, who see government as more of a threat than a protector of their rights as citizens. Villagers in DBG are not sure whether they will be absorbed into the irrigation zone or remain on the edge and suffer the adverse impacts of proximity. The new land law may enable them to claim legal rights over their customary territory, although questions remain about the strength of this protection, when facing powerful interests seeking land. Young men and women face many choices as to their futures, whether to stay in the village, migrate to Bamako, or travel even further. Given women's current status and limited access to effective contraception, population growth is likely to continue, leading to rising pressures on land, water, and soils, and multiplication of small towns and settlements. Although many people have lives beyond the village, their identity is still shaped by this place, landscape, and society.

Taking a forward look, there are a number of foreseeable trends that will determine the prospects people face in making a livelihood in and around DBG, as well as other drivers of change that are less predictable. This final chapter reviews five major factors shaping the options for people in DBG: conflict and insecurity in Mali and the wider Sahel region; demographic growth and likely trends; increased disruption to rainfall and climate patterns; economic growth and investment in DBG and the wider region; and growing pressures on land and grazing. The chapter finishes with a reflection on the impacts of development aid in the life of this and neighbouring villages, before presenting final conclusions on DBG's future.

Conflict and insecurity

Since 2012, Mali and the wider Sahel have been gripped by a worsening set of interlocking conflicts, at local, national, and regional levels, as described in Chapter 1. The current conflict and insecurity span the northern and central regions of Mali, and have spilt over into neighbouring states. There are multiple entangled groups and grievances spread across the Sahel region, from radical jihadist groups seeking Sharia rule, and ethnic groups pushing for greater autonomy or independence, to young people without jobs, and many ordinary people who resent the bad governance, corruption, and centralization of power in the hands of the government in Bamako.[7] Transnational criminal gangs, often closely associated with armed groups, are benefitting from the lawlessness created by conflict, through trade in weapons, drugs, kidnapping, and smuggling of migrants across the desert.[8] Mali and the wider Sahel embody many of the characteristics that typify the 'fragility trap' which has caught some of the poorest countries in Africa.[9] This set of reinforcing factors includes weak economic growth, lack of jobs, diverse groups with strong opposing identities, and a state considered illegitimate and ripe for plunder by those who can seize power through winning elections, or other means. The state has very limited revenue from taxation, relies heavily on aid funds, and has limited capacity to perform its basic functions. The strong exploit the weak and private interests override long-term public purpose. While foreign intervention can buy some time, ultimately, the solutions have to be domestic, generated through simple steps to bring jobs and security, and to re-establish state institutions, collective purpose, and accountable governance systems.[10]

The government in Bamako has found it difficult to re-establish effective control over the north of the country, and, even with the military support of the French Barkhane force, European allies, and the UN's MINUSMA,[11] the government has very limited presence outside the main towns. The Algerian government brokered a peace agreement in 2015, intended to disarm the rebels, integrate their forces into the Malian army, set up joint patrols, and establish interim administrative bodies at Regional and Cercle levels. But to date, very few of the measures agreed have been enacted.

In 2014, five neighbouring Sahelian nations—Mauritania, Mali, Burkina Faso, Niger, and Chad—formed the G5 to coordinate their military strategy and create a joint force, given the interconnected nature of the conflict across the Sahel, and

---

[7] Benjaminsen, T.A. and Ba, B. (2018); International Crisis Group (2016).
[8] Walther, O. (2017); Thiam, A. (2017).
[9] Commission on State Fragility, Growth and Development (2018).
[10] Commission on State Fragility, Growth and Development (2018).
[11] United Nations Multidimensional Integrated Stabilization Mission in Mali. Established by UN Security Council Resolution No. 2100: April 2013.

the great ease with which armed groups criss-cross this vast space. A recent report by the Expert Group on Mali, advising the UN Security Council, flags the close association between jihadist groups and smuggling, identifies several named individuals who are known to be banking large profits from these activities, and proposes a range of sanctions be applied to them.[12] Al Qaeda, the Islamic State, and a range of other foreign jihadists are all present in Southern Libya, the north and centre of Mali, and neighbouring Mauritania and Niger, with financial backing from a number of foreign interests in a shifting set of alliances. Hence, negotiating and implementing a peace agreement for the region would require alignment and coordinated efforts from this diverse mix of interests and state and non-state actors.

Despite the establishment of the G5, there appears little cause to hope these conflicts will rapidly be resolved. While the Malian President Keita has put the re-establishment of peace and security at the top of his agenda, most observers doubt his ability to deliver this promise, since over the 5 years of his first mandate, the conflict has spread much more widely, from the north of the country to cover a far broader area in the centre of Mali. From a largely Tuareg-led insurgency in 2012, the present conflict now involves many communities and groups fighting for access to key resources, settling old scores, and for particular religious ends.[13] A focus on seeking military solutions has tended to dominate Bamako's thinking, in place of a political settlement with the different rebel groups, which would also need to tackle fundamental issues of governance, accountability, and rebalancing the highly centralized political and economic power within the country. The geographical scale of the conflict and its insurgent nature make it impossible to re-establish control through military strength alone. Equally, economic prospects for the large young population are poor, with few businesses setting up in the region and many young school and university graduates unemployed. Jihadist groups are said to offer a monthly wage of 300,000 francs, which is many times what could be earned from most jobs in the formal or informal economy.[14]

Foreign donors have provided substantial military and security support and, as of early 2019, there were fifty-nine countries with more than 12,000 troops, police, and logistical and training personnel in Mali, under MINUSMA. While France has been the principal source of military support, many other EU nations are contributing to the United Nations–led peacekeeping force, alongside the United States, Canada, and a range of Asian and Latin American countries. The French military force was received with great acclaim in the first months of 2013, but

[12] UN Security Council Letter, dated 8 August 2018, from the Panel of Experts established pursuant to Resolution 2374 (2017) on Mali, addressed to the President of the Security Council. UNSC/S/2018/581. International Crisis Group (2018).

[13] Thiam, A. (2017); Benjaminsen, T.A. and Ba, B. (2018).

[14] Equivalent to US$500. Whether or not this figure is accurate, recruits gain status, weapons, and power.

subsequently has been seen by some as too close to the Tuareg, and unwilling to help the Malian government or army re-establish a presence in the Tuareg city of Kidal. At the same time, the Malian army has a reputation for being quick to shoot and ask questions later, and is being investigated for killings of young men of Peul origin, suspected of being members of the Macina Liberation Front.[15] The deployment of European troops to Mali is also the result of the Sahel and Sahara having become critical regions for monitoring movement of people and controlling migration into North Africa and across the Mediterranean. These are very large ungoverned spaces, which are impossible to police effectively, even using drones and air attacks. The conflict is likely to worsen without new thinking and political leadership. The West African Sahel has thus moved from being a 'backwater' of little strategic importance to becoming critical to EU politics and security.

There are multiple consequences of this state of conflict, which affect Mali and its people at all levels, including to some extent the village of DBG. First, there are the direct consequences of the conflict which include a death toll estimated at several thousand over the period 2012–2018 and the damage done to relations between ethnic groups and different communities.[16] It has become, for example, uncomfortable to be of Tuareg origin in Bamako, and many Tuareg have felt it necessary to abandon their traditional clothing. Militia groups, established to provide defence of local communities, have taken to attacking other ethnic groups. The Bambara hunters' associations, known as *donzo*, are now playing this role in some areas, and Peul herding camps are being attacked by militias in a settling of scores and conflicts over access to water and grazing. The Peul have organized themselves to fight back and protect their communities, with some joining the jihadist movement set up by Ahmadou Koufa[17] in 2014, which voices the anger and resentment felt by many pastoral Peul. They have felt politically marginalized and in many areas, have lost access to and control over land, water, and grazing, and they face high levels of corruption when they take land disputes to court. They also accuse the security forces of unfairly targeting all youths of Peul origin, assuming they must be part of the Macina Liberation Front.[18] Second, while donor funding to Mali increased by 20 per cent between 2010 and 2017, an increasing share of this is targeted at military spending, humanitarian aid to displaced people, and measures to stem flows of migration, rather than being

---

[15] A dossier of historic exactions by the Malian army in the north of Mali also exists, covering the period from Independence to 2012, which documents in detail the names, dates, and locations of killings by the army, and confirms the impunity with which the army has operated for many years.

[16] FIDH/AMDH (2018) estimates that 1,200 people have been killed and 30,000 displaced over the period 2016–2018, with more than a million people in the Mopti Region in 2018 in need of humanitarian assistance.

[17] Thought to have been killed in a French/Mali attack on his base in November 2018, he has subsequently reappeared.

[18] Benjaminsen, T.A. and Ba, B. (2018).

invested in the long-term development of institutions and infrastructure needed to build a more effective state and economy. The government budget for military spending has doubled from an average of 10 per cent in the period 2001–2010 to 21 per cent of government expenditure in 2017.

Third, the conflict has led to a recentralization of power and authority in Bamako, in a country twice the size of France, which needs to decentralize decision-making and find ways of shifting power and resources away from central government. Fourth, the state of conflict has discouraged many foreign companies from investing in the country, leaving it open to the less scrupulous parties, which care less about reputational risk. For example, in 2012, South Africa's Illovo company withdrew from its planned sugar cane project in Markala, northeast of Ségou, for multiple reasons including concern for the company brand (being owned by the UK's Associated British Foods), as well as fears for the safety of staff and the project's assets. As a result, the Chinese now dominate the sugar sector and, as seen with the N-Sukala project, have a free hand to behave as they like. Fifth, movement within the country and to neighbouring states has been significantly affected, for traders, herders, and ordinary travellers, for fear of banditry, encountering jihadists, or running into army and police patrols. Bandits operate in many areas away from the principal roads, where they seize vehicles, motorbikes, money, and any other valuables. There have also been more than thirty 'drive-by' assassinations of government personnel in the Mopti Region over the period 2015–2018, by turbaned killers riding on motorbikes,[19] as also happened in April 2016, in Doura, 30 km from DBG. The Governors of Ségou and Mopti Regions regularly impose a ban on use of motorbikes in certain communes, making it hard to get around, visit neighbours, and carry out trade, since there is a major risk of being shot or losing one's motorcycle if caught by the army or police. The villagers of DBG faced such a ban for many months of 2017. Mali's neighbour Burkina Faso has recently installed a similar ban on use of motorbikes in the northeast of the country, between the hours of sunset and sunrise, in an attempt to curb illicit activity.

Sixth, the once-large international NGO sector, which had been an important source of support for many decentralized projects across the country—small-scale energy, credit schemes, and market gardens—has been much diminished. There continue to be Malian NGOs that lead major programmes of work, and Malian staff of large foreign NGOs such as CARE and Oxfam, but the vibrancy and resources of the NGO sector have been greatly reduced. Many international NGOs have closed their doors in Bamako, subcontracting some elements of their portfolio to national organizations. However, many national staff are also unwilling to travel to parts of Central and Northern Mali, so the NGO footprint

---

[19] Described in Chapter 1. Benjaminsen, T.A. and Ba, B. (2018) op cit.

has diminished considerably. Seventh, the tourist sector has completely disappeared. This had been an important source of employment and incomes in major centres like Ségou, Mopti, and Timbuktu with hotels, tour guides, transport, and artisan activities all gaining revenue from tourists. But, since 2013, the number of tourists has fallen to near zero because of fears of attack and kidnapping. Hotels are empty, and events such as Timbuktu's Music in the Desert festival at New Year has been cancelled, while the Ségou festival on the River Niger receives few international visitors.

Malian and international commentators agree that it is vital to re-establish the state's presence and legitimacy, through delivery of basic public services, alongside security from attack. But, in practice many schools, clinics, and government offices remain empty in Central and Northern Mali since any government official is considered a legitimate target by the jihadists.[20] More than half a million of children are estimated to be out of school as a consequence in the Mopti Region.[21] Government staff, having seen their colleagues assassinated, are unwilling to risk their lives in the face of threats from insurgent groups, and have fled to safer places. In DBG, two teachers have stayed, but the rest have left fearing for their safety.

Given its position on the edge of the farming zone, DBG has been visited by army patrols, but it has felt no direct impacts from the spread of conflict in the Ségou region. However, indirectly, the conflict has accelerated the worsening of relations between Bambara and Peul communities, the motorbike ban has greatly hindered movement, and everyone suffers from the poor economic prospects at the national level, which stem from insecurity.

Demography

This study has shown the importance of demographic growth in the village of DBG, the population having tripled over the 35 years from 1981–2016. Population growth for Mali as a whole has been broadly similar, and it is expected that total numbers will rise from 18 million in 2018 to 45 million by 2050, an increase by a factor of 2.5. This prediction assumes a fall in total fertility rates per woman from 6.5 children, to between 3 and 4 by 2050, a pattern which follows recent experience in Kenya, Ethiopia, and Rwanda. Estimates for the Ségou region show that population is expected to rise from 2.7 million today to 4.6 million by 2035, and to 6.5 million by 2050, bringing about a more than doubling of cultivated area by 2035. The current population density for the Ségou region is forty-two people per square km, which could reach seventy-two people per square km by 2035.[22]

---

[20] Benjaminsen, T.A. and Ba, B. (2018).   [21] Thiam, A. (2017).
[22] Sourisseau, J.-M. et al (2016).

A doubling of cultivated area by 2035 would mean that fields occupied 45 per cent of all land. Such rising pressures are likely to generate a number of consequences. First, there will be a larger flow of people to the cities of Ségou, Sikasso, and Bamako, and to destinations further afield. Second, an increase in agricultural intensification is essential to raise productivity and shift to higher-value crops where rainfall allows and market access makes this attractive.[23] Third, there will be further movement north of farming groups into the less densely settled areas, on a seasonal or permanent basis, generating growing hostility and conflict with pastoral communities who need this land for grazing. These issues are explored in more detail in the section Pressures on Land below.

Currently, women bear an average of six to seven children, which is one of the highest rates in the world, and similar to Niger, Burundi, Somalia, Uganda, and Tanzania. This high level is the outcome of poverty, combined with early marriage, widow inheritance, and absence of any effective form of contraception. Levels of education amongst adult women are low, and, in both rural and urban areas, far fewer girls than boys go to school (see Figure 8.1). Hence, there are few

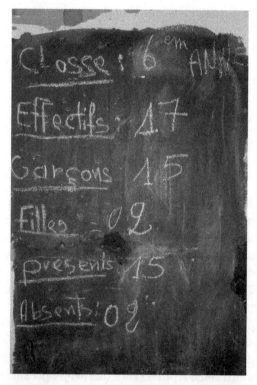

Figure 8.1. Far fewer girls attend school; attendance record, DBG, October 2016

[23] Tiffen, M. et al (1994).

grounds for expecting a slowdown in demographic rates in the near future. Women in town have fewer children than those in rural areas, with the average falling to five for those in urban areas. Many rural women and girls go to Bamako on migration to earn money and, while there, have direct access to new ideas and patterns of life. However, there is little evidence of a change in attitudes amongst women or men over the status of women and girls, and the heavy weight traditionally put on marriage and child rearing.[24] Attempts in 2009 to reform women's status through amendments to Mali's Family Law attracted a very hostile reception from Islamic organizations, and several preachers were able to mobilize large demonstrations in Bamako and elsewhere to pushback on proposals to give, for example, equal inheritance rights to women and men, and a rise in the age for marriage to 18 years. The annual rankings of African countries, established by the Mo Ibrahim Foundation, show Mali to be at midpoint (number twenty-eight out of fifty-four countries) for overall governance, but close to the bottom of the list (number forty-five out of fifty-four) for women's political, legal, and economic status.[25]

Marriage and preparation for a girl's wedding remain hugely important drivers in the life of young women. As was seen in Chapter 7, young female migrants from DBG work very hard for several years to earn the money needed to purchase the substantial portfolio of wedding goods required for a 'good' marriage. The last 35 years have seen much-improved rates of child survival, particularly amongst those under the age of 5 years. The childbirth histories of women in DBG undertaken in 1981 showed almost half of children died before they reached the age of 5.[26] Today, the national figures have fallen to one in eight, and DBG has benefitted from such improvements.[27] This substantial but recent shift in child-survival rates has not been matched by cuts in birth rates in rural areas like DBG. While women do their best to space their births to ensure they do not give birth until the previous child is at least 2 years old and able to walk, a woman is proud of successfully bearing and rearing six or more children to adulthood. Better access to education, improved economic opportunity, and effective contraception might help women and girls to marry later, and space their births further, but the total number of children born is likely to remain high, given women's long conjugal lives.

---

[24] By contrast, see https://www.nytimes.com/2019/01/06/world/africa/niger-divorce-women.html. This article from *The New York Times* describes the rising incidence of divorce, initiated by women, in neighbouring Niger.

[25] Mo Ibrahim Foundation (2018). Ibrahim Index of African Governance (IIAG). The Gender Ranking combines scores for gender parity in primary and secondary schools, women's political empowerment, laws on violence against women, promotion of gender equality, women in the judiciary, and labour-force participation.

[26] Hill, A. et al (1983).

[27] Nationally infant mortality rates for children younger than 5 years old fell from 408 per 1,000 in 1960–1965 to 122 per 1,000 in 2010–2015.

Climate and rainfall trends

Chapter 3 presented past and current rainfall patterns for Ségou and DBG, which show only a partial recovery in terms of total rainfall amounts following the droughts of the 1970s and 80s, and very high levels of variability from year to year. Climate scientists expect the Sahel to receive evermore variable and disruptive rainfall patterns because of warming of the global climate and shifts in large-scale atmospheric processes.[28] Evidence also shows that the Sahara Desert has been heating up more rapidly than the Sahel, provoking a more forceful water cycle, which brings more intense periods of both rainfall and drought. The Intergovernmental Panel on Climate Change (IPCC) Assessment Report of 2014 recognizes the weak database for modelling past and future rainfall in West Africa, attributable to the Sahel's geographical position at the confluence of several large, powerful weather systems. Some climate models say rainfall volume is likely to increase over the next 3 decades, while others predict a decline. Recent modelling makes clear that changes to ocean temperatures are the principal drivers of both drought and heavy rain in Africa, with a warmer south Atlantic relative to the north bringing greater likelihood of drought to the Sahel. Hence, future rainfall in the Sahel will depend on how global warming affects different regions of the Atlantic. The dominance of such large-scale processes is then amplified by human-induced land-use change.[29]

Regardless of the overall quantity of rain falling in the wet season, its increased volatility and shorter season will bring an ever-greater need for risk-spreading strategies and ways to build more resilience into farming and livelihood systems, as discussed in the next section. Sourisseau et al (2016) point to the possibility that the growing season north of the River Niger could fall from the current 50–100 days, to less than 50 days, which would make crop production less and less feasible, even if very short-cycle millet varieties were available. With less reliance on rain-fed crops, farmers and agro-pastoralists would need to diversify into small irrigated plots, and invest greater effort in livestock and a wider range of off-farm activities. Some people would likely set off in search of land and incomes in better-watered southerly regions, as happened in the 1970s and 80s, when severe droughts pushed several million people and their herds from Mali and Burkina Faso into Côte d'Ivoire and Ghana, in search of farmland and grazing. But land has also become scarcer in coastal countries, given the large number of incoming migrants, and this has led to rising hostility towards people of Sahelian origin.

The difficulties in gaining a living from farming discourage young men from continuing the life of their parents. A survey done in 2016 amongst 130 rural

---

[28] Taylor, C. et al (2017), as discussed in Chapter 3.   [29] Giannini, A. (2016).

households in the Ségou region showed that 74 per cent of young men aged between 15 and 24 years said they intended to make their life away from their village, with Bamako the favourite destination.[30] Of these, 28 per cent said they wanted to migrate outside Mali, mainly to Europe. Of young women interviewed, 61 per cent said they expected to live their life away from their home village, of which 97 per cent wanted to go and live in Bamako, or another big city. Chapter 7 described the attraction of migration for all young people in DBG, and the high incidence of people travelling away from home, often for a number of years, partly to gain experience by exploring the world, and partly to earn cash for a range of needs. DBG may retain greater loyalty amongst its young people compared with other villages where land pressures are more intense, and the large Bambara household no longer retains its size and strength. Young migrants from DBG now in Bamako are keen to support their families back home in the village, by sending money and food and investing in the land, but they do not see themselves going back there to live anymore.

Economic development in the Ségou region

Chapter 6 described the shifting pattern of investment in assets in DBG, and uptake of innovations, such as wells, shops, and solar panels. The data illustrate the dynamism of the local economy, the rising value of assets per person in the village, and diversification of capital away from livestock. This section considers economic options for DBG, what new form this dynamism might take over the next 3–4 decades, and how it links into wider economic and technical developments.

Economic opportunities for the people of DBG draw first from the markets and resources immediately available in their territory, second from those within the Ségou region, and third from a range of activities across the wider West African economy, given the links generated through migration. The villagers have identified better roads as a priority for them, and they argue that they could make more money if they were better connected to Ségou. Distance and poor-quality roads mean it takes 2 hours to travel to markets at Ségou and Dougabougou, and consequently, there is a significant price differential between village and town.[31]

Urbanization has been a major spur to economic growth throughout West Africa, with the rapid growth of secondary cities and small towns, as well as burgeoning of capital cities like Bamako, offering markets for many goods and services.[32] Ségou has been an important market town from precolonial times, and currently, it has a population of around 300,000. But it has not maintained

---

[30] Sourisseau, J.-M. et al (2016); Kirwin, M. and Anderson, J. (2018).
[31] A differential which benefits the shopkeepers in the village.   [32] OECD (1998).

its relative importance at national level and, like much of West Africa, it relies on a largely informal economy. The 'informal sector', which includes agriculture, agro-processing and many small-scale manufacturing and service enterprises, employs 75–90 per cent of people nationally, and it cannot be ignored because of its scale and dynamism.[33]

The current modern sector is limited to the *Office du Niger* rice-irrigation scheme and associated milling activities, the Chinese-built cotton textile mill COMATEX, and the sugar mills at Sukala and N-Sukala. Ségou has no significant mining activity, and though cotton ginning used to be important, production and processing have moved away to Sikasso to the south and Kayes to the west. Ségou hosts its own university, and a bridge is due to be built across the Niger to link up with the North Bank. However, its relative proximity to Bamako, and improvement of the 240 km road between the two cities mean that many people with jobs and responsibilities in Ségou actually spend much of their time in Bamako, shuttling between the two cities. People say much of Ségou's wealth is invested in Bamako. However, land in and around Ségou has been rising in value, as property speculation shifts from periurban Bamako to other cities. On the North Bank, wealthier people have been buying up land close to the anticipated site for the new bridge to be built by the Chinese. DBG is too far away and too poorly connected at present to be part of this speculative boom, but at least one household from the village has built a house on the edge of Ségou, to establish a foothold in the urban economy. Construction of the new bridge across the River Niger at Ségou will bring DBG closer to the city, and speed up the river crossing currently done by canoe (see Figure 8.2).

Whether or not the Ségou region does well in future depends in part on resolution of conflicts in the wider country, but also in part on the quality of leadership at city level and its political weight. The Government of Mali has initiated a programme of regionalization which has the espoused aim to shift power and resources to the ten regions of the country. However, resources to fund this process are scarce, and other pressures continue to pull power towards Bamako.

Prosperity in the village has been reliant on migration earnings. Chapters 6 and 7 showed that many household assets in the past have been acquired by young men investing their earnings in a new cart, plough, motorbike, or solar panel. Hence, DBG would do better if its migrants could earn a better income while away and could devote more of it to investment back home. While Mali's GDP has grown by 5 per cent per year since 2010, much of this has been due to rising sales of gold and cotton, Mali's principal commodity exports. There is little employment associated with large-scale gold mining, and few linkages to the wider economy. Cotton production involves an estimated 170,000 farm families

---

[33] Allen, T. et al (2018).

Figure 8.2. Until the new bridge is built, long black canoes continue to ferry people from Ségou to the North Bank, March 2017

in Southern Mali, but they face high input costs and thin margins. And with only 2 per cent of cotton being processed in Mali, there are very limited linkages into jobs and value added. The current political and security situation has discouraged new investment, and expansion of existing firms. In the absence of new investment, migration to coastal West Africa and the Maghreb is likely to grow further.

Some analysts argue that the 'digital economy' offers African countries the chance to leapfrog industrialization and provide a miracle answer to economic growth, by shifting directly to a range of service industries for jobs and growth.[34] Certainly, Africa has shown the highest rate of growth in mobile telephones, with subscriptions in West Africa nearly doubling between 2010 and 2017 to reach a 47 per cent penetration rate, while Internet connections grew from 2 per cent of people in 2005 to 24 per cent in 2018.[35] But others question the scale of likely benefits from the digital economy, and identify as many threats as opportunities. For example, the 'Uberization' of work creates jobs but often on low pay with high levels of precarity. And digital systems will likely lead to mass automation of basic manufacturing and assembly at a global level, with Southeast Asia vulnerable to losing three-quarters of basic manufacturing jobs over the coming decade from automation.[36] Hence, automation could rob African countries of a step in the ladder towards greater industrialization. Others argue that it is important to avoid misleading and alarmist estimates for job losses associated with automation. In practice, there are usually many upsides to technical progress which creates a

[34] WEF (2016).   [35] GSMA (2018).   [36] Lutkenhorst, W. (2018).

range of new opportunities not only in production processes, but also in reshaping how goods, services, and ideas are exchanged. While technical innovation will disrupt lives, the outcome will depend on how change is managed.[37]

Countries like Mali have little industry today and are poorly integrated into global value chains. Tariffs are low, and the CFA franc is over-valued, making it difficult for local producers to compete with imported goods, which are often cheaper and of higher quality than domestic production.[38] China has been able to manufacture and sell goods very cheaply across the world, displacing local manufacturing and leading far more developed African economies to 'premature deindustrialization'.[39] The extensive second-hand clothes business also offers cheap goods for urban customers, but it has displaced domestic textile and clothing industries. In the past, it has been through industrial growth and manufacturing that countries have achieved structural transformation, and built a more diverse economy, with multiple linkages with smaller suppliers up and downstream. Digital services are unlikely to generate high-income jobs for most people: the country will need investment in physical infrastructure, and institutions to support its growth.[40]

The combination of mobile telephones, arrival of 4G services and power from PV cells does provide potential for economic growth and diversification in a village like DBG, which had little prospect of ever getting connected to the electricity grid. The telephone service has been very patchy in the village, especially in the rainy season, with a mobile signal only available at the upper edge of the settlement. The nearest mast was 30 km away at Doura, the commune headquarters. In late 2018, Orange Telecom installed a mast some 15 km farther south, which has improved the network greatly for both calls and 4G services. This will allow villagers easier access to information, get clients for their business, and speak to family and friends elsewhere. Mobile banking, and access to government services should improve, and enable villagers to connect with other settlements facing similar challenges. Gaining access to the Internet could bring a range of benefits for the village school, by enabling pupils to access materials, and teaching could be greatly improved if online lessons were available to bolster current limited capacity.[41] For health needs, the clinic's *matronne* might be able to rely on distant medical colleagues for advice, as well as providing cold storage for drugs that is more reliable. It might also be possible to connect some of the 160 solar panels into a microgrid, which could power larger-scale machinery, for processing crops, metalworking, grinding millet, and pumping water. Women would gain relief from the daily millet pounding, if a mill were available. Thus, there is

---

[37] Commission on Pathways for Prosperity (2018).   [38] Nubukpo, K. (2015).
[39] Rodrik, D. (2016; 2017).
[40] Pilling, D. (2018); Commission on Pathways for Prosperity (2018).
[41] Along the lines of the Orange Digital Schools programme in Guinea.

significant potential to harness this technology, but it will need people from DBG to seize the opportunity. Most probably, it will be people who have spent some time living away, seeing how things are done elsewhere, who will make it happen.

It should be recognized that the impact of these new technologies is not always benign. While digital innovations help 'leapfrog' earlier patterns of economic growth, they have also been helpful to jihadist groups, who have been adept at social media campaigns to spread the insurgency, and to plan attacks, kidnapping, and other criminal activity. There is a lively trade in videos showing attacks by one group on another, while mobile banking apps enable people traffickers to extort funds from those they are transporting.

Pressures on land

The villagers of DBG have experienced a large inflow of people into their territory seeking land to farm, as described in Chapter 4. The proportion of total available land around the village now cultivated has risen from 2.6 per cent in 1980–1982 to 6.2 per cent in 1995, and to 28 per cent in 2018. While part of this growth in farmed area is the consequence of an increase in the village population and extensive use of oxen-drawn ploughs, the main reason for a shift from land abundance to scarcity is the inflow of migrant farmers evicted from their farmland to the south and east of DBG. As described in Chapter 4, this is due to the establishment of a large new sugar cane plantation, which has taken over the land of villages such as Tekena, N'Golobabougou, and Témou. Even where farmers have not lost land directly, devastating bird damage to millet harvests has prompted villagers close to the irrigation scheme to seek farmland elsewhere.

This pressure on land for cultivation has had several consequences. First, there has been a loss of soil fertility, with few nutrients being put back into the soil after harvest. Second, fields have displaced grazing, making it more difficult for herds to move between water and pasture, and leading to growing conflicts over crop damage. Hence, relations between Bambara farmers and Peul herders have worsened considerably in the last 20 years. Third, the people of DBG sense they have lost control over their territory and associated resources because of the large influx of people to farm and graze 'their land'. They can see this is leading to a competitive rush for what valuable resources remain, and they complain of the bush now being filled up with people and livestock. They complain that theft of animals is rising; trees are being felled for charcoal; and wildlife has all but vanished, leaving the hunters' society with nothing left to chase.

The village of DBG lies on the edge of the irrigable zone, under the authority of the *Office du Niger*. Villagers ask themselves whether they should try to acquire land within the irrigation scheme or stay focused on rain-fed crops and livestock. In practice, like villagers displaced by N-Sukala, they may not get any say in the matter although, being on sandy rather than clay soils, they are less likely to be absorbed into a new irrigated sugar or rice scheme. When discussing the development options for villages like DBG, government officials tend to attribute blame for low crop yields on villagers themselves, describing them as victims of their own stupidity, having over-grazed and over-cultivated the land. 'Desertification' is widely used as the narrative to justify neglect of rain-fed areas.[42] Yet, as will be seen in Box 8.2, the Sahel's drylands can be regreened and could become more resilient through a combination of technical and institutional innovations.

Irrigation development and the future of the *Office du Niger*

For regions like the Sahel, faced with low and unpredictable rainfall, irrigated agriculture looks like the obvious answer to secure food and livelihoods.[43] In the last 5 years, there has been a big push from national governments, donors, investors, and development banks for more land in Africa to be put under irrigation, given it currently represents less than 5 per cent of total farmland. Thus, the High Level Sahel strategy meeting of 2013, held in Dakar, Senegal, identified irrigated agriculture as a priority for addressing food security in an era of growing impacts from climate change. Six Sahelian nations announced their aspiration to increase the area under controlled irrigation from 400,000 to 1,000,000 ha by 2020, and called for public and private investment to enable its implementation.[44] But few people stop to ask fundamental questions such as whether the overall resilience of the nation's food system is enhanced through investing scarce capital in irrigated agriculture, especially where it displaces thousands of farmers who must then be resettled, and where it takes out of production many hectares of high-value floodplain grazing and croplands in downstream areas.

For the Government of Mali, the *Office du Niger* has been the primary locus for irrigation investment, based on the dams, canals, and other infrastructure built since its foundation in the 1930s. Today this land grows mainly rice, sugar, and vegetables on 120,000 ha. The Strategic Plan for the *Office du Niger* for the next 10–20 years had predicted growth to a total of 200,000 ha by 2020, through a combination of state funds and private sector investment (see Box 8.1 below).[45] However, such rapid growth at more than 10,000 ha per year, has not been feasible. The revised target of 200,000 ha by 2035 is more realistic and would imply an annual expansion of 4,000 ha. However, this slower rate of expansion does not keep up with growth in the farming population currently in the *Office*, let alone

---

[42] Toulmin, C. and Brock, K. (2016). [43] Malabo-Montpellier Panel (2018).
[44] www.icid.org/decl_dakar.html. [45] Ministère du Développement Rural (2015).

Box 8.1   Attracting large-scale agricultural investment to Mali

The Government of Mali has courted private investors, domestic and foreign, to bring their capital and expertise to help develop irrigated agriculture, as the state has insufficient funds to implement all its plans. In 2004, with support from the World Bank, the government set up an agency to promote international investment (API)[46] with favourable terms to attract investors, such as 30-year tax exemptions and very cheap land. A special unit was also established within the *Office du Niger* to handle allocations of land within the territory it controls. By 2011, more than 500,000 ha of irrigable land had been allocated to investors, many of whom were from overseas, including Libya's sovereign wealth fund, Associated British Foods/Illuvo, and China's N-Sukala, for a range of crops—sugar, fruit and vegetables, jatropha, and rice (see Figure 8.3).

However, by 2017, only one-tenth had actually been put under cultivation, and a number of large schemes, such as Malibya, had collapsed.[47] The jihadist invasion of the north and the subsequent coup d'état, military intervention, and heightened insecurity throughout the centre of the country have

Figure 8.3. Hoarding advertising Libya's 100,000 hectare project (now abandoned) in the *Office du Niger*, outskirts of Ségou, 2011.

(continued)

---

[46] *Agence pour la Promotion des Investissements.*
[47] Malibya aimed to put 100,000 ha of land under rice cultivation for the benefit of Libyan consumers.

Box 8.1 Continued

---

discouraged many investors from committing capital to develop farmland in Mali. By contrast, China remains a staunch presence, and has been welcomed by the government, having got sugar production at N-Sukala up and running in record time. The Chinese have funded a number of other big schemes, such as the third bridge across the River Niger in Bamako, a new hospital and a modern university campus. China's readiness to provide loans and the huge asymmetry in power between the two countries mean that no attempts have been made to ensure Chinese companies comply with the law. Hence, local officials in Ségou complain that N-Sukala does not pay water dues or local taxes on turnover; they do not comply with employment laws affecting sugar mill employees; they have not implemented the results of the Environmental and Social Impact Assessment for the scheme; nor have they paid compensation to farmers who have lost all their land to N-Sukala. Domestic Malian investors, who include *Moulins Modernes du Mali* and *Groupe Tomota*, have also faced challenges from local farmers who seek recompense for loss of land.

Sources: Cotula, L. (2011; 2013); Cotula, L. and Berger, T. (2017); CMAT (2018); Oakland Institute (2011); Nolte, K. and Voget-Kleschin, L. (2014).

---

allow for larger plot size or offer land to incoming farmers.[48] Other options for making better use of existing areas of irrigated agriculture include shifting from rice to higher-value crops, such as fruit and vegetables, and improving operations and maintenance to ensure farmers get water at the right time and place.

There are currently more than twenty dam projects proposed for the River Niger. Upstream in Guinea, President Alpha Condé has declared that the Fomi Dam, on a tributary of the Niger, is a priority for 2019, in order to generate power for Guinea's mining sector and aluminium smelters.[49] The Fomi Dam will be able to store rainy season flood flows and release them during the dry season, enabling a large increase in the availability of water for dry-season irrigation in Mali. It is estimated that an additional 330,000 ha of irrigated land could then be brought into production in the *Office du Niger*, as well as allow double cropping on the existing 120,000 ha. However, there are growing concerns about the consequences

---

[48] The irrigated farmers' union—*Syndicat des exploitants agricoles de l'Office du Niger (SEXAGON)*— argues for at least 0.5 ha per farming family to ensure food security and a surplus for other expenses. However, the current average is only half this amount, which explains current levels of poverty within the *Office du Niger*.

[49] In June 2017, construction of the Fomi Dam passed from the World Bank to a Chinese consortium. It is not clear whether this consortium will abide by the impact assessments undertaken so far by the World Bank, nor their willingness to engage with the broader consultative approach within the River Niger Basin, including downstream Mali.

Figure 8.4. Satellite image showing the *Office du Niger* irrigation scheme (centre left) and Inner Niger Delta (right), Google Earth, 2019.

of diverting such large amounts of water out of the River Niger. Downstream of the Markala Dam, the enormous floodplain of the Inner Niger Delta covers an area of more than 30,000 sq km, providing a livelihood to more than a million people through a combination of fishing, rice farming, and flood retreat grazing, as shown in Figure 8.4. It is also a region of great significance for biodiversity in Africa, second only to the Okavango Delta in Botswana, and a site recognized by Ramsar, offering harbour for billions of migratory birds. Following completion of the Fomi Dam, the new flood regime will mean that in all years, flood height and duration will be reduced. In drought years, a significant proportion of the Inner Niger Delta flood plain will not receive enough water to grow crops or generate reasonable grazing, bringing adverse consequences for many people making a living throughout the delta. It is estimated that the annual cost of the Fomi Dam to livelihoods in the Inner Niger Delta is at least US$100 million.[50] This damage to many herders, farmers, and fisher-folk in Central Mali can only further aggravate resentment towards central government.

Irrigated agriculture offers a powerful vison of what 'modern' agriculture is meant to look like. With its apparent mastery of water and land, and potential rice yields of more than 5 tonnes per ha it would seem to provide the answers. But if you look more closely, the story is less simple. A recent assessment of irrigated agriculture in the Sahel shows that when projects are approved for funding, their costs are systematically under-estimated, and yield projections are far too

[50] www.internationalrivers.org.

optimistic, so that in reality irrigated agriculture turns out to be a very expensive means of growing the Sahel's food supply.[51] Decisions to build more irrigated farming schemes appear blind to the evidence of the recent past, because both the image and the interests associated with large-scale dam projects are very appealing. Experience shows that very few if any of the large number of people displaced by such schemes gain proper compensation, resettlement, or jobs. The net result of this divergence in expected cost and benefit flows is a large and growing deficit for the irrigation scheme, with implications for the viability of the scheme's maintenance, as well as for public sector finances. The government will have taken out a series of loans from donor agencies and financial institutions to fund construction of the irrigation infrastructure. If returns are below expectations, the gap must be bridged through other sources of finance. In many cases, these irrigated agricultural projects become a major financial burden for the state since yields are too low and farmers too poor to fund the costs of maintenance. Hence, the infrastructure deteriorates over time, requiring additional loans to fund its periodic rehabilitation.

Many farmers on irrigation schemes are also finding it difficult to make a living. In the case of Selingué, upstream of Bamako, only one in four farmers is breaking even in financial terms from irrigated farming, and three-quarters of farmers are operating below the official poverty line. Those doing best have a range of irrigated crops on and off-scheme, including in low-lying *bas-fonds* areas outside the main project, where they grow high-value fruit and vegetables. Many of the poorer households divide their time between irrigated plots, rain-fed fields of millet, and grazing livestock in more distant pastures. For these households, an irrigated plot is just one element in a wider portfolio of activities and assets. While the government focuses attention on building new schemes, it pays less attention to the other factors which could make rice farming financially viable: accessible credit, access to equipment (ploughs, oxen, and threshers), viable plot sizes, and reduced competition from cheap imports of rice.

There have also been many damaging spillover effects from irrigated agriculture on wider dryland livelihood systems, which are never taken into account, as is evident from N-Sukala sugar cane plantation. Irrigation schemes and big dams block livestock routes, and eliminate high-value flood plain grazing. Heavy use of pesticides and chemical fertilizer on the irrigation scheme pollutes drinking water and year-round standing water in canals and ponds brings increased risks from malaria, and nesting weaver birds cause devastating damage to neighbouring grain crops. Even when Environmental and Social Impact Assessments are carried out properly, they rarely consider the impacts of the scheme on the broader landscape and its people. In the case of N-Sukala, the eviction of people from their land has generated widespread adverse impacts which reach 50 km or more

---

[51] Bazin, F. et al (2017).

from the site itself, and are in stark contrast to the congratulatory tone of Sukala's report on corporate social responsibility.

Irrigated and rain-fed systems compared

If you visit an irrigation scheme in the dry season, it presents an astonishing vision of vivid greens, a carpet of luxuriant vegetation in a bare, dusty landscape. You can feel the damp, moist air, hear the buzz of insects and frogs, and sense the concentration of life and vegetation in these wet zones. The neighbouring drylands are starkly different for the 6 dry-season months, with fields harvested, grazing in short supply, a hot wind coursing through the bush, and much of the population away earning money in town. But, even at the height of the hot season in March, the careful eye can see that the dryland vegetation is only slumbering and awaiting the life-giving rains. The first signs of renewal can just be detected— with shrubs and trees starting to flower and put forth leaves, such as the wild jasmine shown in Figure 8.5. In the rainy season, the contrast between irrigated and dryland zones is much less striking, but during the rains, visiting researchers, donors, and government officials are few and far between, as the roads are near impassable and 'rural development tourism' comes to a halt.[52] Yet for these 6 months of the year, rain-fed farming areas are transformed into a mosaic of fields greening up with millet and sesame, and extensive pastures hosting stands of perennial and annual grasses. Before dawn, villages are abuzz with people getting an early meal before going out to weed the fields, to make best use of the limited rainfall, and herding animals out to fresh pasture.

Figure 8.5. In May, as the rains approach, wild jasmine puts out fragrant white flowers, May 2016.

[52] Chambers, R. (1979).

Uncertainty in water availability in the Sahel's rain-fed system is at the heart of livelihood and investment strategies, diversification of assets and activities, and role of livestock. Uncertainty, and the vulnerability it generates, can be managed in different ways, either by trying to control the system or by adaptive response.[53] Control strategies assume a mastery of technical issues set within a tractable and predictable context. Such strategies are often based on hierarchical systems and often understate the actual level of uncertainty. By contrast, adaptive strategies adopt a 'learning-by-doing' approach, recognize the benefits of distributed power, and do not seek to 'master' either people or the environment. The complex, risk-prone drylands of the Sahel exemplify inherently unpredictable systems which require a mix of policy and governance tools to support adaptive responses. In order to build greater resilience, diversification needs to be nurtured, and local capacities to innovate encouraged, by strengthening decentralized institutions.[54]

At the same time, the choice between irrigated agriculture and dryland farming can be partially bridged by finding intermediate solutions, such as small-scale irrigation systems, which are under farmer control and have fewer major adverse impacts.[55] Widespread use is made by farmers of low-lying marshy land or *bas-fonds*, where it can be found, for fruit and vegetable growing. Simple forms of rainwater harvesting can also play a valuable role, by providing better conditions for crop growth within the rainy season. Examples include use of planting pits, and construction of stone lines along the contour to slow sheet erosion.[56] Supplementary irrigation from shallow wells and pumps can also ensure sufficient moisture for crops, even if the rains stall midseason or end early.

Sustainable intensification of dryland farming systems: regreening landscapes

If irrigated agriculture provides only a partial answer to future food security in the drylands, how can rain-fed farming offer a more resilient livelihood for millions of rural dwellers across the Sahel? Villages like DBG demonstrate not only the challenges faced but also the energy and innovation at the local-village level which can be drawn upon. Chapters 3 and 4 showed that family-based millet production has not kept pace with population growth, despite a large increase in the

[53] Stirling, A. (2011); Kratli, S. (2015); Behnke, R. et al (1993).

[54] Tari, D. et al (2015) for strengthening the *dedha*, a customary institution for rangeland management in Isiolo County in Northern Kenya, enabling pastoralists to better weather the drought of 2013–2014 than those in neighbouring counties. Also Toulmin, C. et al (2015) Djiré, M. (2004); Hesse, C. et al (2013).

[55] Woodhouse, P. et al (2016).   [56] Reij, C. et al (1996).

area under this crop. There has been a large fall both in yields per hectare and per person, which are attributable to low and uncertain rainfall; loss of soil fertility, especially in the village fields; and the shift of household labour from collective production of millet to higher-value sesame grown by individuals. Trends in crop yields for DBG are mirrored more broadly across the country. For West Africa as a whole, cultivated area has doubled since 1975, and it now represents 22.4 per cent of total area.[57] In Mali, it has expanded at a similar rate, eating into pastoral areas on the northern edge of the farming zone.

As people perceive a growing scarcity of land, it might be expected that they will invest in better soils, vegetation, and landscape management, as has happened in other rain-fed areas of dryland Africa, such as around the city of Kano, Nigeria, and the Machakos District of Kenya.[58] However, such investment requires that people feel confident of gaining returns from the extra effort required, in terms of both higher yields and cash incomes from added harvests, and of sufficiently secure tenure over land and trees to be sure of reaping such benefits. It is not clear (as described below) whether the *Loi Foncier Agricole* will generate greater security in practice.

Elsewhere in the Sahel, a process of 'regreening' of farmland and landscapes has been underway for the last 20 years, and it shows the effectiveness of approaches which combine technical and financial support to smallholder farmers to maintain their farming systems, operating at a landscape level, and strengthening local learning approaches.[59] Regreening involves situations in which:

> significant numbers of farmers, individually or collectively, have developed ways to protect, regenerate, and sustainably manage an increased number of shrubs and trees in their farming systems. This includes an increased density of woody vegetation in cultivated fields as well as the increased protection and improved management of trees at scale, around homesteads, and in individual and community forests. If an agricultural landscape had only a few trees per hectare 20 years ago and there are now 40, 60, or more trees per hectare across large landscapes, we would consider this a regreening success.[60]

Regreening has drawn on farmer-managed protection and management of trees and shrubs that regenerate naturally in fields and fallows. Trees are of great value because they provide households with fuelwood, poles for construction, leaves as soil litter, and edible fruits. They also provide ecological benefits by reducing wind speed and wind erosion, increasing biodiversity, and storing carbon. Policy and

[57] CILSS (2016).   [58] Boserup, E. (1965); Tiffen, M. et al (1994).
[59] Reij, C. and Winterbottom, R. (2015); Toulmin, C. and Brock, K. (2016).
[60] Reij, C. and Winterbottom, R. (2015).

legal issues to improve the enabling conditions are important, such as recognizing local rights over land.[61]

Today, there are reckoned to be at least 5 million ha in Niger which have been regreened, and at least 300,000 ha in Burkina Faso have been transformed through the use of simple soil conservation techniques led by farmers.[62] Initiatives in Mali to follow a similar pathway made good progress for some years, with the reforestation of 500,000 ha in the Seno Plains around Bankass in the Mopti Region.[63] But in Mali, there have been major setbacks because of the current insecurity, deteriorating relations between herders and farmers, and the lack of a neutral arena in which different groups can meet and sort out their problems. Government officials are often seen as favouring particular groups, rather than seeking a fair solution to competition over land, water, and grazing, according to the law. NGOs are often called on to play a more neutral facilitating role, providing a space to experiment with new interventions.[64]

Box 8.2   Measures to regreen rain-fed farming systems in the Sahel

There are multiple actions which help regreen the landscape—re-establishing the *Faidherbia albida* tree cover in the fields surrounding the settlement, to provide shade for animals and leaf litter for the benefit of crops; soil and water conservation investments to improve soil quality and moisture retention, by establishing stone lines, bunds, or vegetative strips to slow down rainfall run-off and limit erosion; water storage through small check dams, and digging out ponds to hold more water for longer in the season, and allow fish farming; and a range of landscape management and woodland protection schemes. A multilevel approach is needed. Some things are best identified and done at field or village level; others at the level of the commune; and yet others, such as protection of livestock routes, to lead herds safely between wet- and dry-season areas over several communes, at the *cercle* or regional level.

Regreening activities cost a small fraction of investment in irrigation, with estimated costs per hectare well below $20 in contrast to $8,500–$17,000 per hectare for controlled irrigation plots.

Source: Reij, C. and Winterbottom, R. (2015); Reij, C. et al (2009); https://www.regreeningafrica.org/.

---

[61] A bit of technical support also helps catalyse the process of regreening. External funding for support of Farmer-Managed Natural Regeneration in Niger's Maradi and Zinder regions since 1985 has been well below US$100 million, which means external investment of well below US$20/ha. Reij, C. personal communication.
[62] Reij, C. et al (2009); https://www.wri.org/our-work/project/re-greening.
[63] CILSS (2016).   [64] Djiré, M. et al (2014).

Bottom-up regreening projects look 'messy' in comparison with the neat vision of a large irrigated plot, but this contrast masks a grounded dynamism in the former approach. Key to regreening success has been letting local people and their institutions take the lead. Institutional arrangements may be invisible, but their strength makes a big difference to how societies cope with change, and act collectively.[65] Success relies on there being a national-level framework to decentralize power and provide space for local initiative.[66] Ways to help include training of local people, mayors, and other community leaders in participatory mapping; using a mix of maps and satellite imagery, to monitor land-use change; time and commitment to work with local community organizations; recognizing and managing the rights of different groups resident and temporarily using the area, such as pastoral herders; seeking formal recognition of villages and camps as having ownership and control over land and natural resources; and ensuring that livestock are properly integrated into the planning process.[67] Whether on grounds of value for money or social justice, dryland grazing and farming areas which cover more than 90 per cent of the Sahel's territory and two-thirds of its people need a fresh approach.

An arena for innovating in local policy and practice: the Daouna project

The village of DBG and surrounding region could benefit greatly from a regreening approach, and a new project offers such potential. A large livestock development project has been identified by the Ségou Regional Council as a high priority for donor funding. Included in the region's Strategic Action Plan of 2012, the project is focused on the extensive grazing lands on the North Bank of the River Niger. A series of project documents and feasibility studies were prepared in 2012–2014, with German government support, and subsequent discussions with the French government have led to the project being incorporated as one major element into the Programme d'Appui au Développement Economique Régionale to be funded by France's Agence Française de Développement, from 2019.[68]

The project seeks to address pressures on grazing attributable to the doubling in livestock numbers since 1990, the northward spread of cultivation into pastoral areas, and the steady rise in crop-livestock disputes, pressures which are

---

[65] Toulmin, C. et al (2015).   [66] Coulibaly, C. (2010).
[67] Chris Reij says, 'In the end the challenge is to create enabling conditions which induce millions of smallholder producers to invest in Sustainable Land Management. In Maradi and Zinder (in Niger) they have done so...and the combination of these individual investment decisions has led to landscape level transformation. But there was never an explicit plan to transform a landscape.'
[68] Covering the Regions of Timbuctoo and Ségou, for total funding of EURO 31 million. The feasibility studies were undertaken for GIZ by a consultancy group based in Bamako, Ingénieurs Conseils en Technique de Développement (ICOTED) (2014).

particularly evident on the northern edge of the farming zone.[69] As described in Chapter 1, the lands on the North Bank of the Niger have long been a meeting place for herds drawn from many different regions, over wet and dry seasons. To the herds and flocks of local Peul and Bambara are added Peul herds moving out of the Inner Niger Delta, needing to find pasture in the rainy season, when the delta is inaccessible because of floods; there are the burgeoning herds of cattle owned by farmers in the *Office du Niger* and traders from Ségou city which come looking for grazing much of the year, and the large dusty red cattle and black sheep trekked southwards by Maures for many months of the long dry season. The Daouna Region, with 200–400 mms average rainfall, has had low population density and limited settlement because of its precolonial history of conflict and raiding, and the deep groundwater table, which has made it difficult to dig wells. Herds must rely on bush ponds for as long as possible, before they turn to village wells. However, the widespread take-up of donkey carts now allows water to be transported longer distances, which has opened up large areas for cultivation and hence, increased tensions between livestock and crops.

Earlier chapters of this book have noted increased conflict between Bambara and Peul around DBG, the withdrawal of herding contracts which used to tie these communities more closely, reduction in manure–water arrangements, and fights over crop damage which have on occasion led to deaths. The Bambara farmers of DBG say the problems worsened 15 years ago, following a deadly affront between farmers and herders at Néguébougou, 20 km to the southwest, in which guns were fired and people died on both sides. A further death of a Peul herder occurred following animals being found in one of DBG's fields, for which two young Bambara men were tried and jailed. Such rising tensions are increasingly common throughout this zone, and are attributed by some to the shift in management of large herds from family-based transhumance to reliance on salaried herders. The latter are socially isolated, a long way from home, responsible for too many animals, and armed.[70] The emergence of Peul jihadist groups, such as the Macina Liberation Front, both are the product of such conflicts and further aggravate disputes between these groups.

The chairman of the Ségou regional herders' association nevertheless is sure that herders and cultivators have enough of a shared interest to find common ground.[71] But they need an over-arching arena in which to discuss how they will manage their shared resources. Under the Daouna project, investments are planned in six communes of the North Bank, comprising livestock water points, vaccination sites, slaughter and market facilities, milk processing plants, local road building, and irrigated vegetable gardens. To address the encroachment of fields into grazing lands, four pasture zones have been planned, covering 200,000

---

[69] Turner, M. et al (2016).   [70] Turner, M. (2009).
[71] Interview, 10 July 2017, in Ségou.

ha intended exclusively for grazing herds and within which no cultivation is to be allowed.

There are numerous potential benefits which the Daouna project could confer on the wider region, by providing a means to plan and agree how livestock and crops can best be accommodated in the wider landscape, but it faces a number of difficulties. These include being spread over six communes, and two *cercles*, so there are a number of *Maires* and *Préfets* to align behind the project. There are also questions about whether establishing large reserves exclusively for grazing is the best answer to protecting forage resources for pasture. Two of the four grazing reserves proposed in the original project have provoked serious protests as they are located in areas where there are existing fields. In the case of the first grazing area, farmers were very concerned to see the project team driving big concrete pillars into the ground to establish the boundaries to this zone, which would have displaced a large number of farmers, and aggravated disputes between crops and livestock.[72] The other two pastoral grazing zones in the Daouna project are further to the north, in areas of lighter settlement and thus may be easier to set up. A new form of land privatization is also taking place, with the appearance of private boreholes in areas expected to be within the Daouna project. These are mainly the actions of rich herd owners from Bamako, Ségou, and Niono, who are in effect privatizing the grazing around such water points. This process of anarchic privatiztion is leading to a reduction in common grazing lands traditionally open to all, and growing tensions between traditional pastoralism and this new form of appropriation.

The Daouna project will also need to take into account the presence of irrigated farming schemes, like N-Sukala, which generate major impacts on the wider landscape because of the eviction and forced migration of farmers and the need to move cattle away from the sugar cane. The layout of irrigation zones largely ignores the livestock sector, and their requirements for fodder and water, despite many farmers relying on work oxen to plough the land, and investment of wealth in cattle herds. Since the *Office du Niger* plans to develop further irrigated areas, many more people in surrounding villages and camps are likely to be evicted. The consequent rush for soils and pastures in the area to the north and west of N-Sukala has provoked growing antagonisms between Peul and many farmers, both resident and incomers. Most of all, design and management of the Daouna project need to move away from a top-down approach in which commune mayors are told by government officials what will happen, with no possibility of feedback, to one in which local people are brought together to discuss ways to address increasing pressures on land and grazing.

---

[72] Fortunately, the Danish aid agency, which had agreed to fund this first grazing area, was willing to recognize the damage it would cause, abandoned the installation of this grazing zone, and restricted their funds to support of an abattoir, and water point.

Implementing the *Loi Foncier Agricole*

The *Loi Foncier Agricole* has revised the centralized, state-led ownership of land, and it recognizes for the first time local user rights over land, water, grazing, and woodland. Promulgated in April 2017, the law modifies the framework for managing land and natural resources, through the creation of land committees at the level of the village or camp (*Commissions Foncières villageoises et de fractions* (COFOs)).[73] These are intended to be arenas within which to sort out disputes, as well as manage land. As noted in Chapter 4, the Decrees outlining how such COFOs are meant to be constituted have now been issued, and they specify their composition and functions, the procedure for registering land transactions, and the establishment of a national observatory on land rights.[74] The COFO will provide conciliation services for disputes over land, before parties take the dispute to formal structures; build-up an inventory of customary practice; participate in the setting up of a cadastral survey at commune level; participate in putting land management into practice at the commune level; and give a view on all relevant tenure questions. While the COFO is a big step forward in transferring responsibilities to local institutions, there will need to be a commune-level structure to ensure management of land and common property resources which surpass the reach of a single village or camp. Putting COFO into place in the six communes of Daouna would require an understanding of the process by the people of the commune and the mayor, identifying suitable people to be COFO members, and their training in the tasks involved.

The Agricultural Land Law of 2017 (*Loi Foncier Agricole*) also recognizes the legal status of *Conventions Locales* for pastoral grazing lands, such as those prepared for the Communes of Bellen and N'Koumandougou. Thus, there is much the new law can offer for clarifying and confirming different land rights holders, and establishing the village or camp as the principal arena for resolving disputes. However, progress with implementation is slow. Several pilot areas have been identified, but government is hoping for donor funding to take such pilots forward. At the same time, the current insecurity in the centre of the country has inflamed relations between different groups, with access to land, water, and grazing at the heart of this conflict. Consequently, implementation of the new law will be taking place in a highly charged political atmosphere.

What difference has development assistance made to DBG?

Development aid flows have been a major source of funds for the Government of Mali, accounting since the 1970s for 12–15 per cent of the country's gross national

---

[73] Loi numéro 2017/001 du 11 Avril 2017.
[74] Décret no. 2018 0333/P-RM du 4 avril 2018. Décret no. 2018 0334/P-RM du 4 avril 2018.

income, and half the government budget. Mali has received a total of $30 bn since 1970, averaging US$600 m/year, with annual receipts varying over the years, depending in part on donor trends. Major projects, such as the *Office du Niger*, have sucked up a large share of the money, and health and education have both been significant recipients from the 1990s onwards. Since the 2012 crisis, a greater share has gone into military and security-focused activities. The principal donors to Mali are the EU, the United States, France, Germany, the World Bank, the African Development Bank, and China. China's assistance takes the form of loans for large infrastructural projects, such as the proposed new bridge over the River Niger at Ségou, and current construction of the Taoussa Dam east of Timbuktu.[75]

While villages like DBG, distant from major centres, have seen some benefits from this longstanding flow of aid to Mali, they have also suffered the consequences of the donor focus on irrigated agriculture. In terms of actual development projects, the German agency GIZ set up a solar power charging station in DBG in 2006, but this was after several villagers had already purchased their own solar panels and were earning money from charging-up devices and batteries.[76] The project shut its doors after 5 years because the services it offered were being sold more cheaply by villagers' own energy businesses. However, it reopened in 2017, when the villagers were presented with a large freezer cabinet, being run from the solar panels. Currently the man given responsibility for managing the solar station has been making iced lollies for sale. In the 1990s, a Saudi organization dug a couple of deep wells for drinking water, and today CARE-Mali is supporting the creation of women's saving associations in this and neighbouring villages. The German aid organization GIZ, based its local government support programme in Ségou (PACT), but the commune of N'Koumandougou was not targeted by their activities. However, the neighbouring commune of Bellen has benefitted from a number of schemes, such as development of fish farming and design of a *Convention Locale* to manage herd movements within the commune, both of which DBG has now followed.

While DBG has benefitted little from direct aid, donor agencies have been very influential in terms of shaping government policy. For example, in the early 1980s, the World Bank launched a set of structural adjustment programmes across Africa, forcing big reductions in government spending, abandonment of state interventions in grain markets, cuts in agricultural extension, and privatization of state-owned enterprise. This was beneficial for DBG because the villagers no longer had to deliver a quota of millet to the parastatal agency OPAM at a price well below market levels.[77] DBG has never received any visits from agricultural

---

[75] One senior official said to me, 'The Chinese are even worse than the jihadists. They creep about in secret and then you find they're everywhere.' Bamako, October 2016.

[76] Through its decentralization-support project, Projet d'Appui aux Collectivités Territoriales PACT-GIZ, Ségou.

[77] Office pour les Produits Agricoles du Mali.

extension services and, therefore, did not miss their abolition. The push for decentralized local government in the 1990s, advocated by many Malian politicians and NGOs following re-establishment of democratic government in 1992, was strongly supported by the donor community, and is seen positively by most people in DBG. In the 2000s, donors focused government attention on poverty-reduction strategies, and latterly, many big donors have pushed the government to pass the *Loi Foncier Agricole*. This new law is the outcome of a long process of research, engagement, and policy debate largely supported by the French government, to recast land rights away from assertion of state domain and towards 'customary' land users. Implementation of this law entails a loss of power and patronage for government; hence, it is said that the legislation only passed because of heavy pressure from several donors, including the World Bank, who made its passage conditional for other funding. This measure could be of great benefit to DBG and the surrounding neighbourhood if it both clarifies the strength of local user rights relative to the state and establishes an arena within which competing claims can be resolved.

The overall impact and consequences of development assistance have long been contested.[78] Its proponents point to rapid improvements in health and education; a greater focus by governments on addressing poverty and setting up safety nets; large-scale relief of suffering during humanitarian emergencies; and greater services focused on women and girls. While not denying the contributions made to delivery of key public services, critics point to the political consequences of transferring large amounts of money to central government. These include further worsening the already weak accountability felt by the executive branch of government towards its citizens, weakening domestic opposition, and postponing essential changes in policy.[79] In the current political climate, Lebovich asserts that presidents across the Sahel have recognized clearly how to use concerns about terrorism and migration to consolidate their own position, and attract more money to central government.[80] Easterley notes that any country with attractive incentives for investment does not need aid. Poor accountability undermines democracy and the rule of law, and generates conditions in which corruption can flourish.[81] Collier argues that the future of aid will be in helping the least successful countries catch up, in part, by encouraging firms to set up and start generating incomes and jobs in high-risk locations, and, in part, by focusing on specific things, such as eradicating malaria, providing scholarships for poor children, or investing in key public infrastructure.[82] Illicit financial flows out of the continent are significant for Africa as a whole, estimated at $80 billion a year, broadly equivalent to the flow of remittance income. The figure for Mali is not

---

[78]   Bauer, P. (1972); Sachs, J. (2005); Commission for Africa (2005); Easterly, W. (2007).
[79]   Van der Walle, N. (2012).   [80]   Lebovich, A. (2018).   [81]   Easterly, W. (2007).
[82]   Commission on State Fragility, Growth and Development (2018).

known, but use of the CFA franc, which is linked to the Euro zone, makes it easy to transfer money abroad.[83]

West Africa was described until recently as a 'backwater', of low geo-strategic importance, with few resources which cannot be found elsewhere.[84] However, over the last decade, growing conflict across West Africa, the rise of jihadism, and high levels of migration from this region to Europe have brought the region much greater attention. Finding jobs for young people and controlling migration have become twin objectives for many European donors. In 2017, the Sahel Alliance was launched to pool and coordinate the principal donors to the Sahel—France, Germany, the EU, the World Bank, the African Development Bank, and UNDP.[85] They have pledged a total of 9 billion euros over the period 2018–2022, and outlined six priority areas which aim to provide security, increase energy access, provide training and generate employment for young people, develop solutions for rural areas, fight against climate change, and strengthen governance. Today the presidents of Niger and Mali call for financial support by saying their countries represent a dam which, if it breaks, will unleash terror across a much wider region. Recent evidence shows that increased overseas development assistance is unlikely to curb migration flows and, to the extent that overseas development assistance brings faster economic progress, may amplify rather than reduce the desire and ability to migrate.[86] Rather than seeking to cut migration levels per se, perhaps aid could help shape and manage migration better, by developing safe, lawful channels for movement; by better matching of skills and job opportunities; and by finding ways of supporting diaspora linkages.

In conclusion

How to tell the story of DBG over the next 35 years? Clearly, it is not possible, since life always throws up unexpected happenings. There are, however, more optimistic and more sombre directions which this community and region might take. Previous chapters have described the major forces which have shaped livelihood options for people in DBG, such as pressures on land, falling millet yields, shifting patterns of migration, worsening relations between farmers and herders, and the erosion of collective household production. This final chapter has presented current challenges facing the village because of conflict and insecurity across the region, more uncertain and erratic rainfall, the neglect of rain-fed farming in favour of large-scale irrigated agriculture, and political governance which is both centralized and unaccountable to the large majority of the population.[87]

---

[83] OECD, Paris. (2018).   [84] Turner, M. (2009).
[85] https://www.alliance-sahel.org to which have been added Denmark, Italy, Luxemburg, Netherlands, Spain, and the UK.
[86] Clemens, M. and Postel, H. (2018).   [87] Mara, M. (2019).

Taking the less optimistic direction for each of the factors outlined in this chapter would lead to a worsening of the conflict, with growing mayhem in the centre of the country, and repeated tit-for-tat massacres between ethnic groups and their various militias.[88] Continued large-scale land allocations by government to commercial investors for irrigation purposes will displace ever-larger numbers of people from their land, pushing them further to compete for land in areas of grazing.[89] This can only generate greater hostility amongst livestock-keeping groups, and resentment amongst those who have been thrown off their land, with no prospect of compensation. Where government is unable to invest in providing basic health and education services for village people, the flow of young migrants to Bamako, digging for gold, and travel farther afield will continue. In the absence of attractive job opportunities within the country, young people will be tempted by the money and power associated with recruitment for illicit activities. Where the ties between migrants and their village family stretch and break, the benefits which money, ideas, and new technology bring to more marginal regions will wither. And as individualism ousts the more traditional values of collective activity, mutual help, and risk-spreading within the domestic group, so people who have been less successful will find themselves evermore vulnerable to the shocks of climate, demography, and impoverishment.

A more promising picture for the future would see action at local, national, and regional levels. Within Mali, government needs to play a more active and accountable role to support decentralized activities, through empowering communes and village-level associations to plan and manage their own development. With support from the donor community, this could involve provision of decentralized finance to build more resilience to climate extremes, as shown by pilot examples in Mali's Fifth Region.[90] If the government was more ready to explore political solutions to the conflict in North and Central Mali, they would be less reliant on military might, and this would reduce the damage caused by an army that inspires fear amongst those who encounter its soldiers. If the government also took responsibility for bringing several militias in line, there would be fewer grounds for armed escalation between ethnic and religious groups. The new land law would need a careful rollout to ensure that arenas are created where the complex historic conflicting claims to valuable resources of land, water, soils, and grazing

---

[88] As I write, news has just emerged of the massacre of 134 Peuls in a village near Bankass in Central Mali, likely perpetrated by a militia group supported and given weapons by the army. March 2019. http://en.rfi.fr/africa/20190419-mali-prime-minister-and-government-resigns-over-public-anger-dealing-massacre.

[89] At the March 2019 Gulf Conference on Food Production, representatives of the Malian government have offered large-scale land allocations within the Office du Niger zone to private companies, leaving little doubt that more evictions of farming villages and herders' camps are on the way. http://maliactu.info/economie/rehabilitation-du-canal-de-macina-et-du-fala-de-bokywere-loffice-du-niger-en-quete-de-26-milliards-de-fcfa.

[90] Near East Foundation (2016).

can be resolved peacefully, location by location. Renewed attention to dryland farming could work with farmers to achieve better integration of livestock into cropping systems, to maintain soil fertility, identify and spread short-cycle seed varieties, and promote a regreening of landscapes across the country. A restatement of collective values, shared well-being, and mutual accountability articulated and espoused by those in leadership positions could help shift the current ideology away from individualism to approaches that are more collective. If more irrigated agriculture is considered essential, regardless of cost, then better processes of compensation should be set up for those adversely affected, such as providing them with access to their own irrigated plots. Strengthening ties between the migrant diaspora and their home villages would enable less favoured regions to benefit from sending their sons and daughters away. If projects such as the proposed Daouna scheme brought significant tangible local benefits, such as better roads, investment in boreholes and market gardens, and a platform to discuss and plan the future for the North Bank, this would demonstrate a willingness in government to listen to and support local priorities. Overall, a positive virtuous cycle could be established, recognizing the value, culture, and knowledge of communities such as DBG, and which helps reinvest in the landscapes that will need to sustain them and their descendants for decades to come.

The worsening conflict at the level of the whole West African region requires a multinational strategy combining military, political, and economic approaches, to unpick the interests—geopolitical, ideological, and financial—which are generating increased mayhem across the Sahel. Europe has a very strong interest in helping the region develop along a peaceful and sustainable pathway, helping to generate the growth in jobs, education, and prospects for well-being that will encourage young people to stay in the region, rather than trek to Libya and attempt the risky sea crossing to an increasingly hostile shore.

Glossary of Bambara terms

Ba	Mother
Badenya	Mother-childness, meaning the warm and co-operative relationship associated with children of the same mother
Balanzan	*Faidherbia albida* tree, also known as Gao, found in farmlands around Ségou, drops its leaves in rainy season, seeds and leaves used as fodder
Basi	Cous-cous
Bélé	Gravelly land or soil
Béné	Sesame
Benke	Mother's brother, uncle
Béré	*Boscia senegalensis*, bears a berry which used as famine food
Bi te	Today not. Meaning a long time ago.
Blon	Entrance hallway to a compound
Bwa	Clay soil.
Cencen	Sand, sandy soil
Changara	*Combretum glutinosum*, a common shrub used for dyeing cloth and medicines
Cha-tigi	Chief of the work-team
Dasiri	Sacred grove
Dah	*Hibiscus sabdariffa*, used as a condiment
Dégé	Sour millet porridge, eaten with milk and sugar in the afternoon
Denke	Male child
Denmuso	Female child
Denw	Children
Diji	Honey, lit. bee water
Dogoke	Younger brother
Du	Compound, family
Dugu	Town, village
Dugule	*Ficus gnapharlorcarpa*, shade tree
Dugura	*Cordyla pinnata*, bears edible fruit
Dugutigi	Chief of town, village
Dutigi	Chief of compound, family
Fa	Father
Fadenya	Father-childness, meaning the competitive rivalry considered typical of children of the same father but different mothers
Fama	Those holding power, such as president, government, army, ruler
Fantan	Those without power
Fini	Fonio, also cloth
Finimugu	Home-spun and woven cotton cloth
Fogo-fogo	*Calotropis procera*
Foroba	Large field, meaning activity done collectively

Foroba flaw	Peuls "owned" and settled by Segou kings on grazing lands around the city to care for cattle, in 18th and 19th centuries
Fufafu	Great-great grandfather/mother
Gala	*Pterocarpus lucens*, used to dye cloth
Gwa	Hearth, cooking fire and hence household
Gwatigi	Chief of household
Gwélé	*Prosopis juliflora*, tree with very hard wood used for mortars
Horondugu	Town, village of "noble" people (i.e. non-casted)
Jaatigi	Person who acts as landlord, protector of an incomer
Jamu	Family name
Jon	Slave, captive
Jonforo	Field given to slave to farm, meaning individual activity carried out in spare time
Komo	Secret society
Koroke	Older brother
Manyo	Maize
Moke	Grandfather
Momuso	Grandmother
Moni	Porridge gruel
Ncin	*Panicum laetum*, wild grass harvested for its seed
Nyamakala	Casted people, with special knowledge and access to spiritual world
Nyé-nyé	Husks around millet seed
Nyo goshi	Millet threshing
Nzamara	*Cenchrus biflorus*, Cram-cram, an annual grass
Paki	Farming technique, using a long-handled hoe, for making small holes across unploughed land where millet seed can be dropped, allowing for rapid sowing over a large area
Sanji	Rainfall, lit. year-water
Sanyo	Bush-field millet, long-cycle
Ségé	*Striga*, parasitic weed found on millet, also known as witch-weed
Senankunya	Joking relationship between cousins, and lineage groups
Sho	Cowpeas, *Vigna unguiculata*
So	House, usually the dwelling of a woman/wife
Soforo	House-field, village-fields around the settlement
Sogo	Annual festival at harvest-time
Sotigi	Chief of the house, husband
Souna, sunan	Village-field millet, short-cycle
Taafi fin	Cloth dyed indigo
Tiga-nkuru	*Vigna subterranea*, Bambara earthnut
Tô	Thick millet porridge eaten with sauce, at midday or evening
Ton	Association, youth group
Tonjon	"Soldier-slave" from Ségou kingdom
Tubabu-muso	White woman
Tulomasama	Great-grandparent
Wa	Perennial grass, for fodder and weaving mats and granaries, *Andropogon gayanus*
Wuluku	Grass used for sweeping brushes, *Schoenfeldia gracilis*.

References

Adamczewski Hertzog, A. (2014) *Qui prendra ma terre? L'Office du Niger, des investissements internationaux aux arrangements fonciers locaux.* Doctoral thesis. l'Université Montpellier Paul Valéry, Montpellier III. HAL ID tel-01080286v2.

Allen, T., Heinrigs, P., and Heo, I. (2018) *Agriculture, Food and Jobs in West Africa.* West African Papers No. 14. Paris: OECD Publishing. https://doi.org/10.1787/dc152bc0-en.

Ba, A.K. (1987) *L'Epopée de Ségou. Da Monzon: Un pouvoir guerrier.* Paris: Favre. ISBN: 2828902501 978-2828902506.

Bâ, A.H. (1994) *Oui mon Commandant !* Arles, France: Actes Sud. ISBN: 2742701168 9782742701162.

Batterbury, S. (2001) Landscapes of diversity: A local political ecology of livelihood diversification in south-western Niger. *Ecumene* 8(4): 437–464. https://doi.org/10.1177/096746080100800404.

Bauer, P. (1972) *Dissent on Development.* Cambridge, MA: Harvard University Press. OCLC No. 249335319.

Bazin, F. Hathie, I. Skinner, J., and Koundouno, J. (Eds.) (2017) *Irrigation, Food Security and Poverty – Lessons from Three Large Dams in West Africa.* Global Water Initiative West Africa. London: IIED; Paris: IRAM. ISBN:978-1-78431-527-6.

Bazin, J. (1970) Recherches sur les formations socio-politiques anciennes en pays bambara. *Notes Maliennes* 1: 29–40. ISSN: 0378-2034.

Bazin, J. (1975) Guerre et servitude à Ségou. In: Ed. C. Meillassoux. *L'esclavage en Afrique précoloniale*, pp. 135–182. Paris: Maspéro. OCLC: 1364470.

Bazin, J. (1988) Princes désarmés, corps dangereux. Les 'rois-femmes' de la région de Segu. *Cahiers d'Etudes Africaines* 28(11/112): 375–441. https://doi.org/10.3406/cea.1988.1658.

Becker, L.C. (2013) Land sales and the transformation of social relations and landscape in peri-urban Mali. *Geoforum* 46: 113–123. https://doi.org/10.1016/j.geoforum.2012.12.017.

Becker, L.C. (1996) Access to labor in rural Mali. *Human Organisation* 55(3): 279–288. Journal ISSN: 00187259.

Becker, L.C. (1990) The collapse of the family farm in West Africa? Evidence from Mali. *Geographical Journal* 156(3): 313–322. https://doi.org/10.2307/635532.

Behnke, R. and Mortimore, M. (Eds.) (2016) *The End of Desertification? Disputing Environmental Change in the Drylands.* Berlin: Springer-Verlag. https://doi.org/10.1007/978-3-642-16014-1.

Behnke, R., Scoones, I., and Kerven, C. (Eds.) (1993) *Range Ecology at Disequilibrium: New Models of Natural Variability and Pastoral Adaptation in African Savannas.* London: ODI. ISBN: 0850031958 https://doi.org/10.1002/ldr.3400050108.

Benjaminsen, T.A. and Ba, B. (2018) Why do pastoralists in Mali join jihadist groups? A political ecological explanation. *Journal of Peasant Studies* 46(1): 1–20. https://doi.org/10.1080/03066150.2018.1474457.

Berry, S. (1993) *No Condition is Permanent. The Social Dynamics of Agrarian Change in Sub-Saharan Africa.* Madison: University of Wisconsin Press. ISBN: 9780299139346.

Bertrand, M. and Djiré, M. (2016) Monopoly foncier au Mali. *Sciences du Sud. Le journal de l'IRD* 83: 5. https://www.ird.fr/la-mediatheque/journal-sciences-au-sud/les-numeros/n-83-juin-a-octobre-2016/sciences-au-sud-no-83-partenaires. Accessed 24 April 19.

Bliss, C. and Stern, N. (1982) *Palanpur. The Economy of an Indian Village.* Oxford: Clarendon Press. https://doi.org/10.1017/S0026749X00014505.

Boserup, E. (1965) *The Conditions of Agricultural Growth: The Economics of Agrarian Change under Population Pressure.* London: Allen and Unwin. https://doi.org/10.4324/9781315131450.

Brock, K. and Coulibaly, N. (1999) *Sustainable Rural Livelihoods in Mali.* Falmer, UK: IDS Research report issue 35. ISBN: 1 85864 269 8.

Brockington, D. and Noe, C., (forthcoming) *Prosperity in Rural Africa? Insights from Longitudinal Studies in Tanzania.* Oxford: Clarendon Press.

Brockington, D. and Howland, O. (2018) Economic growth, rural assets and prosperity: exploring the implications of a 20-year record of asset growth in Tanzania. *Journal of Modern African Studies* 56(2): 217–243. https://doi.org/10.1017/S0022278X18000186.

Chambers, R. (1979) *Rural Development Tourism – Poverty Unperceived.* Paper presented to the Workshop on Participatory Rural Appraisal, Institute of Development Studies, Brighton, UK, 4–7 December 1979. http://opendocs.ids.ac.uk/opendocs/handle/123456789/867.

Chauveau, J.-P. (2001) *Question foncière en Côte d'Ivoire. Ou: comment remettre à zéro le compteur de l'histoire.* Drylands Programme Issue Paper No. 95. London: IIED. ISBN: 978-1-904035-54-1. ISSN: 1357 9312.

Chayanov, A.V. (1966) *The Theory of Peasant Economy.* Homewood, IL: Richard D. Irwin, Inc., for the American Economic Association. ISBN: 0719018633.

CILSS (2016) *Landscapes of West Africa: A Window on a Changing World.* Garretson, SD: U.S. Geological Survey. https://doi.org/10.5066/F7N014QZ.

Cissé, M. and Hiernaux, P. (1984) Impact de la mise en valeur agricole sur les ressources fourragères. Etude de cas : les jachères de Dalonguebougou (Mali central), *CIPEA Document de Programme AZ96,* International Livestock Center for Africa. Bamako, Mali. Available at: https://hdl.handle.net/10568/11085. Accessed 20 August 2019.

Clemens, M.A. and Postel, H.M. (2018) Deterring emigration with foreign aid: an overview of evidence from low-income countries. *Population and Development Review* 44: 667–693. doi:10.1111/padr.12184.

CMAT (2018) *Déclaration finale du Village des Sans Terre, Ségou le 26-27 mars 2018.* Convergence malienne contre les accaparements de terres. Bamako, Mali. Coordination Nationale des Organisations Paysannes, CNOP. Available at : https://africaconvergence.net/IMG/pdf/declaration_village_sans_terre_2018_vf.pdf. Accessed 20 August 2019.

Commission for Africa (2005) *Our Common Interest.* London: Penguin. ISBN: 0141024682 978-0141024684.

Commission on Pathways for Prosperity (2018) *Charting Pathways for Inclusive Growth. From Paralysis to Preparation.* Oxford: Blavatnik School of Government.

Commission on State Fragility, Growth and Development (2018) *Escaping the Fragility Trap.* Oxford: Oxford Blavatnik School of Government; London: LSE.

Condé, M. (1984) *Ségou: Les murailles de terres.* Paris: Pocket. ISBN: 2253037117 9782253037118.

Conrad, D.C. and Fisher, H.J. (1982) The conquest that never was: Ghana and the Almoravids, 1076. *History in Africa* Published online by Cambridge University Press: 13 May 2014. 10: 21–59; [1983] 10: 53–78. https://doi.org/10.2307/3171598.

Cooper, B.M. (1997) *Marriage in Maradi. Gender and Culture in a Hausa Society in Niger. 1900–1989.* New Haven, CT: Heinemann.

Cotula, L. (2013) *The Great African Land Grab? Agricultural Investments and the Global Food System.* London: Zed Books. ISBN: 9781780324203.

Cotula, L. (2011) *Land Deals in Africa: What Is in the Contracts?* London: IIED Report. ISBN:978-1-84369-804-3.

Cotula, L. and Berger, T. (2017) *Legal Empowerment in Agribusiness Investments: Harnessing Political Economy Analysis*. LEGEND Analytical paper. London: ODI.

Coulibaly, C. (2010) *La décentralisation au Mali : le transfert de compétences en difficulté*. Comité Technique Foncier et Développement. Paris: AFD.

Dieterlen, G. (1952) *Essai sur la religion Bambara*. Paris: Presses Universitaires de France.

Direction Nationale de la Statistique et de l'Information (2008) *Manuel de l'Agent Recenseur, Quatrième recensement général de la population et de l'habitat 2009*. Direction Nationale de la Statistique et de l'Information (DNSI), Bamako, Mali. http://microdata.worldbank.org/index.php/catalog/2099.

Djiré, M. Polack, E., and Cotula, L. (2014) *Developing Tools to Secure Land Rights in West Africa: A 'Bottom Up' Approach*. IIED Briefing. London: IIED.

Djiré, M. (2007) *Les paysans maliens exclus de la propriété foncière? Les avatars de l'appropriation par le titre foncier*. Drylands Programme Issue Paper No. 144. London: IIED. ISBN: 978-1-84369-660-5. ISSN: 1357-9312.

Djiré, M. (2004) *The Myths and Realities of Local Governance in Sanankoroba, Mali*. Drylands Programme Issue Paper No. 130. London: IIED. ISBN: 978-1-84369-535-6. ISSN: 1357-9312.

Easterly, W. (2007) Was development assistance a mistake? *The American Economic Review* 97(2): 328–332. DOI:10.1257/aer.97.2.328.

Echenberg, M. (1985) '*Morts Pour la France*': The African Soldier in France during the Second World War. *Journal of African History* 26 (4): 363–380. https://doi.org/10.1017/S0021853700028796.

Fairhead, J. and Leach, M. (1998) *Reframing Deforestation: Global Analyses and Local Realities: Studies in West Africa*. Milton: Routledge. https://doi.org/10.4324/9780203400340.

Fauvelle, F.-X. (2018) *The Golden Rhinoceros. Histories of the African Middle Ages*. Princeton, NJ: Princeton University Press. ISBN 9780691181264.

Faye, A. et al. (2001) *Policy Requirements for Farmer Investment in Semi-Arid Africa. Région de Diourbel: Synthesis*. Drylands Research Working Paper No. 23e. Crewkerne, UK: Drylands Research. http://hdl.handle.net/10068/616772.

Fernández-Rivera, S. Hiernaux, P. Williams, T.O. Turner, M.D., and Schlecht, E. (2005) Nutritional constraints to grazing ruminants in the millet–cowpea–livestock farming system of the Sahel. Coping with feed scarcity. In: Eds. A.A. Ayantunde, S. Fernández-Rivera, and G. McCrabb, *Coping with Feed Scarcity in Smallholder Livestock Systems in Developing Countries*. Nairobi, Kenya: International Livestock Research Institute, pp. 157–182. ISBN 92-9146-167-9.

FIDH/AMDH (2018) *Dans le centre du Mali, les populations prises au piège du terrorisme et du contre-terrorisme*. Fédération Internationale des Droits de l'Homme/Association Malienne des Droits de l'Homme. Report no. 727. Nairobi, Kenya: ILRI.

Fulton, D. and Toulmin, C. (1982) *A Socio-Economic Study of an Agro-Pastoral System in Central Mali*. Report to the International Livestock Center for Africa. Addis Ababa, Ethiopia: ILRI.

Galliéni, J.-S. (1885) *Voyage au Soudan français (Haut Niger et pays de Ségou), 1879–1881*. Paris: Hachette. ISBN: 2012631991 / 978-2012631991.

Garrity, D. et al (2010) Evergreen agriculture: a robust approach to sustainable food security in Africa. *Food Security* 2(3): 197–214. https://doi.org/10.1007/s12571-010-0070-7.

Giannini, A. (2016) 40 years of climate modelling: the causes of late 20th century drought in the Sahel. In: Eds. R. Behnke and M. Mortimore, *The End of Desertification? Disputing*

Environmental Change in the Drylands, pp. 265–292. Berlin: Springer-Verlag. https://doi.org/10.1007/978-3-642-16014-1_10.

Giannini, A. et al (2013) A unifying view of climate change in the Sahel linking intra-seasonal, interannual and longer time scales. *Environmental Research Letters* 8(2): n.pag. https://iopscience.iop.org/article/10.1088/1748-9326/8/2/024010.

de Gobineau, H. (1953) *Noblesse d'Afrique*. Paris: Présence Africaine. ISBN: 2708708376 / 978-2708708372.

Goody, J. (1958) *The Development Cycle in Domestic Groups*. Cambridge: Cambridge University Press. ISBN: 978-0521096607 / 9780521096607.

Gorer, G. (1945) *Africa Dances*. Harmondsworth: Penguin. ISBN: 0140095020 / 9780140095029.

GSMA (2018) *The Mobile Economy. West Africa*. London: GSMA.

GTZ (Ed.) (2000) *Codes Locaux pour une Gestion Durable des Ressources Naturelles. Recueil des expériences de la Coopération technique allemande en Afrique francophone*. Eschborn, Germany: GTZ.

Guyer, J. (1997) *An African Niche Economy. Farming to Feed Ibadan 1968–88*. Edinburgh: International African Library. ISBN: 0748609318.

Guyer, J. (1981) Household and community in African Studies. *African Studies Review* 24 (2–3): 83–137. https://doi.org/10.2307/523903.

Haaland, R. (1980) Man's role in the changing habitat of Méma during the old kingdom of Ghana. *Norwegian Archaeological Review* 13(1): 31–46. https://doi.org/10.1080/00293652.1980.9965328.

Hart, K. (1982) *The Political Economy of West African Agriculture*. Cambridge: Cambridge University Press. ISBN: 0521240735.

Haywood, M. (1981) *Evolution de l'utilisation des terres et de la végétation dans la zone soudano-sahélienne du projet CIPEA au Mali*. Addis Abéba: CIPEA. Available at: https://hdl.handle.net/10568/10971. Accessed 20 August 2019.

Hesse, C. Anderson, S., Cotula, L., Skinner, J., and Toulmin, C. (2013) *Managing the Boom and Bust: Supporting Climate Resilient Livelihoods in the Sahel*. Issue Paper. London: IIED. ISBN 978-1-84369-977-4.

Hiernaux, P. and Gerard, B. (1999) The influence of vegetation pattern on the productivity, diversity and stability of vegetation: the case of "brousse tigrée" in the Sahel. *Acta Oecologica* 20(3): 147–158. https://doi.org/10.1016/S1146-609X(99)80028-9.

Hill, A., Randall, S., and v.d. Eerenbeemt, M.-L. (1983) *Infant and Child Mortality in Rural Mali*. Working Paper 83–5, Centre for Population Studies. London: London School of Hygiene and Tropical Medicine. ISBN: 0902657089 / 978-0902657083.

Hill, P. (1972) *Rural Hausa: A Village and a Setting*. Cambridge: Cambridge University Press. ISBN: 0521082420.

Hill, P. (1977) *Population, Prosperity and Poverty. Rural Kano 1900 and 1970*. Cambridge, Cambridge University Press. ISBN: 0521215110 / 9780521215114.

Himanshu, Lanjouw, P., and Stern, N. (2018) *How Lives Change: Palanpur, India, and Development Economics*. Oxford: Clarendon Press. ISBN: 9780198806509 / 9780191844102 / 9780192529060.

Hudson, P. (2015) *Under an African Sky. A Journey to the Frontline of Climate Change*. Oxford: New Internationalist. ISBN: 9781780261799 / 1780261799.

Hugot, H.-J. (1974) *Le Sahara avant le Désert*. Paris: Hespérides. ISBN: 2855880017 9782855880013.

Ingénieurs Conseils en Technique de Développement/ICOTED (2014) *Etude de Faisabilité du Projet d'Aménagement de Quatre Sites Pastoraux dans la Zone de Daouna, Région de Ségou*. Rapport de synthèse. Bamako, Mali.

Institut Nationale de la Statistique du Mali (INSM) (2018) *Consommation, pauvrété et bien-être des ménages*. Avril 2017–mars 2018. Bamako, Mali.

International Crisis Group (2016) *Central Mali: An Uprising in the Making?* Report no. 238/ Africa. New York.

Jackson, M. (2011) *Life within Limits. Well-being in a World of Want*. Durham, NC: Duke University Press. ISBN: 978-0-8223-4915-0 / 978-0-8223-4892-4.

Jerven, M. (2013) *Poor Numbers. How We Are Misled by African Development Statistics and What to Do about It*. Ithaca, NY: Cornell University Press. ISBN: 0-8014-5163-9 / 978-0-8014-5163-8.

Jerven, M. (2015) *Africa. Why Economists Get It Wrong*. London: Zed Books. ISBN: 9781783601325 / 9781783601332.

Kirwin, M. and J. Anderson (2018) *Identifying the Factors Driving West African Migration*. West African Papers No. 17. Paris: OECD Publishing. https://doi.org/10.1787/eb3b2806-en.

Kratli, S. (2015) *Valuing Variability. New Perspectives in Climate Resilient Drylands Development*. London: IIED. ISBN: 978-1-78431-157-5.

Lanjouw, P. and Stern, N. (1998) *Economic Development in Palanpur over Five Decades*. Oxford: Clarendon Press. ISBN: 0198288328 / 9780198288329 / 9780198831952 / 0198831951.

Leach, M. and Mearns, R. (Eds.) (1996) *The Lie of the Land. Challenging Received Wisdom on the African Environment*. London: International African Institute. https://doi.org/10.1002/1099-145X(200007/08)11:4<393::AID-LDR389>3.0.CO;2-P.

Lebovich, A. (2018) *Halting Ambition: EU Migration and Security Policy in the Sahel*. European Council on Foreign Relations. Brussels, Belgium: ecfr.eu.

Levtzion, N. and Hopkins, J.F.P. (Eds.) (2000) *Corpus of Early Arabic Sources for West African History*. Princeton, NJ: Markus Weiner. ISBN: 1558762418 / ISBN: 978-1558762411.

Lewis, J.v.D. (1978) *Descendants and Crops. Two Poles of Production in a Malian Peasant Village*. Yale University, PhD Thesis.

Lovejoy, P. (1986) *Salt of the Desert Sun. A History of Salt Production and Trade in the Central Sudan*. African Studies Series 46. Cambridge: Cambridge University Press. ISBN: 0521301823.

Lutkenhorst, W. (2018) *Creating Wealth without Labour? Emerging Contours of a New Techno-Economic Landscape*. Discussion Paper, November 2018. Bonn, Germany: German Development Institute. DOI: 10.23661/dp11.2018.

MacDonald, K.C. (2012) 'The least of their inhabited villages are fortified': the walled settlements of Ségou. *Azania: Archaeological Research in Africa* 47(3): 343–364. https://doi.org/10.1080/0067270X.2012.707478

MacDonald, K.C., Camara, S., Canós Donnay, S., Gestrich, N., and Keita, D. (2011) Sorotomo: A forgotten Malian capital? *Archaeology International* 13/14(2009–2011): 52–64. http://dx.doi.org/10.5334/ai.1315.

Magasa, A. (1978) *Papa-Commandant a jeté un grand filet devant nous. Les exploités des rives du Niger 1902–1962*. Paris: Maspéro. ISBN: 2707109797.

Malabo-Montpellier Panel (2018) *Water-Wise. Smart Irrigation Strategies for Africa*. Dakar, Senegal. December 2018.

Mann, G. (2006) *Native Sons: West African Veterans and France in the Twentieth Century. Politics, History, and Culture*. Durham, NC: Duke University Press. ISBN: 978-0-8223-3768-3.

Mara, M. (2019) *La guerre au Mali est d'abord une guerre contre nous-mêmes*. Available at: www.moussamara.com. Accessed 20 August 2019.

Martin, M. (1984) *Food Intake in two Bambara Villages in the Ségou Region of Mali*. Unpublished MSc thesis, Department of Human Nutrition, London School of Hygiene and Tropical Medicine, London.

Mathieu, P. Zongo, M., and Paré, L. (2002) Monetary Land transactions in Western Burkina Faso: commoditisation, papers and ambiguities. *European Journal of Development Research* 14(2): 109–128. DOI: 10.1080/714000431.

Maydell, H.-J. von, (1986) *Trees and Shrubs of the Sahel. Their Characteristics and Uses*. Eschborn: GTZ. ISBN : 3880853185.

Mbajum, S. (2013) *Les combattants africains dits « Tirailleurs Sénégalais » au secours de la France (1857–1945)*. Paris: Riveneuve Editions. ISBN: 9782360131761 / 2360131761.

McIntosh, R.J. (1998) *The Peoples of the Middle Niger: The Island of Gold*. Oxford: Blackwells. ISBN 10: 0631173617.

Meillassoux, C. (1975) *Femmes, greniers et capitaux*. Paris: Maspéro. ISBN: 2707107816.

Meillassoux, C. (1991) *The Anthropology of Slavery*. Chicago: University of Chicago Press. ISBN: 9780226519128.

Ministère du Développement Rural (2015). *Étude du Programme d'Aménagement Hydro-Agricole (PAHA) de la zone Office du Niger (ON)*. Cellule de Planification et de Statistique du Développement Rural (CPS/SDR). Projet d'Accroissement de la Productivité Agricole au Mali (PAPAM). Phase 1 (Etat des lieux). Rapport de synthèse. Bamako, Mali.

Moore, H. (2018) Prosperity in crisis and the longue durée in Africa. *Journal of Peasant Studies* 45:7, 1501–1517. DOI: 10.1080/03066150.2018.1446001.

Mortimore, M. (2009) *Dryland opportunities. A New Paradigm for People, Ecosystems and Development*. Gland: IUCN, IIED, UNDP. ISBN 978-2-8317-1183-6.

Mortimore, M. (1989) *Adapting to Drought. Farmers, Famines and Desertification in West Africa*. Cambridge: Cambridge University Press. ISBN 0 521 323126.

Mortimore, M. et al (2001) Synthesis of long-term change in Maradi Department, Niger 1960–2000. *Drylands Research Working Paper* No. 39e. Somerset, UK: Crewkerne. http://hdl.handle.net/10068/617069.

Moser, C. (2009) *Ordinary Families, Extraordinary Lives. Assets and poverty reduction in Guayaquil, 1978–2004*. Washington, DC: Brookings Institution Press. ISBN: 9780815703273.

Mushongah, J. and Scoones, I. (2012) Livelihood change in rural Zimbabwe over 20 years. *Journal of Development Studies* 48(9): 1–17. https://doi.org/10.1080/00220388.2012.671474.

Near East Foundation (2016) *Decentralising Climate Adaptation Funds in Mali*. NEF, BRACED, IED-Afrique, IIED. Available at: http://www.neareast.org/download/materials_center/Decentralisation-Mali.pdf. Accessed 20 August 2019.

Netting, R.McC. (1993) *Smalholders, Householders: Farm Families and the Ecology of Intensive, Sustainable Agriculture*. Stanford, CA: Stanford University Press. ISBN: 0804721025 / 9780804721028.

New York Times (2019) Hearing Divorce Cases on a Sidewalk in Niger, as Women Assert Their Power. 6 January. Available at: https://www.nytimes.com/2019/01/06/reader-center/niger-divorce-women.html. Accessed 20 August 2019.

Nolte, K. and Voget-Kleschin, L. (2014), Consultation in large-scale land acquisitions: an evaluation of three cases in mali. *World Development* 64: 654–668. https://doi.org/10.1016/j.worlddev.2014.06.028.

Nubukpo, K. (2015) Le franc CFA, un frein à l'émergence des économies africaines? *L'économie politique* 68(4): 71–79. https://doi.org/10.3917/leco.068.0071.

Oakland Institute (2011) *Comprendre les Investissements Fonciers en Afrique*. Rapport – Mali. Oakland, CA: Oakland Institute.

OECD (2018) *Illicit Financial Flows. The Economy of Illicit Trade in West Africa*. Paris: OECD. https://doi.org/10.1787/9789264268418-en.

OECD (1998) *Préparer l'Avenir de l'Afrique de l'Ouest – Une Vision à l'Horizon 2020. Etude des perspectives à long terme en Afrique de l'Ouest*. Paris: OECD. https://doi. org/10.1787/9789264263727-fr.

Pageard, R. (1961a) Note sur le peuplement du pays de Ségou. *Journal de la Société des Africanistes* 31(1): 83–90. https://doi.org/10.3406/jafr.1961.1931.

Pageard, R. (1961b) La marche orientale du Mali (Ségou-Djenné) en 1644, d'après le Tarikh es-Soudan. *Journal de la Société des Africanistes* 31(1): 73–81. https://doi.org/10.3406/ jafr.1961.1930.

Park, M. (2003) *Travels into the Interior of Africa*. London: Eland Press. ISBN: 0907871046 / 978-0907871040.

Pilling, D. (2018) African Economy: The Limits of "Leapfrogging." The Big Read Innovationa. *Financial Times* 13 August. Available at: https://www.ft.com/content/ 052b0a34-9b1b-11e8-9702-5946bae86e6d. Accessed 20 August 2019.

Raimbault, M. and Sanogo, K. (1991) *Recherches archéologiques au Mali. Les sites protohistoriques de la Zone lacustre*. Paris: ACCT-Karthala. ISBN: 2865372855.

Randall, S.C. (1984*) A Comparative Demographic Study of Three Sahelian Populations: Marriage and Child Care as Intermediate Determinants of Fertility and Mortality*. PhD thesis, London School of Hygiene & Tropical Medicine. https://doi.org/10.17037/ PUBS.01620624.

Randall, S., Coast, E., and Leone, T. (2011) Cultural constructions of the concept of household in sample surveys. *Population Studies* 65(2): 217–229. https://doi.org/10.1080/00324 728.2011.576768.

Randall, S. and Coast, E. (2016) The quality of demographic data on older Africans. *Demographic Research* 34: 143–174. DOI: 10.4054/DemRes.2016.34.5.

Raynaut, C. (Ed.) (1997) *Sahels. Diversité et dynamiques des relations sociétés-nature*. Paris: Karthala. ISBN 2-86537-791-1.

Reij, C. and Winterbottom, R. (2015) *Scaling up Re-greening. Six Steps to Success*. Washington, DC: WRI. ISBN: 978-1-56973-861-0.

Reij, C., Tappan, G., and Smale, M. (2009) *Agro-Environmental Transformation in the Sahel. Another Kind of 'Green Revolution'*. IFPRI Discussion Paper No. 914. Washington, DC: IFPRI.

Reij, C., Scoones, I., and Toulmin, C. (1996) *Sustaining the Soil: Indigenous Soil and Water Conservation in Africa*. London: Earthscan.

Richards, P. (1989) Agriculture as a performance. In: Eds. R. Chambers, A. Pacey, and L. Thrupp, *Farmer First: Farmer Innovation and Agricultural Research*, pp. 39–42. London: Intermediate Technology. http://opendocs.ids.ac.uk/opendocs/handle/ 123456789/701.

Roberts, R.L. (1987) *Warriors, Merchants and Slaves. The State and the Economy in the Middle Niger Valley 1700–1914*. Stanford, CA: Stanford University Press. ISBN: 0804713782 /978-0804713788.

Rochegude, A. and Plançon, C. (2009) *Décentralisation, acteurs locaux et foncier. Fiches pays*. Comité Technique «Foncier et Développement» Paris: AFD.

Rodrik, D. (2017) Growth without industrialisation? *Project Syndicate*. 10 October. Available at: https://www.project-syndicate.org/commentary/poor-economies-growing-without-industrializing-by-dani-rodrik-2017-10?barrier=accesspaylog. Accessed 22 July 2017.

Rodrik, D. (2016) Premature de-industrialisation. *Journal of Economic Growth* 21(1): 1–33. https://doi.org/10.1007/s10887-015-9122-3.

Ruthenberg, H. (1980) *Farming Systems in the Tropics*. Oxford: Clarendon Press. ISBN: 019859481X / 9780198594819 / 0198594828 / 9780198594826.

Sachs, J. (2005) *The End of Poverty: Economic Possibilities for Our Time*. New York: Penguin Press. ISBN 9780143036586.

Scheele, J. (2012) *Smugglers and Saints of the Sahara: Regional Connectivity in the Twentieth Century*. Cambridge: Cambridge University Press. ISBN: 9781107022126 / 1107022126.

Smith, M. (1981) *Baba of Karo. A Woman of the Muslim Hausa*. New Haven, CT: Yale University Press. ISBN: 0300027346 / 9780300027341 / 0300027419 / 9780300027419.

Smith, M.G. (1955) *The Economy of Hausa Communities of Zaria*. Colonial Research Series No.16. London, HMSO. ASIN: B0000CJ51P.

Sourisseau J.-M., Soumaré M., Bélières J.-F., Guengant J.-P., Bourgeois R., Coulibaly B., and Traoré S., (2016) *Diagnostic territorial de la région de Ségou au Mali*. Paris: AFD. http://agritrop.cirad.fr/580517/.

Stirling, A. (2011) From sustainability, through diversity to transformation: towards more reflexive governance of vulnerability. In: Eds. A. Hommels, J., Mesman, and W.E. Bijker, *Vulnerability in Technological Cultures: New Directions in Research and Governance*, pp. 305–332. Cambridge, MA: MIT Press. ISBN: 978-0-262-52580-0.

Swift, J.J. (Ed.) (1984) *Pastoral Development in Central Niger*. Niamey Ministère du Développement Rural and USAID. Niamey, Niger: USAID.

Sy, O. (2009) *Reconstruire l'Afrique, vers une nouvelle gouvernance fondée sur les dynamiques locales*. Paris: Éditions Charles Léopold Mayer. ISBN: 9782843771491 / 2843771498 / 9995210061 / 9789995210069.

Tari, D., King-Okumu, C., and Jarso, I. (2015) *Strengthening Local Customary Institutions: a Case Study in Isiolo County, Northern Kenya*. Research Paper. Nairobi, Kenya: Adaptation Consortium.

Taylor, C. et al (2017) Frequency of extreme Sahelian storms tripled since 1982 in satellite observations *Nature* 544(7651): 475. https://doi.org/10.1038/nature22069.

Thiam, A. (2017) *Centre du Mali: Enjeux et dangers d'une crise négligée*. Geneva, Switzerland: Humanitarian Dialogue.

Tiffen, M. (1976) *The Enterprising Peasant. Economic development in Gombe Emirate, North-Eastern State, Nigeria 1900–1968*. London: Ministry of Overseas Development Overseas Research publication No. 21. ISBN: 0118806890 : L8.00 / 9780118806893.

Tiffen, M., Mortimore, M., and Gichuki, F. (1994) *More People, Less Erosion: Environmental Recovery in Kenya*. Chichester, UK: Wiley. ISBN: 0471941433 / 9780471941439.

Togola, T. (2008) *Archaeological Investigations of Iron Age Sites in the Méma Region, Mali (West Africa)*. Cambridge Monographs in African Archaeology, No. 73. Oxford: Hadrian Books. https://hdl.handle.net/1911/16676.

Toulmin, C. and Brock. K. (2016) Desertification in the Sahel: local practice meets global narrative. In: Eds. R. Behnke and M. Mortimore, *The End of Desertification*, pp. 37–54. Berlin: Springer Verlag. https://doi.org/10.1007/978-3-642-16014-1_2.

Toulmin, C. et al (2015) Investing in institutional "software" to build climate resilience. *Anglejournal.com*. Available at: https://anglejournal.com/article/2015-06-investing-in-institutional-software-to-build-climate-resilience/. Accessed 22 July 2019.

Toulmin, C. (2009) *Climate Change in Africa*. London: Zed Press. ISBN: 9781848130159 / 9781848136281 / 9781780326115 / 9781848130142.

Toulmin, C. et al (2000) *Diversification of livelihoods: Evidence from Mali and Ethiopia*. IDS Research report 47. Brighton, UK: IDS. ISBN: 1858643244.

Toulmin, C. (1992) *Cattle, Women and Wells. Managing Household Survival in the Sahel*. Oxford: Clarendon Press. ISBN: 0198290063.

Toulmin, C. (1988) Smiling in the Sahel. *New Scientist* 12: 69.

Toulmin, C. (1987) *Changing Patterns of Investment in a Sahelian Community*. D. Phil thesis (1987) Faculty of Social Studies, University of Oxford.

Traoré, A. and Soumaré, S. (1984) Supplementation alimentaire des boeufs de labour du système agro-pastoral du mil à Dalonguebougou: resultats préliminaires. *CIPEA Document de Programme AZ 111*. Bamako, Mali: ILCA. https://hdl.handle.net/10568/10983.

Turner, M. et al (2016) Variation in vegetation cover and livestock mobility needs in Sahelian West Africa. *Journal of Land Use Science* 11(1): 76–95. https://doi.org/10.1080/17 47423X.2014.965280.

Turner, M. (2009) Capital on the move: the changing relation between livestock and labor in Mali, West Africa. *Geoforum* 40: 746–755. https://doi.org/10.1016/j.geoforum.2009.04.002.

van der Walle, N. (2012) *Has Aid Been a Good Thing? Foreign Aid in Dangerous Places: The Donors and Mali's Democracy*. WIDER Working Paper *2012/61*. http://hdl.handle.net/10419/80969.

Walther, O. (2017) *Wars and Conflicts in the Sahara-Sahel*. West African Papers No. 10. Paris: OECD Publishing. https://doi.org/10.1787/8bbc5813-en.

de Weerdt, J. (2010) Moving out of poverty in Tanzania: evidence from Kagera. *Journal of Development Studies* 46(2): 331–349. https://doi.org/10.1080/00220380902974393.

WEF (2016) *Connecting Africa's Resources through Digital Transformation*. Geneva, Switzerland: World Economic Forum.

Whitehead, A. (2006) Persistent poverty in North East Ghana. *Journal of Development Studies* 42(2): 278–300. https://doi.org/10.1080/00220380500405410.

Wilson, R.T., de Leeuw, P.N., and de Haan, C. (1983) (Eds.) *Recherches sur le systèmes des zones arides du Mali: résultats préliminaires*. Addis Ababa, Ethiopia: ILCA/ILRI. https://hdl.handle.net/10568/11107.

Woodhouse, P. et al (2016) African farmer-led irrigation development: Re-framing agricultural policy and investment? *Journal of Peasant Studies* 44(1): 213–233. https://doi.org/10.1080/03066150.2016.1219719.

Wooten, S. (2009) *The Art of Livelihood. Creating Expressive Agri-Culture in Rural Mali*. Durham, NC: Carolina Academic Press. ISBN: 978-1-59460-731-8.

Young, A. (2012) The African growth miracle. *Journal of Political Economy* 120: 696–739. https://doi.org/10.1086/668501.

Index